NIGERIAN CHILDREN:
Developmental
Perspectives

NIGERIAN CHILDREN: Developmental Perspectives

EDITED BY

H. Valerie Curran

Routledge & Kegan Paul
London, Boston, Melbourne and Henley

First published in 1984
by Routledge & Kegan Paul plc

39 Store Street, London WC1E 7DD, England

9 Park Street, Boston, Mass. 02108, USA

464 St Kilda Road, Melbourne,
Victoria 3004, Australia and

Broadway House, Newtown Road,
Henley-on-Thames, Oxon RG9 1EN, England

Set in Century 10/12 pt
by Columns, Reading
and printed in Great Britain
by The Thetford Press Ltd,
Thetford, Norfolk

Library of Congress Cataloging in Publication Data

Nigerian children.
Includes index.
1. Child development – Nigeria – Addresses, essays,
lectures. 2. Infants – Nigeria – Addresses, essays,
lectures. I. Curran, H. Valerie.
HQ792.N5N53   1984   305.2'3'09669   83-22764

ISBN 0-7100-9515-5 (pbk.)

FOR ALICE AND DENNIS

Contents

Figures

Plates

1 Sideview of male Lagos baby aged 40 days in Stage 1.2. He is looking at the ball in his right window and extends his right arm and fingers towards it. The patterning of his fingers is suggestive of reaching and grasping *pages 20-1*

2 and 3 Comparison of Lagos male aged 33 days and Cambridge male aged 39 days. Both exhibit the fixed gaze of Stage 1.2. The Cambridge photograph was taken through the baby's right-hand window, with a mirror reflecting the image of the ball in the other window. The Lagos photograph was taken from video-tape showing pictures through both windows presented adjacently on a split-screen monitor *pages 20-1*

4 to 13 Sequential photographs of trajectory tracking and cross-looking in American male aged 76 days and Nigerian male aged 90 days. Photographs at approximately $\frac{1}{2}$ second intervals. In top picture of each sequence, baby is looking at ball in his right window. In pictures 2 and 3, baby's gaze follows upward path of ball that has been withdrawn from his view. In picture 4 baby's gaze has shifted over and down to his left window; no ball has yet arrived, and in picture 5 he cross-looks into the other window *pages 22-7*

Tables

Contributors

Ibinabo Agiobu-Kemmer
Psychological Laboratory, University of St Andrews, Scotland, and Department of Psychology, University of Lagos.

Robert Bundy
Department of Psychology, University of Lagos.

H. Valerie Curran
Institute of Psychiatry, University of London.

Brenda Meldrum
Thomas Coram Research Unit, University of London, Institute of Education.

Penny Milner
Psychological Laboratory, University of St Andrews, Scotland.

Alastair Mundy-Castle
Department of Psychology, University of Lagos.

Anya Oyewole
Department of Child Health, University College Hospital, Ibadan.

Christopher A. Saunders
Hertfordshire College of Higher Education, Watford, Herts.

Andrew Whiten
Psychological Laboratory, University of St Andrews, Scotland.

1 Introduction

H. Valerie Curran

This book brings together some of the major studies of Nigerian children. In writing it, we had in mind the university or college student whose courses incorporate child development: students of psychology, education and teaching. Anyone carrying out research with Nigerian children will find this book especially useful, both for the data it provides and for its treatment of a wide range of research techniques and methods.

Further, we would like to think that this book will be read by those actively involved with education in Nigeria. Each author has drawn out the educational implications of the results of his or her own study. These will interest not only the 'professional' educators who work in educational administration and planning or who teach in schools. They will also concern those who educate the child long before he enters a classroom – his parents and caretakers. Indeed several of the chapters stress that the major influences on a child's future achievement are not what happens to him in school after he is six years old. Rather, the main determinants are to be found long before that in the learning opportunities provided by his social and physical environment since he was born.

Nigerian children

When I told a non-psychologist friend of mine that I was editing this book, she asked me why it was just about Nigerian children. On reflection, her question was not so strange. After all, most books on child development do not have titles referring to the nationality of the children whose development they talk about.

Usually their titles refer to 'child development' in general; or to aspects of it, such as socialisation, perception or cognition; or to the particular approach taken to describing development, such as ethological, Piagetian or psychoanalytic. These books do not say they are *about* Swiss children or *about* middle-class North Americans or whoever were the actual children originally used in the research under discussion.

The obvious point is that such texts are generally based on the behaviour of Western children. And, moreover, their studies are usually based on the behaviour of Western children in very contrived situations which often bear little relation to those children's familiar environments. In the past decade, many psychologists have questioned the relevance and generalisability of such research to Western children's normal, everyday behaviour (e.g. Donaldson, 1978; Curran, 1980). How much more questionable, then, is its relevance to the behaviour of children in countries outside the West?

On that basis alone there is clearly a need for the Nigerian student and the Nigerian educator to have books on child development which are based on Nigerian children.

There is a second reason why we feel it is important to bring together these studies of Nigerian children. Nowadays virtually everyone accepts that a child's development reflects her complex and changing interactions with her particular social and physical environment. It follows from this that different environments may differentially affect how the child develops. So developmental variations may be found between children of, say, a small Nigerian village and urban Ibadan. Such variations are probably not in the social and intellectual abilities or competences of the two cultural groups. Indeed it is likely that such competences are universal (cf. Cole and Scribner, 1974; Dasen, 1977; Curran, 1980). Rather, cultural differences in *performance* appear to reflect differences in the ways those competences are organised and used for the particular task in hand.

I discuss this issue later on in more detail. It suffices here to simply make the point that once we accept the notion of organism-environment interaction, we also accept that different environments may differentially affect a child's development. Therefore we need to study the development of Nigerian children within Nigerian environmental and cultural contexts.

Third, it can be argued that just as aspects of people's behaviour reflect the particular culture in which they grew up, so too do *theories* of child development reflect aspects of the cultures in which they originated. As Ibinabo Agiobu-Kemmer points out in Chapter 4, the most popular theories of child development, having been formulated in the West, reflect Western philosophical thought. She notes, for instance, that Western psychologists divide man up into components – distinguishing his rational or cognitive aspects from his emotional or affective aspects. In contrast, many traditional African and Eastern approaches would emphasise the continuity and interdependence of these aspects of man.

That theories reflect the cultural preoccupations of their origins can be illustrated by Piaget's theory. This, the major theory positing *universals* in children's intellectual development, is almost totally concerned with *logical* abilities. It sees the child's development as culminating in those logical operations which are required for Western scientific thought.

Other cultural traditions would clearly have very different views of what constituted any endpoint of development. Rather than logical abilities alone, other cultures would probably place equal, if not more, stress and value on social and emotional aspects of maturation. Russian approaches, for example, emphasise the social and historical origins of man's thought processes (cf. Luria, 1976). Or again, much Chinese research has taken its framework from the Maoist theory of human conflict (cf. You-Yuh, 1976). Such studies are often neglected in the West mainly because they are investigating different issues from different perspectives and asking different questions about the growing child. Students should therefore study theories of child development from the viewpoint that they, like the children they are based on, have specific cultural origins. By working with children in their familiar cultural contexts, we can more clearly perceive the cultural relativeness of existing theories.

It also follows from this line of argument that current theories may not encompass aspects of development which are important outside the West. In other words, our cultural preoccupations may also restrict the comprehensiveness of our theories of development. Piaget (1972) himself mentioned the possibility that new mental structures may yet be discovered. And beyond such possibilities, we actually know that some cultures provide opportunities for learning and development which simply do not exist in the West and therefore are not considered by the predominant theories. Training in altered states of consciousness is one example (cf. Price-Williams, 1975). Another, which I discuss later (Chapter 5), relates to tone languages. Even though a majority of the world's languages are tone languages (cf. Fromkin, 1978) we know virtually nothing about them from a developmental viewpoint. Indeed, this fact in itself reflects cultural boundaries in the range of existing theories of development.

Finally, we would like to stress firmly here that in talking about 'Nigerian Children', we do not mean to neglect the vastly rich physical, social and linguistic variations in environments within Nigeria. Nigeria has many cultural groups and the studies reported in this book have involved very few of them. We hope that future researchers will be able to extend studies all over Nigeria, exploring both similarities and variations in the development of Nigeria's children. That will involve an extensive research effort, not the least because many cultural groups today are experiencing such rapid social change that their environmental influences will be very different a few years hence.

Developmental perspectives

Having emphasised the importance of studying Nigerian children within Nigerian cultural contexts, I now need to outline the developmental perspectives which have been used by the studies in the following chapters.

In studying child development, our main aim is to describe the changing nature of the child's interactions with her environment as she grows from birth to maturity. Many different perspectives may be taken in doing this: different in the methods and designs used; different in the aspects of development which are focussed on; different in the emphases placed on describing the nature of the child himself, the nature of his experiences in his environment, and the inter-relations between the two.

The *methods* which the studies use span a wide spectrum from, at one extreme, experiments in controlled, laboratory conditions to, at the other extreme, observations of children in their everyday, home environment. Interviews, surveys and questionnaires are also used in one or other study. This range of approaches is important in itself. As I implied earlier, it reflects the growing consensus in psychology that behaviour should be studied in a wide variety of settings and contexts, using a range of methods (cf. Blurton-Jones, 1972; Cole, 1975; Fodor, 1976; Curran, 1980). This is crucial when we view development as involving changes not only in the child's abilities, but also in the contexts in which she employs them. And clearly, the more varied our data sources, the more we are able to support and generalise the inferences we make from them.

The *designs* of different studies include a variety of group comparisons besides experimental ones. Children of different ages are compared either cross-sectionally or longitudinally (as in Anya Oyewole's research which follows the same group of children from one year until nineteen years of age). Children of different environments are compared, either across cultures or across less extreme divides such as urban versus rural habitats.

Where cross-cultural comparisons are made between Nigerian and non-Nigerian children, they have not been for any simple-minded reasons of seeing who performs better or worse. The misinterpretation of such group differences in performance hindered the progress of cross-cultural psychology for far too long (cf. Cole and Bruner, 1971; Curran, 1980). Rather, the purpose of cross-cultural comparisons is first to test how general our theories are – do they apply to children from diverse cultural backgrounds or are they restricted to particular cultural groups? This does not mean concentrating only on ways in which children are the same. A truly general theory should be able to predict both similarities and differences in children's psychological development. Second, because most of us accept the idea of organism-environment interaction it makes sense to look at how different environments affect child development. By allowing significant variation in the environments of the children we study, cross-cultural research can elucidate the nature of children's interaction with their social and physical surroundings. Third, on a more practical level, different cultures stand to learn a few lessons from each others' ways of caring for their children. For some examples of this point, the reader is referred to Chapters 3 and 4 in which Andrew Whiten and Penny Milner, and Ibinabo Agiobu-Kemmer, discuss how Nigerian and British mothers and caretakers could teach each other some lessons about interacting with their children.

The studies taken as a whole do not form any structure in terms of which aspects of child development they focus on. In no way does the book attempt any global coverage of social, emotional and cognitive growth; nor any chronology of development from birth to adulthood. The studies were selected for their careful research on issues in child development. Research which aims only to test children for assessing individual differences is excluded because it is not concerned with child development. (This type of research has, until recently, formed the bulk of work with Nigerian children, presumably because of perceived educational needs for standardised tests.) In introducing the following chapters in this book, I will look at which aspects of both the child and his experiences of his environment each study examines.

Two chapters (2 and 5) have taken perspectives on development which focus on the child and his changing abilities. Robert Bundy and Alastair Mundy-Castle (Chapter 2) use an experimental technique in controlled, laboratory conditions to study visual attention in infants. They are able to identify several stages in the child's acquisition of looking strategies. Those stages are qualitatively the same, and are acquired in the same sequence, by infants in both Nigeria and North America. The only cross-cultural differences found were in the ages at which infants entered certain stages. In trying to explain these, the authors consider differences in the environments of Nigerian and North American infants.

When speculating about environmental sources of differences in performance, it is useful to distinguish three senses of 'environment': first, the child's familiar, everyday environment; second, the environment in which the child's performance was examined; third, the relation between the first and second.

All three senses of 'environment' are considered in Bundy and Mundy-Castle's discussion. The first – differences in the two groups' everyday environments – is obviously a long list (cf. Campbell, 1961). The authors focus on differences in levels of visual stimulation or 'enrichment' for the two groups of infants. The second – differences in the experimental environment of the two groups – are treated carefully, but most importantly in terms of how those differences may have interacted with differences in their everyday environments (i.e. the 'third' sense of environment). For example, demand feeding by Nigerian mothers may have affected their infants' levels of arousal during the experiment.

Although no cross-cultural comparisons were involved, the same distinctions between environments were also important in my own study (Chapter 5). I had to consider how the situations in which I asked a child to perform various tasks related to her more everyday environment and its task demands. My study also focusses on children's abilities and how those change with age. It investigates the development of memory of children from six to twelve years of age. All the children involved were attending state primary schools in Ibadan.

Three perspectives were used to look at memory and this meant giving three distinct types of memory problems in different contexts. I used interview techniques as well as experiments. But my 'laboratory' was just a bench and table in the quietest place the school had available at the time. Based on children's performance in the different kinds of memory tasks, I conclude that children do not simply remember 'more' as they grow older. Rather, they remember more *because* they impose more meaning on, and extract more meaning from, what they are remembering. Age differences in memory performance depend on the meaningfulness of both the particular task and the context in which it is given. I end the chapter by discussing how schools could enhance children's memory performance.

In both Chapters 2 and 5, the authors concentrate on how children actively construe particular situations. By doing this, they could characterise developmental changes. However, when it came to interpreting differences in performance in terms of children's everyday environments, the authors could only speculate.

If any causative links between children's abilities and children's environments are to be made, then clearly we must start by studying *both* sides of the interaction.

This task was the aim of perhaps the two most ambitious studies in the book: Chapter 3 by Andrew Whiten and Penny Milner and Chapter 4 by Ibinabo Agiobu-Kemmer. These chapters report two parallel research projects, both with groups of 6-15-month-old infants in Nigeria and Britain. Each project involves direct observation of infants in their home environments and each uses Piagetian tasks to assess cognitive abilities.

In the introduction to their chapter, Andrew Whiten and Penny Milner give a clear and succinct account of the enormous problems involved in studying infant-environment interaction: first in recording the child's experiences of his environment; second, in adequately and reliably assessing his range of abilities; and third in relating the first to the second. Their chapter is primarily concerned with the infant's experiences and especially those seen as 'educational' – those which support his cognitive development. Whiten and Milner have developed a hierarchical classification of these experiences which relates subjective and objective categories of behaviour. On the basis of this classification, they discuss similarities and differences in the experiences of Nigerian and British infants, pointing out how both Nigerian and British parents have lessons to teach to and learn from each other.

A similar conclusion is drawn by Ibinabo Agiobu-Kemmer in Chapter 4. From direct observations of infants in their home environments, she reports cultural differences in children's playful interactions. These are qualitative rather than quantitative and are described in terms of three categories of play which she calls social, technical and socio-technical. These differences appear to affect the child's development differently at different ages. The young infant seems to benefit from traditional Nigerian child care practices, such as travelling on his mother's back. The older infant seems to gain from larger proportions of technical play involving objects, which was more a characteristic of the British infant's experiences.

Agiobu-Kemmer also argues that emotional factors may be as, if not more, important than cognitive factors for intellectual development during infancy. As Whiten and Milner's results also implied, there is a complex interaction between cognitive and affective aspects of early childhood development.

Both Chapters 3 and 4 highlight interesting issues for the young child's pre-school 'teachers' – his parents, siblings and other caretakers. For example, a recurrent theme, also noted in Chapter 2, is the breadth and richness of the social environment in which the Nigerian child lives. This is a very positive advantage, especially for the young child who can learn from the older children around him as well as from the adults. Whiten and Milner report how older children were often as creative, if not more so, as adults when they were showing infants what could be done with different objects. They go on to point out how this has educational potential and could be used to promote early learning in child-to-child based teaching programmes. Play-objects for such programmes could be made from cheap or free local materials and need not involve any sophisticated manufactured toys. Interestingly, Ibinabo Agiobu-Kemmer remarks that in her study the more toys there were around, the more adults played technical games with their infants. This could, however, mean that manufactured toys primarily increased the adults' (rather than the infants') interest in the interaction. Whichever way round the motivation lies, it would not detract from the author's argument for creating a cheap toy industry in Nigeria.

In Chapter 6, Anya Oyewole takes a very different approach to looking at children's interactions with their environments. Rather than directly observing children and recording their experiences, she collates data on specific factors in their environments. These factors she calls collectively the child's 'micro-ecology'. They include his levels of nutrition and health, the stability of his caretaking and certain socio-economic variables. She examines how those factors relate to children's later success at school.

Anya Oyewole's study is remarkable in using data on a large group of children who have been followed through from one to nineteen years of age. Her results have important educational implications, especially in showing the major disadvantage suffered by children who start school later than average. Oyewole concludes that although free primary education may mean that all children have equal access to schools, it does not mean that they have equal educational opportunity.

Anya Oyewole reports some disturbing findings on malnutrition among her sample of children from a traditional area of Ibadan. In the following chapter, Brenda Meldrum looks at the child-rearing practices (including the feeding and health care) of a group of mothers from that very same area.

Studies of child-rearing are commonly criticised because, in looking only at what is done *to* the child, one implicitly assumes that the child is a passive recipient of socialisation rather than a very active modifier of his environment. In this way such studies appear to neglect the child's major role in his interaction with his environment.

One case to which this criticism cannot be applied fully is the feeding and health care of the young infant. Obviously, the infant is active in these things – after all, he does the eating. His crying, sucking and sleeping patterns moderate the duration and frequency of feeding and so on. But he does not have quite such a major role as his caretaker in deciding whether to be breast or bottle fed, or what his first solids should be, or when and how to take medicines or be innoculated. It is therefore important to understand the caretaker's practices, attitudes and beliefs about those things – and crucially so when malnutrition results. As Brenda Meldrum argues, economic factors are not the only ones affecting a child's nutrition.

Her findings point to the positive aspects of traditional child care as compared with some of those imported from the West – as did the very different studies of Whiten and Milner and Agiobu-Kemmer. Despite obvious contrasts in their approaches, all those authors would therefore accord in warning parents against any indiscriminate adoption of Western types of childcare.

Clearly, the study of child development is not only about how a majority of children grow to maturity. There is a very important minority of children in every country who, due to a variety of factors, will either not follow typical developmental progressions or who will need special help in order to do so. Chapter 8 by Christopher Saunders is concerned with Nigerian children who have special needs.

Christopher Saunders reports a detailed survey of children in Plateau State which was carried out to estimate how many children had mental and/or physical handicaps. Clearly, if those children's special needs are to be met we have to know what their particular needs are and how many children require help. In doing this, Christopher Saunders also gives detailed discussions of the practical problems of carrying out surveys in Nigeria and the ways in which he coped with them. On the basis of his survey results, he is able to make some very concrete recommendations for both types and numbers of facilities which handicapped children need.

Finally, all the authors have been concerned to make this

book directly relevant to Nigerian students. And we all wanted to publish our work in a form which is easily obtainable and accessible. I would like to have included a lot more carefully carried out studies of Nigerian children, but was frustrated by the limited amount of such research available. I can only hope that this book will stimulate students and researchers to carry out their own studies of Nigerian children.

References

Blurton-Jones, N. (1972), 'Characteristics of ethological studies of human behaviour', in N. Blurton-Jones (ed.), *Ethological Studies of Child Behaviour*, Cambridge University Press.

Campbell, D.T. (1961), 'The mutual methodological relevance of anthropology and psychology', in F.L.K. Hsu (ed.) *Psychological Anthropology*, Dorset Press, Homewood, Ill.

Cole, M. (1975), 'An ethnographic psychology of cognition', in R.W. Brislin, S. Bochner and W.J. Lonner (eds), *Cross-cultural Perspectives on Learning*, Halstead Press, New York.

Cole, M. and Bruner, J.S. (1971), 'Cultural differences and inferences about psychological processes', *American Psychologist*, 26, pp. 867-76.

Cole, M. and Scribner, S. (1974), *Culture and Thought: a Psychological Introduction*, Wiley, New York.

Curran, H.V. (1980), 'Cross-cultural perspectives on cognition', in G.L. Claxton (ed.), *New Directions in Cognitive Psychology*, Routledge & Kegan Paul, London.

Dasen, P.R. (1977), 'Are cognitive processes universal? A contribution to cross-cultural Piagetian psychology', in N. Warren (ed.), *Studies in Cross-Cultural Psychology*, Academic Press, New York.

Donaldson, M. (1978), *Children's Minds*, Fontana, London.

Fodor, J.A. (1976), *The Language of Thought*, Harvester Press, Hassocks, Sussex.

Fromkin, V.A. (1978), *Tone: A Linguistic Survey*, Academic Press, New York.

Luria, A.R. (1976), *Cognitive Development, its Cultural and Social Foundations*, Harvard University Press.

Piaget, J. (1972), 'Intellectual evolution from adolescence to adulthood', *Human Development*, 15, pp. 1-12.

Price-Williams, D.R. (1975), 'Primitive mentality – civilised style', in R.W. Brislin, S. Bochner and W.J. Lonner (eds), *Cross-cultural Perspectives on Learning*, Halstead Press, New York.

You-Yuh, K., (1976), 'China', in V.S. Sexton and H.K. Misiak (eds), *Psychology around the World*, Brooks Cole, Belmont, California.

2 Looking strategies in Nigerian infants: a cross-cultural study

Robert Bundy and Alastair Mundy-Castle

Introduction

Although most mothers might claim that their newborn children have some rudimentary form of vision, quite what it is that a baby can see, and how much he is in control of incoming stimulation, remain matters for speculation and research. At birth the neurophysiology of the visual system is immature, but develops rapidly during the first five months of life (see Trevarthen 1980). However, both observation and research indicate that varying degrees of visual awareness are present and developing from the moment of birth. Furthermore, experiments involving the presentation of human faces indicate that a baby can recognise his mother's face as distinct from that of a stranger as early as two weeks of age (e.g. Carpenter 1975). In this instance the child is not only responding differentially to varieties of stimulation, he is also exhibiting an ability to interpret information – he is perceiving.

Apart from the interpretation of a stimulus pattern, a second important feature of visual perception is the extent to which an infant can control incoming stimulation by attending to selected aspects of his sensory environment. Visual attention involves the ability to distinguish figure from ground in the visual field, and also the visuo-motor co-ordination necessary to look at an object of interest in the right place at the right time. Thus the early development of perception involves an intimate association between both physiological and cognitive processes.

Since infants cannot describe what they are seeing, a variety of methods have been developed which rely on the direct observation of behaviour to indicate the state of their visual development. A smile, a frown, a startled expression, the frequency and duration of looking at a visual display, and others have been used by researchers to measure such variables as acuity, discrimination, identification and interest. Although many of these studies had dealt at length with the development of recognition, depth perception, colour discrimination and spatial relationships in the visual field, little attention had been paid to spatial-temporal relationships until the early 1970s. The development of the ability to appreciate changes in a visual display in terms of time as well as space was relatively unexplored.

In this respect, a particularly fruitful method was developed by Mundy-Castle and Anglin (1974), in which infants were seated in front of a screen containing two windows into which bright shiny balls could be lowered according to a programme. A ball was presented in either left or right window in an alternating sequence of thirty trials, with the exceptions of trials 15 and 28 where the presentation was repeated in the same window, thus providing two 'violation trials' (see Mundy-Castle, 1970). The sequence and duration of looking into the windows was recorded using a multichannel pen recorder by two observers, each positioned behind a one-way mirror behind either left or right window, as shown in Figure 2.1. This method allows observation of the development of the co-ordination of both spatial and temporal aspects of a changing visual display, including the ability to anticipate, and is the methodological basis for the research reported in this chapter.

Results of their study carried out in Cambridge (Massachusetts, USA) on 135 infants ranging in age from 10 days to $8\frac{1}{2}$ months led Mundy-Castle and Anglin to identify three developmental stages of looking in the experiment context. Stage 1 was characterised by long periods of fixation in which the babies were apparently 'oblivious of the fine structure of events' (1974, p. 715) in their visual field. They tended to stare fixedly into one window, paying little attention to the ball. In the second stage, infants paid direct attention to the balls, anticipating their appearance and 'co-ordinating their behaviour with the pattern of events' (p. 717). Stage 3 was characterised by active visual search of both windows and other phenomena in the visual field. Stage 3 infants would look at the balls, check empty windows

Figure 2.1 *Cross-section diagram showing one observer (o) of the two who watch the baby (b) each through a one-way mirror (m), their heads covered by a dark cloth (d) to aid one-way vision. The baby watches the ball (s) which is raised and lowered automatically through windows (w) in screen (c). The observers control the balls and signal when the baby is looking through their window by means of a switch (p) connected to the recording device (r) and automatic presentation control box (a) in a separate room (x)*

and search around and above the windows frequently and with apparent purpose.

The appearance of the three stages was independent of sex, and roughly correlated with age: youngest infants used the Stage 1 looking strategy, while Stages 2 and 3 were acquired at approximately 1-2 months and 2-3 months respectively. The qualitative identification of the three stages was reinforced by quantitative data in terms of (a) the 'number of looks' at a ball or at the window where a ball was most recently presented, (b) the number of 'cross-looks' at the window opposite that of presentation, and (c) 'average fixation time'.

Continued experimentation from 1974 to the present, with 90 Nigerian babies ranging in age from five days to ten months, in Lagos, has led to the refining of the three stages.

Firstly, it was observed that some children exhibited more

Table 2.1   *Stages and sub-stages of looking in the experimental context*

Stage	Characteristics	Sub-stage	Characteristics
1	long periods of fixation little or no attention to the balls themselves oblivious to the fine structure of visual events	1.1	fixation usually on lower edge of one window no apparent attention to the balls
		1.2	fixation in window rather than on edge attention occasionally attracted to the balls
2	looks into windows match sequence of visual events (appearance of balls) anticipation of ball's appearance	2.1	little anticipation
		2.2	frequent anticipation attention still restricted to balls and windows occasional cross-looking
3	Stage 2 characteristics plus: active visual search coverage of whole visual field (peripheral phenomena as well as balls and windows)	3.1	frequent cross-looking *or* trajectory tracking
		3.2	frequent cross-looking *and* trajectory tracking

than one stage of looking behaviour. Looking strategies are acquired in a developmental sequence. But one strategy does not necessarily replace another. An infant is assessed at his most sophisticated stage of looking, but may still employ a less sophisticated looking strategy from time to time. Secondly, each stage is recognised as comprising two sub-stages (see Table 2.1).

The first sub-stage of Stage 1 involves long periods of fixation, usually on the lower edge or corner of one window. Prolonged looking is also observed in the second sub-stage, Stage 1.2, although looking is now directed more towards the ball itself, and from time to time towards the ball appearing in the other window. In both Stage 1.1 and 1.2 the baby's fixation remains singularly constant. If the mother moves the baby's head, the direction of gaze adjusts to retain the same point of fixation, and distress may result if the baby is forced to look somewhere else.

In Stage 2, attention is paid directly to both balls. The first sub-stage, Stage 2.1, involves a looking strategy closely linked to the appearance of the balls, with some evidence of anticipation. In Stage 2.2 anticipation is frequent: as soon as a ball disappears the gaze rapidly switches to the other window to await the arrival of the ball. Anticipation in this stage is maintained even if the arrival of the next ball is unusually delayed.

Whereas Stage 2 looking is largely confined to the balls themselves, Stage 3 is characterised by active search of the visual field, where objects outside the windows may attract the baby's attention from time to time. Furthermore, frequent cross-looking is observed, whereby both windows (and ball if present) are monitored in quick succession. From time to time the infant may watch the ball disappear about the top margin of the window, and follow the imaginary path of the ball on upwards with his gaze. At the highest point the gaze may cross over and down to meet the appearance of the ball at the top of the other window. This phenomenon is termed 'trajectory tracking'. In Stage 3.1 *either* cross-looking *or* trajectory tracking is observed, although cross-looking appears to characterise the majority of Stage 3.1 infants observed. However, an infant may be said to have acquired Stage 3.2 when both cross-looking and trajectory tracking appear in the same experimental session.

Although the acquisition of these stages and substages is roughly correlated with age, new acquisitions are not considered to imply the discarding of old strategies. For example, although an older infant may appear to use Stage 3.2 most of the time, he still might use less differentiated stages of looking from time to time, even Stage 1.1.

Comparison of data from Nigeria and USA

The Cambridge babies were from middle-class white American families. These infants were habitually exposed to visually exciting influences such as television, mobiles strung across cots and baby-carriages, and other 'creative playthings'.

In contrast the Nigerian babies came from lower-income Yoruba and Ibo families in the Idi-Araba, Itire, Lawanson and Mushin areas of Lagos. Home visits revealed that these infants were rarely exposed to the so-called visually enriching stimulation of their American counterparts. They did, however, experience a high level of stimulation from parents, members of their families, peers and others. Mobiles were never encountered, toys were scarce, and none had television. Cots and baby-carriages were not observed, infants usually sleeping with their mothers and spending most of their waking hours being carried or cared for by both adults and young children. Thus the Lagos environment might be described as more social and less technical than the Cambridge environment (see Agiobu-Kemmer's chapter in this volume).

The procedure of the Cambridge study was effectively replicated, except that, due to technical difficulties, no violation trials were included in the presentation sequence. As in Cambridge, mothers and offspring were allowed to become accustomed to the laboratory before the test period. Testing involved at least thirty presentations of $6\frac{1}{2}$ seconds each, with inter-trial intervals of $3\frac{1}{2}$ seconds. Often, when the baby's interest was maintained, more than thirty presentations were given, although only the first thirty were used for analysis. Dr (Mrs) Odiakosa of the Institute of Child Health, Lagos University Teaching Hospital, was on hand to confirm that the babies were in good health.

Results

As in Cambridge, the stimulus situation held the attention of the Lagos infants adequately in almost all cases. A small number of the older infants cried, but most completed the thirty trials, their attention being held even with tears in their eyes. Plate 1 shows a male aged forty days watching a ball in a window and extending his hand towards it.

The looking strategies of subjects were categorised according to the three stages and their sub-stages, while numbers of looks, cross-looks, and average fixation times were quantified from the chart of the pen recorder. Figure 2.2 shows some typical chart records illustrating the three main stages; these recordings are

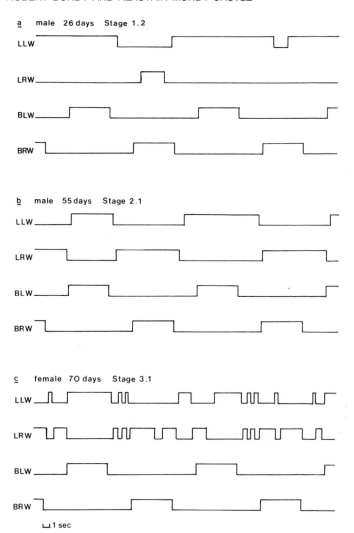

Figure 2.2 *Sample recordings of three looking strategies*
There are four tracings in each of the above three samples. LLW
indicates looking into baby's left window, LRW indicates looking into
baby's right window, BLW indicates ball in baby's left window, BRW
indicates ball in baby's right window. Sample *a*: Stage 1.2, gaze directed
mostly into left window with one look to right window. Sample *b*: Stage
2.1, matching of looks with appearance of balls, two instances of
anticipation. Sample *c*: Stage 3.1, frequent cross-looking especially
during the inter-trial intervals. No trajectory tracking was observed.

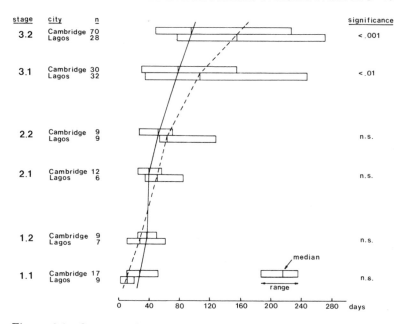

stage	city	n
3.2	Cambridge	70
	Lagos	28
3.1	Cambridge	30
	Lagos	32
2.2	Cambridge	9
	Lagos	9
2.1	Cambridge	12
	Lagos	6
1.2	Cambridge	9
	Lagos	7
1.1	Cambridge	17
	Lagos	9

significance:
< .001
< .01
n.s.
n.s.
n.s.
n.s.

Figure 2.3   *Stages and ages – Cambridge and Lagos*

very similar to those of Cambridge infants published by Mundy-Castle and Anglin (1974, p. 717). In general, looking strategies were observed to be the same in Lagos as Cambridge. This is further supported by Plates 2 and 3, and 4-13, which show photographic comparisons of Nigerian and American infants in Stages 1.2 and 3.2 respectively.

Figure 2.3 shows a graphic comparison of quantitative measures from Nigeria and USA. It shows that the age composition of each stage and sub-stage follows the same trend for both Cambridge and Lagos infants. However, application of the median test indicates that age differences at the 1 per cent level of significance appear with Stage 3 (age composition corrected for differences in upper and lower margins of age ranges in Stages 3.2 and 1.1 respectively). The age composition of Stage 3.1 is relatively older for Lagos infants, while more younger infants in Cambridge are to be found in Stage 3.2 than in Lagos. This implies that Cambridge infants use the strategies of Stages 3.1 and 3.2 at earlier ages than Lagos infants.

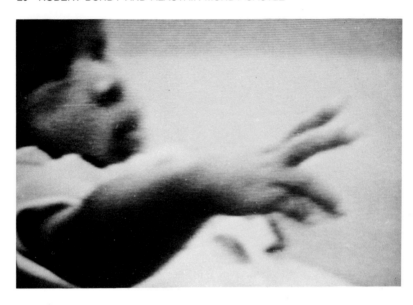

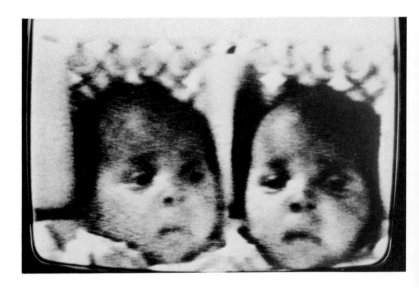

1 Sideview of male Lagos baby aged 40 days in Stage 1.2. He is looking at the ball in his right window and extends his right arm and fingers towards it. The patterning of his fingers is suggestive of reaching and grasping

2 and 3 Comparison of Lagos male aged 33 days and Cambridge male aged 39 days. Both exhibit the fixed gaze of Stage 1.2. The Cambridge photograph was taken through the baby's right-hand window, with a mirror reflecting the image of the ball in the other window. The Lagos photograph was taken from video-tape showing pictures through both windows presented adjacently on a split-screen monitor

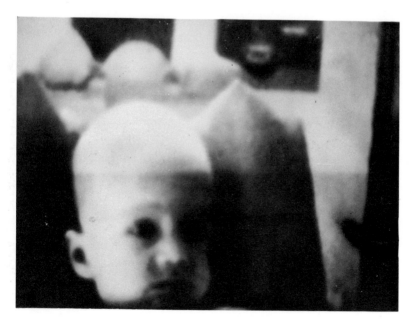

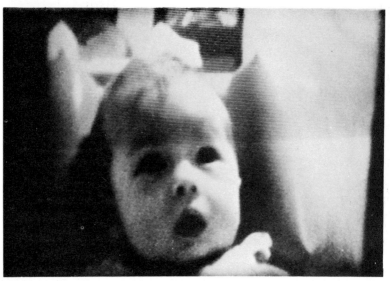

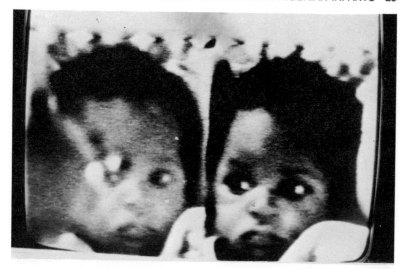

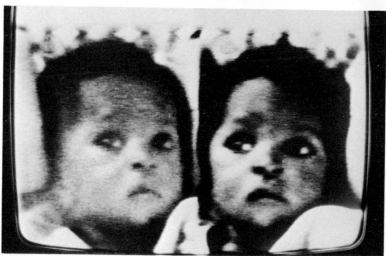

4 to 13 Sequential photographs of trajectory tracking and cross-looking in American male aged 76 days and Nigerian male aged 90 days. Photographs at approximately ½ second intervals. In top picture of each sequence, baby is looking at ball in his right window. In pictures 2 and 3, baby's gaze follows upward path of ball that has been withdrawn from his view. In picture 4 baby's gaze has shifted over and down to his left window; no ball has yet arrived, and in picture 5 he cross-looks into the other window

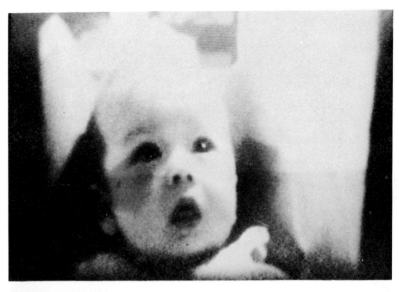

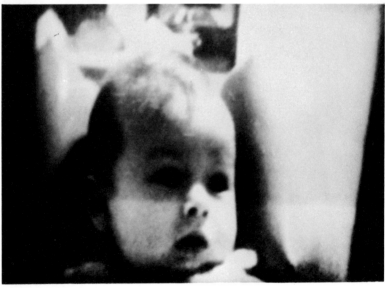

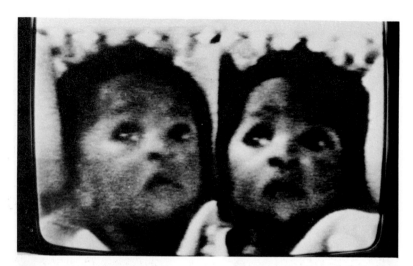

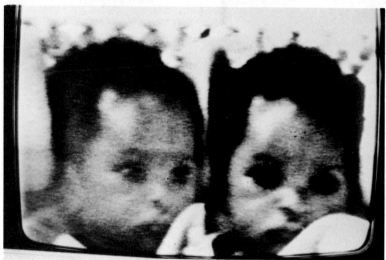

A similar result can be inferred from Figure 2.4, where infants are grouped according to their ages. A few Cambridge infants of less than one month of age were observed in Stage 2, while all of the same age Lagos infants were in Stage 1.1 or Stage 1.2. From five months of age, a greater percentage of Lagos infants were in Stage 3.1 and by seven months, although some Lagos infants were in Stage 3.1 all of the Cambridge sample had acquired Stage 3.2. This again suggests an earlier transition from Stage 3.1 to Stage 3.2 in the Cambridge sample.

A further look at Figure 2.4 indicates that the most important transitional age is 1-2 months for both groups of babies. At this age we observe infants in almost all the stages. It appears that this is a period where individual differences in the use of looking strategies are most marked in both samples.

The foregoing results are based on observational categorisation of looking behaviour into stages and sub-stages. These stages are identified by observation and classified by qualitative criteria such as cross-looking and anticipation. We then made a quantitative comparison in terms of number of looks, number of cross-looks and average fixation time.

A subsample of Lagos infants was matched for age with Mundy-Castle and Anglin's (1974) sample from less than one

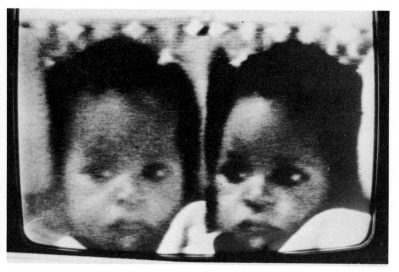

month of age to eight months of age. Figure 2.5 indicates that older infants in Cambridge looked more frequently, and correspondingly had lower average fixation times than their Lagos peers. This difference is significant after the age of five months. However, there is little difference in the number of cross-looks between the two groups except at the age 1-2 months.

Two further observations were noted in the Lagos sample that corresponded closely with observations from the Cambridge sample. First, during the experimental period some infants occasionally changed their looking strategy from one stage to a lower stage, particularly from Stage 2.1 to Stage 1.2. Second, chart records of looking after the presentation sequence had finished typically showed that infants in Stages 2.1 and 2.2 anticipate the appearance of the ball that never comes – and await its arrival long after the time when it should have appeared. Infants who have acquired the cross-looking of Stage 3 rapidly check back and forth from window to window for a considerable period following the final stimulus.

Taken together, this analysis appears to indicate that:
(a) infants in both Cambridge and Lagos use similar looking strategies occurring in the same developmental sequence;
(b) Cambridge infants appear to be more visually active in the

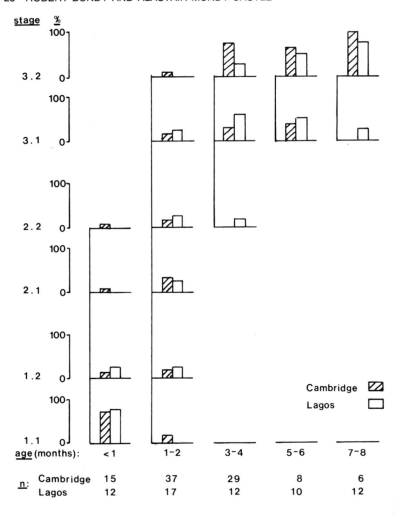

Figure 2.4 *Percentages of stages in each age group*

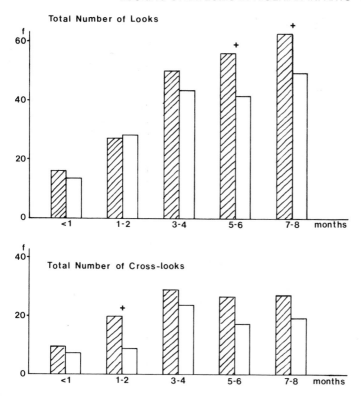

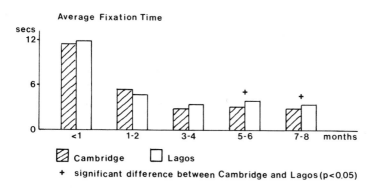

Figure 2.5 *Looking data – age group averages*

context of the experiment, using the strategies of Stage 3 at a slightly younger age than Lagos infants. This difference appears to emerge from about the fifth month onward, in the transition from Stage 3.1 to Stage 3.2.

Discussion

The results of this comparison between Lagos and Cambridge samples indicate that infants in both Nigeria and America use the same looking strategies, and acquire them in the same order. Thus it appears likely that there are universal patterns of infant looking behaviour. Intercultural differences, if any, relate to the age, rather than the order, of acquiring these patterns.

The differences observed after the fifth month might be derived from the visual enrichment given by middle-class American mothers to their children, absent among their Lagos counterparts. However, the comparison under consideration does not allow a firm conclusion if we take into account possible differences in arousal between the two groups at the time of testing.

Although the acquisition of looking strategies appears to be roughly correlated with age, the observation that infants sometimes revert from one looking strategy to a lower one – possibly associated with sleepiness – indicates that arousal may also be a salient factor in the level and quality of visual activity at any given moment. Indeed there appears to be a similarity between the Stage 1.1 of a three week old baby, and the 'fixating without focussing' or 'staring into space' that adults sometimes experience either when absorbed in reflective contemplation or during times of relaxed wakefulness. Furthermore differences in levels of arousal might be expected to have more effect on looking behaviour when active visual search is part of the repertoire (Stage 3) than with the less differentiated looking strategies. And it is in Stage 3 that differences are significant between the two groups.

The most likely arousal factor is the inclusion of violation trials in the Cambridge stimulus sequence, which were not present in the Lagos programme. Violation trials, included to guard against habituation, would act as an arousal agent, especially in Stage 3 where both windows are monitored in quick succession. Any departure from the established pattern of presentation is likely to increase the frequency of cross-looking, and therefore encourage more visual activity. This is particularly so at the more active level of Stage 3 where the differences between Lagos and Cambridge were observed. Violation trials at earlier stages of looking are unlikely to be noticed, as is implied by looking behaviour after the termination of the presentation sequence. Stage 2 infants appear quite happy to await the ball that never comes, and do not check back at the other window. Stage 3 infants on the other hand search rapidly in both windows until, after a while, other events in the visual field claim their attention.

A further possibility derives from the observation that Lagos mothers fed their children on demand. It was quite common to observe mothers giving breast to their infants while awaiting their turn in the laboratory. Thus it is possible that the Lagos babies were more satisfied and less aroused than the Cambridge babies. If this is true, it is likely that fewer Lagos than Cambridge babies were excluded from the study through over-arousal leading to persistent crying.

While the reason for the differences in the age of acquisition of Stage 3 remains in question, the nature of the looking strategies appears confirmed, lending support to the developmental significance of each strategy. Commenting on the work of Mundy-Castle and Anglin (1974), Bower (1979) gives evidence to show that infants below the age of 5 months can appreciate an object in terms of either its place or its movement, but not both at the same time. The observation of trajectory tracking is evidence of the child integrating both place and movement simultaneously. Mundy-Castle (1980), in agreement with Bower, points out that Stage 1 babies are 'perceptually absorbed in a unitary place', while Stage 2 babies are aware of the 'existence and location of two separate places, but not of movement between them'. Stage 3 then represents the mental co-ordination of place and movement (p. 244).

Mundy-Castle (1970) also pointed out that the mental co-ordination of place and movement is a prerequisite for the appreciation of causal relationships. Such a co-ordination represents the beginnings of the ability to understand space-time relationships, and serves as a basis for predictive interpretation of the world around us. This major developmental step, evidenced by the acquisition of the looking strategy of Stage 3.2, is sometimes taken as early as two months of age, both in Cambridge and Lagos.

Postscript

Preliminary analysis of results from a similar experiment testing the alternative hypotheses raised in this chapter to explain observed differences between Cambridge and Lagos babies indicates that neither the presence of violation trials nor general state of arousal relate to looking performance in the experimental context. It therefore seems likely that 'visual' enrichment' may be responsible for the earlier age of acquisition of Stage 3 by Cambridge babies. However, the concept of 'visual enrichment' needs to be refined. Although Lagos babies may not experience mobiles, television, toys and suchlike, they do experience a profusion of movement and colour. When carried on the back of their mother, aunt or sister, Lagos babies experience the bright colours and shapes of the cloth against which they are held, and also are exposed to the colourful, dynamic environment in which their families live. When being cared for and awake, the absence of toys does not preclude household objects, and, of course, people. The concept of 'visual enrichment' requires a greater degree of definition and understanding than is presently available. Until this is achieved, and the relation between social and non-social aspects of the environment and their effects on development are better understood, it would be premature to make pronouncements on the 'proper' way to raise an infant.

Acknowledgments

The research in Lagos was supported by a grant from The Nuffield Foundation, to whom we express our gratitude. Thanks are also due to our many collaborators, notably Dr (Mrs) O. Odiakosa, Mr E. Kayode, Miss E. Akinsola, Mrs N. Darnton and Dr Hajia R. Abdullahi.

References

Bower, T.G.R. (1974), *Development in Infancy*, Freeman, San Francisco.
Bower, T.G.R. (1979), *Human Development*, Freeman, San Francisco.

Carpenter, G. (1975), 'Mother's face and the newborn', in R. Lewin (ed.), *Child Alive*, Temple Smith, London.

Mundy-Castle, A.C. (1970), 'The descent of meaning', *Social Science Information*, 9, pp. 125-142.

Mundy-Castle, A.C. (1980), 'Perception and communication in infancy', in D.R. Olson (ed.), *The Social Foundations of Language and Thought*, Norton, New York.

Mundy-Castle, A.C. and Anglin, J.M. (1974), 'Looking strategies in infants', in L.J. Stone, H.T. Smith and L.B. Murphy (eds), *The Competent Infant*, Tavistock, London.

Trevarthen, C. (1980), 'Neurological development and the growth of psychological functions', in J. Sants (ed.), *Developmental Psychology and Society*, Macmillan, London.

3 The educational experiences of Nigerian infants

Andrew Whiten and Penny Milner

Introduction

We all know that a child's interactions with its environment influence its development, don't we? From developmental scientists to parents, who would doubt it?

But think for a moment just how we know. To be more specific, how would we know that specific experiences in everyday life have particular effects on the developing child?

First of all, we have to describe and record the experiences, and there are a number of difficulties here. For one thing, there is more to any one experience than can be perceived by the observer of the child's interaction with his environment; incoming information is interpreted by the developing brain on the basis of past experiences (e.g. Kagan *et al.*, 1978, p. 5) and its storage involves integration with these. What is superficially the same set of environmental inputs may constitute different experiences for different children, or for the same child at different ages. To put this same point the other way round, the *same* category of experience may be provided for different children by *different* environmental configurations. In addition, there is no reason to think that this process of integration of experiences is not continuous during the child's waking, and possibly sleeping or dreaming, life. Recording of experiences thus presents a considerable practical problem. Most research on child-rearing practices has not even attempted to record these through direct observation but has relied on interviews with parents such that White *et al.* (1979) can list just five studies which have seriously attempted to directly sample significant portions of the stream of developing children's experiences.

There are many other difficulties to surmount in recording experiences (White *et al.*, 1973, 1978; Whiten, 1977), but those already mentioned are sufficiently fundamental to emphasise that this first task is not straightforward. The second task is to record outcomes, and the favourite of developmental psychologists is, of course, the intelligence quotient. Testing IQ has its own difficulties which I shall not discuss here; Lewis (1976) may be consulted for a general critique, and Vernon (1969) and Le Vine (1970) for discussions of the use of American and European tests in Africa. There has been little attempt to go beyond this to meet Lewis and Coates' (1976) demand for a framework which would 'allow us to compare specific interactions with specific outcomes'. White *et al.*'s (1973, 1978, 1979) valiant attempt to do so, by exploring the origins of a range of intellectual and social competencies, very honestly acknowledges the many serious difficulties this involves. For brevity just one may be mentioned as an illustration: nobody has yet designed tests which assess the manifest sophisticated competencies of children in the sphere of social interaction at all adequately, despite the importance of this in everyday life. And, of course, the alternative to this, assessing children's spontaneous performances, is likely to be influenced by differences in the uncontrolled context of such performances.

The third task in assessing developmental effects is to relate the recorded experiences to the outcomes. The most common technique is that of statistical correlation: are children who have had more of some experience more likely to show a particular outcome? However, such correlations can never demonstrate cause and effect in development. If it were found that children who were beaten as infants tended to be more aggressive when they grew up, this would not prove that the beating caused this particular developmental outcome. Both characteristics may have been independently caused by something else. Examples of possible alternative explanations of the correlation might be that children of parents who beat their infants genetically inherit a tendency to grow up aggressive, or that aggressive people behave in infancy in such a fashion as to elicit beating.

The only way to prove cause and effect is by experimentation. If we took a sample of parents and randomly assigned them to two groups, one of which we got to beat their children, then, with a specifiable confidence, we could say that any greater tendency to aggression when the children grew up must have been caused by the beating. The alternative explanations discussed in the previous example cannot now apply.

However, there are a number of problems in conducting experiments in child-rearing. In the first place there is an ethical question of course; one does not want to perform an experimental manipulation which may have harmful effects, yet, as argued above, until it has been done one cannot know if that will be the case. Always there is the doubt that some desirable developmental outcome is effected only at the expense of some other achievement, which is not under study. Even when the manipulation is suspected to be beneficial, the experiment may not be easy to implement. In particular it is difficult to be sure that the only difference between control and experimental groups is the experience intended; White et al. (1979) found that a major influence in their experiment was the mere visiting of the home by the experimenters rather than the precise experiences provided!

All this should serve to emphasise that reliable knowledge about whether and how specific experiences in everyday life have particular effects on the developing child is not easy to come by. It is the product only of a long and carefully conducted research effort. I hope that much of what passes for such knowledge will be critically scrutinised before acceptance, particularly by those students newly embarked upon exploration of developmental science to whom this chapter is principally addressed.

The natural history of children's experiences: two studies

In this chapter we shall be concerned mainly with attempts to do some justice to the first task – description of infants' everyday experiences – but in discussing the significance of these all the above cautions should be borne in mind.

Both studies have involved British and Nigerian infants, but not in order to make any simple comparisons of which were 'best'. Rather, such a broad cultural sample can support the theoretical side of developmental research through the use of its diversity to both generate and test hypotheses (Leiderman et al., 1977). And at a more pragmatic level, we wished to explore whether the parents of each culture might learn something about child-rearing from those of the other. It is on this basis that the results to be discussed from study 1 concern distress and comfort, where British parents may learn from Nigerian mothers; and infant education, where Nigerian parents may have something to learn from the British parents. Study 2 goes on to examine the latter topic in more detail.

Study 1: Infancy in Eluama, Nigeria and Oxford, England

1.1 RATIONALE

In Britain one of the biggest problems faced by parents with small infants is crying (Dunn, 1977). Picking the infant up and holding it is the most efficient way to stop this (Bell and Ainsworth, 1972) but many parents fear that this will 'spoil' the baby; that is, the infant will subsequently cry more and demand greater attention (Newson and Newson, 1963). In contrast, commentators on Nigerian infancy have noted that 'the child is fondly and warmly carried' (Durojaiye, 1976), 'all its needs are completely and promptly met' (Biesheuvel, 1959) and 'the African infant's experience seems to be ideal. His needs are better catered for than usually obtains in Western Europe, and it would seem that there is much to be said for adopting African practice in dealing with babies for the first few months of life' (Carothers, 1953). The apparent contradiction between such opinions about Nigerian child-rearing and the British concern with 'spoiling' led us to go beyond subjective impressions and quantify certain relevant categories of behaviour in both cultures. Our initial questions were simply: 'What *are* the differences in patterns of contact between infants and their caretakers in Britain and Nigeria?' and 'Which group of infants exhibits most crying?'

1.2 STUDY LOCATIONS AND METHODS

The twelve British infants lived around the Oxford area in England, and the fifteen Nigerian infants in the kindred of Eluama in an Igbo village, Owerri Ebeiri near Orlu. The latter study was conducted in collaboration with a Psychology Department undergraduate of Lagos University, A.E. Ibeh, in his own village. Background sample characteristics are shown in Table 3.1 (page 63).

Mothers were interviewed about a wide range of questions on child-rearing and child development, but the data summarised here are based on direct observation in the infants' everyday environments. Shorthand symbols for behavioural categories of the infant, its mother and other social companions were entered sequentially into a checksheet grid divided into ten-second time blocks, paced by an electronic timer delivering signals to a small ear-piece. A wide range of behaviour, including sequential relationships between infant behaviours and those of others, can be reconstructed from such analogue records.

Data for the British infants were collected in 50 hours of observation during 1973-5. The Nigerian data are derived from 56 hours of observation during a two-month period in 1975.

1.3 FINDINGS ABOUT DISTRESS AND COMFORT

Recall our first question about patterns of contact: the answer is expressed in Figure 3.1. At three months of age and whether awake or asleep, the Eluama infants spent much more time in contact with someone (Mann-Whitney U-test, $p < 0.001$). This included carrying the infant, but also sitting or lying with it on the lap or at the breast. Eluama infants also spent more of their time within the mother's reach when out of direct physical contact ($p < 0.001$). Which group of infants showed most distress? Figure 3.2 shows that at the age of three months, it is the Oxford infants who fussed ($p < 0.01$) and cried ($p < 0.025$) more. To this extent Carothers' opinion seems to be supported, so we went on to ask if there were any associated differences in the ways in which the Britons and Nigerians responded to infant distress. Figure 3.3 shows that the percentage of both cries ($p < 0.01$) and fusses ($p < 0.001$) which were ignored was smaller for the Eluama infants; also, Eluama caretakers responded slightly more quickly to the first signs of distress ($p < 0.025$). These latter data give the impression that caretakers in both cultures responded pretty quickly, in less than 15 seconds. This is true but slightly misleading in that the responses concerned are not distinguished. Figure 3.4 shows that in fact the profiles of responses are different, notably in that Oxford caretakers tended to respond more by talking than did the Nigerians ($p < 0.001$)

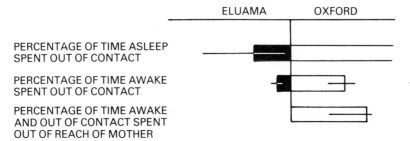

Figure 3.1 *Contact patterns*
Medians and interquartile ranges are shown for the percentage of time
infants spent out of body contact when asleep or awake, and the
percentage of the latter for which they were out of reach of the mother
(>3′), at three months of age.

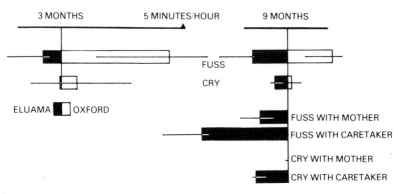

Figure 3.2 *Infant distress*
Medians and interquartile ranges are shown for the amount of fussing
and crying in minutes per hour at (a) three months and (b) nine months
of age. At nine months the Nigerian data are further dissected
according to whether the infant was in the care of its mother or a child
caretaker.

whereas Eluama caretakers responded 'physically' (p < 0.001),
that is, by picking up, rocking, patting or carrying.

To summarise: the Eluama caretakers responded more often,
more quickly and with contact rather than speech. All these
constitute 'spoiling' according to some British caretakers, yet
our data show that at three months the Eluama infants showed
less distress.

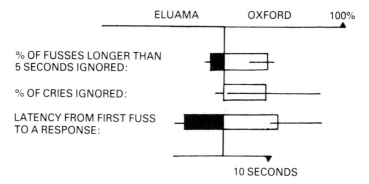

Figure 3.3 *Responsiveness of caretakers*
Medians and interquartile ranges are shown for the percentage of
fusses more than five seconds long and cries ignored, and the latency of
a first response to infant fussing, for infants three months of age.

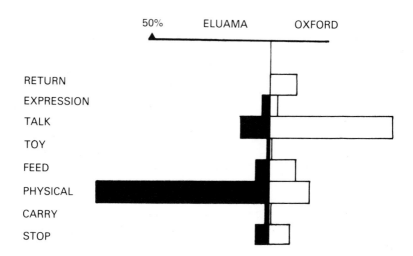

Figure 3.4 *Response profiles*
Each of several different types of response to infant fussing is shown as
the mean percentage of all responses made by caretakers of infants
aged three months. The responses are: RETURNS (approaches to
within reach), EXPRESSION (smiles or laughs), TALK (talks), TOY
(shows or provides manipulable object), FEED (milk or spoonfeed),
PHYSICAL (cradle, bounce, rock, pat, tickle, or pick up), CARRY (carry
along) and STOP (terminate activity causing distress, like dressing
infant).

But does this difference continue? Figure 3.2 shows that it does not, for at nine months there is no significant difference in either fussing and crying. However, this can be further analysed within the pattern of care at this age, and one of the values of observational fieldwork lies in making us aware of realities such as, in this case, the amount of time the infant now spends with a child caretaker. This caretaker would often take the infant into a mixed age group of children at play or working in the fields, and our impression was that this often rough environment explained much of the distress. This is borne out by the breakdown presented in Figure 3.2, of distress behaviour shown per unit time spent either with mother or child caretaker. When with the child caretaker, the infants actually showed more fussing ($p < 0.05$) and crying ($p < 0.05$) than Oxford infants. When with their mothers they showed less crying ($p < 0.05$) but not significantly less fussing than their Oxford counterparts.

Our conclusion is therefore double-edged. On the one hand the Eluama infants exposed to a 'spoiling' pattern of care showed less, rather than more, distress behaviour. Now what British mothers may learn from these Nigerian mothers is not that this pattern is necessarily better than theirs in any absolute sense. It cannot necessarily be transferred successfully from one culture to another, for we do not know what factors it may need to interact with for success – factors which may not be present in the foreign culture. What we can say is that British mothers do not need to worry so much as they seem to: it *is* possible to treat infants in the fashion of the Eluama mothers and, up to the age we have studied, have an infant who cries little. Similarly, there seems no reason why Nigerian mothers prone to Westernising their child-rearing patterns should embrace the notion of 'spoiling' at the expense of their traditional approach.

On the other hand, we are able to present hard data which, particularly for nine months of age, show that Nigerian infants do show distress and indeed, at the lower level of fussing, show not significantly less than British infants. This reality differs from the anecdotes and impressions which inspired this research, such as Biesheuvel's description of African infancy as a 'state of blissful security'.

Just how far these findings for Eluama can be generalised in Nigeria or indeed sub-Saharan Africa we cannot know; in particular it is difficult to know how 'traditional' is the pattern described above, in which by nine months the infant is spending nearly half its time with a child caretaker rather than with its mother. In contrast, Lambo's (1969) account of traditional ways was that 'in the early months, and sometimes up to the age of fifteen months, the child is inseparable from his mother who carries him on her back and feeds him at the slightest whimper'. However, the growing role of the child caretaker as the infant develops appeared to us not to be a means of coping with new, but rather traditional, forms of work which our rural mothers undertook away from home – notably farming and market trading. If this pattern is indeed related to agriculture, then it may have a history of thousands of years.

Research on child-rearing in hunting and gathering cultures of the kinds which characterised the prior and major part of human history has demonstrated a pattern much more like Lambo's description, but which often continues to weaning at three years of age without a role for child caretakers (Draper, 1976; Konner, 1977).

Findings about infant education

Although in this study we started out with specific questions, fieldwork of this kind often throws up new ones which had not been thought of before the observations were made. One set of behaviours which raised such questions are those we may call educational.

By infant education we do not mean nursery classes or playgroups. By the time children come to these, let alone school, they have learned a lot, and not totally by their own efforts. Some things they learn because of the behaviour of others. One category of such behaviour was called 'create possibilities', defined as 'performing an act intended to create a possibility for some action by the infant on an object'. It thus enhances the scope for an infant's interaction with objects. Now Figure 3.5 shows that this behaviour was more common in Oxford. This cannot be explained simply by lack of manufactured toys. Defining a toy as any manipulable object, the frequency with which different toys were manipulated was not significantly different for the two cultures, and the tendency for caretakers to offer a toy was greater for Eluama, although not significantly so.

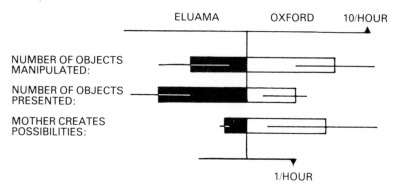

Figure 3.5 *Object play and infant education*
Medians and interquartile ranges are shown for the frequency per hour
at which nine-month-old infants manipulate different objects, and at
which caretakers provide manipulable objects or create possibilities.

The difference was rather in the more elaborate types of infant
education characterised by 'create possibilities'.

Whiten *et al.* (1980) speculated that:

> each of these styles of childrearing has been adaptive in
> relation to the wider culture, at least until recently. The
> Oxford infant, through the variety of teaching play we have
> referred to, is equipped with an elaborate repertoire of flexible
> and rather abstract skills which may eventually facilitate the
> transition to formal education and induction into a complex
> technological culture. He glimpses only small parts of the way
> the adult society earns its living.

> The Eluama infant's experience has, until recently, been
> different, for the ways of earning a living, the adult ecology,
> involved a set of relatively limited skills which could be
> picked up largely through direct observation. These are still
> acquired and practised by young children, and infants are
> involved early on in these groups where they can see 'adult'
> tasks, some done by children 'for real' and others incorporated
> into play. They have not needed to be extensively educated in
> a more abstract way in a separate home environment.

Durojaiye (1976) summarises the success of formal education
in Africa tersely: 'the wastage rate is alarming in every African

country's educational effort'. There are probably many reasons for this and several are suggested in Durojaiye's admirably conceived book. The above data suggest that one of them may lie in a pattern of child-rearing which has been adaptive but, in respect of early education, is becoming less so as the culture changes, and changes rapidly.

Accordingly, we made a second and more detailed study of this topic.

Study 2: Infant education in Eruwa, Nigeria

2.1 RATIONALE

There were two principal reasons for this study. One was the cross-cultural difference indicated by the data from Study 1, and its educational implications. The other was simply the lack of description and analysis in the developmental literature of the sorts of behaviour covered by or associated with the category 'creates possibility'. This project therefore aimed first of all to develop a classification for such behaviour, and then to quantify it for developing British and Nigerian infants.

2.2 STUDY LOCATIONS AND METHODS

For the most part we shall be concerned with some of our initial analyses of data from the Nigerian study, conducted in the Yoruba town of Eruwa. The main reason for expanding our research from a rural to an urban location was that we were now less concerned with studying traditional child-rearing, but rather with the current status of early education in the most common environment of the small town, midway between the sort of village in Study 1, and cities where something more like the British data might be expected. The British infants came from the Cupar and St Andrews areas in Scotland, two towns of similar size to Eruwa. It would, however, be a vain attempt to try to find locations in any other sense 'comparable' in the two countries (cf. Table 3.2, page 64).

The Nigerian data were collected over a six-month period in 1978. Having found it worked so well in Study 1, we repeated the practice of having in both countries one British and one Nigerian native language speaker conduct observations side by side, the latter in this case concerned with a separate but related topic of research (Agiobu-Kemmer, this volume).

The longer period of fieldwork allowed each infant to be studied longitudinally, being visited up to eight times at intervals of two weeks for $1\frac{1}{2}$-hour observation sessions. In this paper, however, we shall be concerned only with the mean of all sessions for each infant. There were eight infants in each of three age groups, $6-9\frac{1}{2}$, $8\frac{1}{2}-12$ and $11-14\frac{1}{2}$ months.

As in Study 1, mothers were told that we wanted to learn about how normal infants developed, and would be writing down what they did and what happened to them. They should therefore carry on as they would have if we were not there. It is unlikely that they did this perfectly, but we feel that after the first one or two sessions behaviour seemed to be fairly 'natural'. Data were recorded by pen and paper using the same system as for Study 1. However, the categories were different and their nature requires some explanation.

2.3 DESCRIBING THE EDUCATIONAL ENVIRONMENT OF INFANTS

The principal problem which we address concerns what we can loosely distinguish as *objective* versus *subjective* descriptive categories. Each of these has its special advantages, but severe disadvantages too. Description in subjective terms tends to lack precision and objective replicability, as Blurton-Jones (1972) made clear. For example, a category of maternal behaviour described as 'warm' is likely to be interpreted in different ways by independent observers (and high inter-observer agreement between particular collaborators in one study doesn't solve this problem of transfer to a new independent study – the real challenge of objectivity). On the other hand, using an objective measure such as frequency of a particular type of smile to assess a mother-infant relationship, although more scientific, neglects much that we as human beings know to be significant in the relationship, such as that conjured up by 'warmth'.

One answer to these problems is to use a mixture of relatively subjective and objective categories. But this only means that one's categories have a mixture of different flaws. To attempt a real reduction in flaws, we have adopted a hierarchical classification of forms of support to cognitive development which explicitly relates relatively objective and subjective behavioural categories in such a way as to capitalise on the better points of each. In this classification, clusters of categories at one level represent different ways of achieving the category at the level above them. Thus in Figure 3.6 PROVIDE STABLE BASE and SUPPORT MANIPULATION are alternative ways of achieving SUPPORT INTERACTION, and the latter and MODIFY INTERACTION are in turn alternative ways of doing CREATE POSSIBILITY. Such high-level categories tend to refer to relatively general functions served by them with respect to the infant's cognitive development. Low-level categories tend to be more concrete, defined as far as possible by their physical form.

The fact that such different types of category are combined in one system means that, on the one hand, the superficial subjectivity and vagueness of the high-level categories is avoided by their explicit relationship with the lower-level objective ones, yet, on the other hand, the potential triviality of the latter is avoided by their inclusion in the higher categories which are of wide functional significance.

Lindsay and Norman (1977) point out that definitions usually contain three components: the *class* to which the concept belongs, the *properties* which distinguish it from other members of that class, and concrete *examples*. Now, note that any *instance* of behaviour will be classed in one category of every level in the hierarchy (e.g. in Figure 3.6 it is the *same behaviour* which is classed as PROVIDE STABLE BASE and SUPPORT INTER-ACTION). Thus each category, besides its own explicit definition which corresponds to Lindsay and Norman's 'properties' in distinguishing it from its neighbours on that level, draws on all those definitions of categories connected to it at higher levels, which constitute its 'class', and all those definitions of categories beneath it, which provide ever more concrete 'examples'.

The present classification is the result of a slow evolution during about 500 hours of direct observation in Britain, 200 hours in Nigeria, and more detailed and repeated observations of 30 hours of play between British mothers and infants recorded on videotape.

In this paper we shall not describe all the categories. A full catalogue and more extensive explication of its nature is available from the authors (Whiten *et al.*, 1979 and in prep.). We would not, of course, claim that the classification is more than

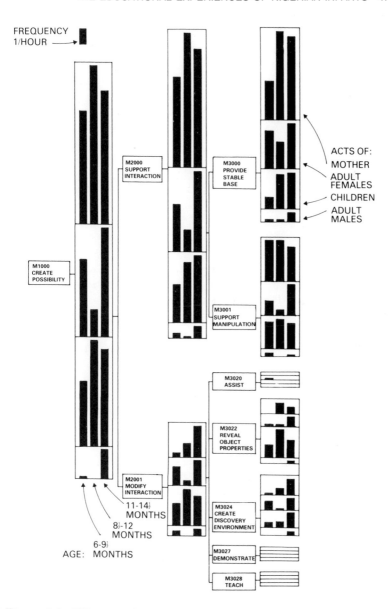

Figure 3.6 *Who provided infant education in Eruwa*
Median frequencies per hour for the major categories of CREATE
POSSIBILITY are distinguished according to four major classes of
people interacting with infants in each of three age groups.

one amongst an infinite number possible for the same phenomena. In many ways, too, it must be regarded as provisional, and in our current research it is being extensively revised. Nevertheless, we did find that nearly all examples of CREATE POSSIBILITY we observed during quantitative data collection in Nigeria were covered by the subcategories discussed below.

2.4 THE CONTENT OF THE MAJOR FUNCTIONAL CATEGORIES

Having outlined the nature of the system, some flavour of what sort of behaviour it covers may be given by a brief account of the major categories of levels 1-3. Complete definitions are given in the appendix. The concept of CREATE POSSIBILITY (Figure 3.6) has been broadened since Study 1. It includes all parental behaviour which creates the potential for enhancement of infant cognitive development through play with objects, and can be achieved in two ways distinguished at level 2. In SUPPORT INTERACTION, M (any individual who interacts with the infant) makes it more likely that B (the infant) will play with things but doesn't influence *what* B may learn – this depends only on interaction between the powers of B and the object's properties. At level 3, this involves either maintaining B in a state which makes play possible (PROVIDE STABLE BASE) or promoting contact with objects (SUPPORT MANIPULATION).

In the second level 2 category, MODIFY INTERACTION, M goes beyond simply increasing the likelihood of B interacting with objects; *what* B learns may be influenced by her behaviour. At level 3, this can be achieved by helping B (ASSIST), providing him with information (REVEAL OBJECT PROPERTIES), providing an environment in which he will discover things (CREATE DISCOVERY ENVIRONMENT), or teaching B how to do things, with or without further support of his own attempts (TEACH and DEMONSTRATE respectively).

2.5 THE EDUCATIONAL ENVIRONMENT OF INFANTS IN ERUWA

We can now proceed to examine the occurrence of these categories in the experience of the Nigerian infants, concentrating on the relative importance of the different categories at each level, developmental changes in the frequency of categories, and differences in who within the infant's world is responsible for them.

Figure 3.6 shows the frequency of high-level categories for each of the three age groups, broken down in terms of whether they are performed by the mother, other adult females, child caretakers, or adult males. Figure 3.7 gives more detail about the distributions for two interactants which earlier discussion drew attention to: mothers and child caretakers.

Note in Figure 3.6 that it is these two who accounted for more of the instances of CREATE POSSIBILITY, although other adult females (grandmothers, co-wives, neighbours and so on) together accounted for nearly as much as the children. Adult males, including the father, did very little of such behaviour, particularly in the infant's first year. However, our sampling tended to fall at times when men were away at work.

At level 2 (Figure 3.7) we see that most of CREATE POSSIBILITY is made up of SUPPORT INTERACTION, and the mother does most of this – particularly its subcategory PROVIDE STABLE BASE, concerned with the infant's motivational state. In contrast it is the child caretaker who does more of the educationally more elaborate MODIFY INTERACTION.

It is PROVIDE STABLE BASE which is responsible for any developmental changes in SUPPORT INTERACTION. The simple notion that a decreasing need for external support of non-distressed motivational state would be reflected in a corresponding gradual drop in PROVIDE STABLE BASE was denied by the low frequency for the younger age group. In fact if we look at this category in a little more detail (Figure 3.8), the frequency of the category COMFORT, concerned specifically with the emotion of distress, was highest for the middle age group, $8\frac{1}{2}$-12 months of age. This category demonstrated the biggest difference in mother and child caretaker roles, and was expressed mainly in terms of the categories CHANGE B's POSITION (M7020) and DISTRACT WITH TOY (M7030). Here may be the clue to the developmental change in COMFORT, for these acts can compensate for the infant's frustration when motoric incompetence interferes with access to and manipulation of objects in the middle age range; at a later age such incompetence is less common, and at the earlier age this particular type of exploratory motivation is less common. The two other sub-

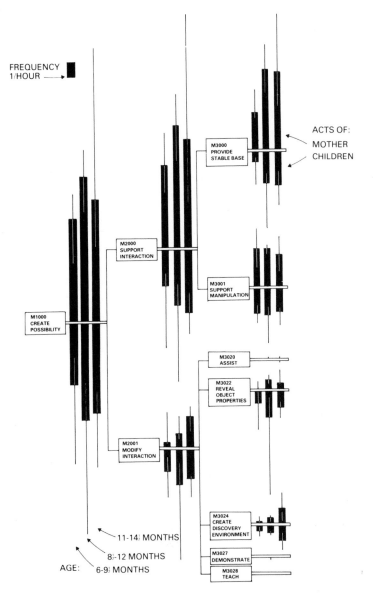

Figure 3.7   *The roles of mother and child caretaker in infant education
– CREATE POSSIBILITY*
As Figure 3.6 but contrasting mother and child caretaker roles,
expressed as medians with interquartile ranges. This format is
maintained in Figures 3.8 and 3.9.

categories of ELIMINATE UNDESIRABLE BEHAVIOUR –
MAINTAIN IN FIELD and RESTORE ATTENTION – did, in
contrast, exhibit a progressive increase which probably reflects
the infant's exploratory progression.

The low frequency of BACKGROUND PARTICIPATION
(M4001) is misleading in that it does not draw on two important

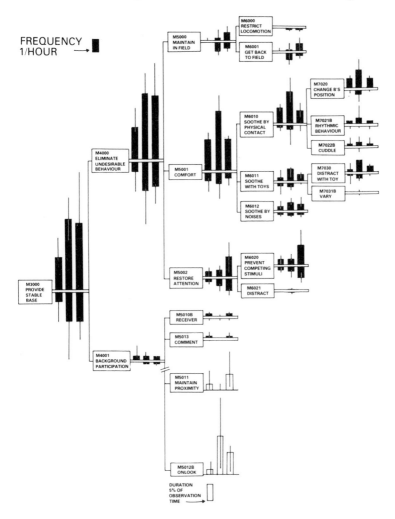

Figure 3.8 *The roles of mother and child caretaker in infant education
– PROVIDE STABLE BASE*
The format of Figure 3.7 is continued.

subcategories which are not easily expressed as event frequencies, but rather as the durations of states. It was possible to collect data on these for the mother only. ONLOOK (M5012B), in which the mother is simply watching the infant's play, like COMFORT followed a U-curve, being more common for the middle age range, whereas MAINTAIN PROXIMITY (M5011), where the mother moves close to the infant such that she could play with him, showed the opposite developmental change. Thus in these terms BACKGROUND PARTICIPATION took a more remote form for the middle age group. It seems possible that this fits a phase of infant play which is relatively solitary. In the later age group, more (and more elaborate) joint play of the mother-infant-object type is possible, although only the category CREATE DISCOVERY ENVIRONMENT (M3024) indicates an expression of this. In the younger age group we might expect that closeness of the mother would reflect infant dependence, but that the data for COMFORT contradict this. That is not necessarily so; the overall pattern for the middle age group may be to reduce, for these less dependent infants, the relatively direct participation of MAINTAIN PROXIMITY, monitoring the infant's independent exploration through ONLOOK and then with COMFORT coping with the frequent distress engendered.

SUPPORT MANIPULATION (Figure 3.9) was expressed mainly in terms of PROVIDE OBJECT (M5051), done equally by mothers and child caretakers. SUPPORT APPROACH (M4011) was rare, but notice that, as a subcategory of SUPPORT MANIPULATION, it must be concerned with objects; crawling and walking were often supported in their own right, with no objects involved. Of the two common subcategories of PROVIDE OBJECT, BRING NEAR (M6063B) appeared to become less necessary as the infant's locomotory prowess developed, but OFFER OBJECT (M6061B) continued. Our initial image of this latter category (indeed of SUPPORT CONTACT in general) as one only important for the youngest infants was thus (like other categories already discussed) corrected by the quantitative data.

Turning to the deeper intervention of MODIFY INTERACTION (Figure 3.7), we see that the child caretaker's greater role lay in REVEAL OBJECT PROPERTIES (M3022), whereas mother and child frequencies were mirror images for the only other common subcategory, CREATE DISCOVERY ENVIRON-

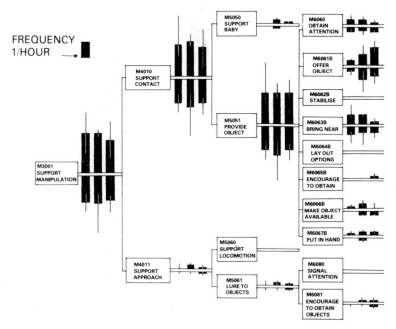

Figure 3.9 *The roles of mother and child caretaker in infant education – SUPPORT MANIPULATION*
The format of Figure 3.7 is continued.

MENT (M3024). The latter, which includes sophisticated interactions like playing games (it is very similar to the original, more restricted use of 'create possibilities' in Study 1), increased gradually through all age groups. REVEAL OBJECT PROPERTIES shows a trend towards an earlier peak, but this is not a significant difference and the data for all interactants combined indicates a continued increase (Figure 3.10).

2.6 CROSS-CULTURAL DIFFERENCES

British and Nigerian data are contrasted in Figure 3.10 for the major categories. This is sufficient to illustrate where some of the most significant differences may lie, although as will be apparent from prior discussion this does not mean that inspection of inferior categories would not reveal greater contrasts.

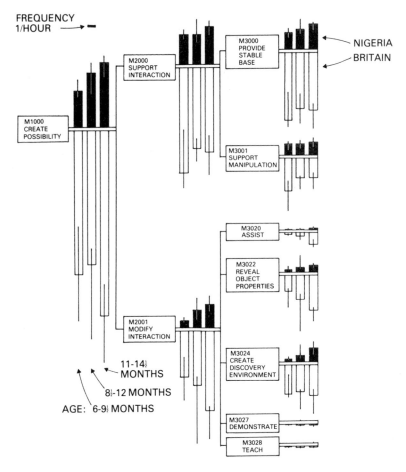

Figure 3.10 *Infant education in Eruwa, Nigeria, and Cupar and St Andrews, Britain*
The format of Figure 3.7 is maintained except that frequencies of CREATE POSSIBILITY for all classes of caretaker combined are contrasted for Nigeria and Britain.

On the basis of the sort of differences found in maternal responsiveness in Study 1, PROVIDE STABLE BASE might have been expected to show a higher frequency for the Eruwa sample than for the British, but the reverse was the case. Inspection of categories beneath those shown in Figure 3.10 reveals that this was due less to ELIMINATE UNDESIRABLE

BEHAVIOUR than to BACKGROUND PARTICIPATION. For the oldest age group the former category shows no difference, and the greater frequency for the British infants at earlier ages was due more to RESTORE ATTENTION than to COMFORT. The similarity of the latter in the two samples was also reflected in Agiobu-Kemmer's results. Note that this category is not a measure of responsiveness and so does not conflict with the results of Study 1; it is possible that the similar scores could be generated by a higher responsiveness in one sample counter-balanced by a lower incidence of distress. The greater frequency of BACKGROUND PARTICIPATION for the British sample was accounted for mainly by the category of COMMENT, in which the mother gives a verbal comment on what B is doing.

The overall frequency of CREATE POSSIBILITY is higher for the British infants of Cupar and St Andrews, replicating the findings of Study 1 which generated the present project. The differences are greater for MODIFY than for SUPPORT interaction, and greatest for the youngest age group; that is, support for cognitive development, particularly of this more elaborate kind, seems to be shown much earlier in the British sample. Of the subcategories, it is CREATE DISCOVERY ENVIRONMENT which repeats this pattern most clearly, although the overall difference between the cultures is maintained in all categories.

General discussion

Several aspects of the data have already been discussed in passing. In particular we have offered speculations on how certain differences in caretaker behaviour might be explained by interaction with differences in infants, in a way that is open to test. To some extent further analysis of our own data may achieve this.

However, some further general comments can be made.

1 THE PATTERN OF THE EDUCATIONAL ENVIRONMENT IN INFANCY

In the foregoing we have concentrated on discussing differences. Yet similarities are just as striking in Figures 3.6-3.10. If we rank the frequencies of the seven level 3 categories, we find that at *every* age and for *both* cultural samples, PROVIDE STABLE BASE is the most common, and DEMONSTRATE and TEACH the least common, followed by ASSIST (Figure 3.10). For the Nigerian sample SUPPORT MANIPULATION is consistently followed by CREATE DISCOVERY ENVIRONMENT, which almost overtakes it; and then REVEAL OBJECT PROPERTIES. Only for the British sample is this consistency broken by the predominance for each succeeding age group of SUPPORT MANIPULATION, CREATE DISCOVERY ENVIRONMENT and finally REVEAL OBJECT PROPERTIES. In the broadest terms, then, one might say that the British and Nigerian caretakers showed a rather similar *pattern*, with one sample simply showing a higher rate of output overall.

Also, although there are many developmental changes, there are perhaps rather more *consistencies* across age differences than one might expect, given that we are dealing with infants developing from their first clumsy manipulations of objects to the achievement of what in Piaget's terms constitute intelligent and symbolic levels of operation. The frequency of CREATE POSSIBILITY, for example, changed little between age-groups two and three for the Nigerian sample, or between age-groups one and two for the British sample. What seems to be happening is that the major functions defined in the categories of levels 1-3 continue to be important throughout the period under study, but are expressed in different ways at different points in development. Within the framework of our classification, these are differentiated by successively lower categories.

DEMONSTRATE and TEACH are exceptions to this conclusion, particularly for the Nigerian sample. We are clearly describing their origins at this stage of development. Although we do not know how adequate the functions of level 3 are for describing support of later childhood development, we may guess that TEACH (defined more broadly) will increase and perhaps level off, although the frequencies of subcategories representing its content will, like our own, change over time. Perhaps SUPPORT INTERACTION would eventually decline to the levels of TEACH shown in this study.

Although the hierarchical classification outlined makes some progress in describing the complexity of differences in the way such functions are achieved, it is important to be aware of what else needs to be examined for a deeper understanding of how social experiences influence cognitive development. The present study gives an outline of this, but does not really get to grips with certain potentially important differences in the ways these categories may be performed. It does not, for example, explicitly differentiate the extent to which the acts are integrated with, or appropriate to, the child's behaviour of the moment, or its current cognitive competencies. Also, to make our first project manageable, we put aside cognitive development concerned with talking and other social competencies not concerned with the world of objects. Expanding our description to cope with these issues is the goal of our current research effort.

2 COGNITIVE DEVELOPMENT AND THE MANAGEMENT OF MOTIVATIONAL STATE

Although we had thought that SUPPORT INTERACTION, and particularly PROVIDE STABLE BASE, would be important (that is, occupy much of the caretaker's time) for small infants, its consistent predominance up to 14 months requires further comment.

First, it is this finding which justifies the title of this chapter, starting as it does with a discussion of distress and comfort. Although while it is distressed the infant may be learning *something*, it will clearly be gaining little sensorimotor information about the world of objects, and Figures 3.7 and 3.8 show that within the broad concept of support to cognitive development provided by CREATE POSSIBILITY, the COMFORT of distress is a major activity right through the ages studied.

Thus quite apart from its significance for the infant's emotional behaviour, comfort and the exact nature of its relationship to cognitive development deserves further study. In Chapter 4 Agiobu-Kemmer expands on the start made on this issue by Bell (1970) with respect to the restricted cognitive achievement of object permanence.

That the mere presence of a familiar caretaker can encourage exploratory activity by an infant was also emphasised by Ainsworth et al. (1971). This lowest level of intervention we have explored further in BACKGROUND PARTICIPATION. Note that only frequencies of the mother's role in MAINTAIN PROXIMITY and ONLOOK are given. In fact it was rare for the Nigerian infants to be unaccompanied by anybody, so the total frequencies of these categories would clearly be much higher than those shown in Figure 3.8. These categories, apart from the role they serve as BACKGROUND PARTICIPATION, allow the monitoring of the infant's activities such that the more directly interventive categories may be applied as appropriate. The superficial commonness and banality of these types of PROVIDE STABLE BASE should not be allowed to encourage neglect of the significant role in the infant's educational environment which their very commonness indicates.

3 CROSS-CULTURAL DIFFERENCES IN INFANT EDUCATION

In view of the points just made, the discussion under Study 1 of what British parents may have to learn from Nigerian parents about the lack of dangers in responsive comfort behaviour may be cited again, but will not be repeated under the present heading.

Here we shall discuss the lower frequency of the more elaborate MODIFY INTERACTION categories in the Nigerian sample. The first question must be whether this apparent lower level of educational experience really does have the implications for cognitive development implied by the way we have defined the categories. Two answers must be given.

The first is derived from other studies, of which there is a significant corpus demonstrating through both correlations and experiments that differences in educational experiences do influence early cognitive development. Experimental studies have mostly involved the intervention of providing extra educational experience for pre-school children at a disadvantage in terms of the normal levels of such experiences in their own homes. There has been tremendous variation in success here, but the fact that the more successful ones share characteristics which can be drawn together to provide guidelines for future attempts (Bruner, 1971, 1975; Bronfenbrenner, 1976; Kellaghan, 1977) indicates that this is not random. There have been relatively few attempts to perform such studies in infancy, presumably because of the assumptions that there is little opportunity for education at this stage of development and that the greatest impact on equality at school will be achieved by intervention in the immediate pre-school period. However, the massive Harvard Preschool Project, on the basis of naturalistic observations, concluded that differences in both social and technical competencies at age six were already apparent by age three (White *et al.*, 1973). They therefore focused research on the period one to three years, and on the basis of multiple correlations between earlier experiences and competence at three years, concluded both that 'children who turn out well at three years of age clearly begin to reveal their future success before they turn 15 months old' and that

> the data we gathered on the process of development between 12 and 15 months of age are the best data for us to look at in our attempt at identifying those learning experiences that contributed maximally to the achievement of high levels of competence. . . . In retrospect we invested too heavily in gathering of comparable data on children beyond that age . . . We believe we might have been wiser in executing this study had we arranged to gather task data on children from the time they were seven or eight months of age. (White *et al.*, 1978)

Accordingly, White *et al.* (1979) designed an experimental programme in which, for infants between the ages of five and 18 months, one group of parents was encouraged to modify their behaviour according to the guidelines developed from the correlational studies. This was apparently by no means easy to do, and the children's future competence scores were enhanced only when the parents concerned had not already raised children. This indication that parents' behaviour is not easily modified, particularly when well-practised, forces us to interpret the rather limited differences shown in outcomes between experimental and control children as a demonstration of the influence, rather than impotence, of social experiences in early cognitive development.

As emphasised in our introductory comments, such experimental work is important in providing hard evidence of a causal relationship between particular experiences and developmental outcomes, and that just reviewed indicates that the sort of differences depicted in Figure 3.10 would predict lower levels of performance in some areas of future cognitive performance. It tells us little about just what those areas are likely to be.

However, it is important to note that at the same time that

intervention studies have demonstrated effects of experience, they and other research have shown that many effects are reversible (Clarke and Clarke, 1976; Dunn, 1976). The differences in cognitive performance produced by the educational interventions already mentioned generally fade away within a few years of the intervention ending (Kellaghan, 1977). And, on the other side of the coin, children reared in a modern residential nursery who at two years of age were retarded in language development had by four years caught up with a comparable home-reared sample (Tizard and Rees, 1974). This potential reversibility is important, but equally so is the recognition that that potential is often unlikely to be realised. In the normal course of events, for example, the tested IQ performance of British school children from upper and lower social classes has been shown to widen progressively (Douglas, 1964; Douglas et al., 1968).

Aside from experimental studies, a correlational one particularly relevant to the interpretation of the significance of Figure 3.10 is Carew's (1977) finding that IQ tested at age three years 'is much more strongly related to intellectual experiences provided to the child by his human environment than to similar experiences that the child constructs for himself'. This is true for experiences right up to the age of $2\frac{1}{2}$ years after which experiences initiated by the child become more important.

However, the second answer to the question of what implications the cross-cultural differences of Figure 3.10 may have, based upon our own data, is not as clear as the findings quoted above would predict. In our testing of infants to obtain some measures of cognitive competencies we rejected conventional tests which award to the infant a single IQ or DQ score; we wanted to assess the infant's various skills differentially and relate these to the various categories of the hierarchy. This does not leave much choice of available tests, and we decided to use Uzgiris and Hunt's (1975) scales, since these not only provide six separate sub-scales, but base them upon the fundamental competencies described within the single coherent framework of Piaget's research.

Now these tests tended to show very few differences between the samples and those which were significant were small in magnitude (see Agiobu-Kemmer, Chapter 4, for more details). Overall the Nigerian infants tended to be ahead, and even if allowance were made for the influence of the Nigerian infants' faster motor development, the British infants would not be shown to be at an advantage proportional to the differences in their experiences indicated in Figure 3.10.

Does this mean that experiences were unimportant? We think not; rather it is the case that the tests, chosen before we started the project, do not adequately assess the range of competencies we have since observed and which may be influenced more by the behaviour described in CREATE POSSIBILITY. Goldberg (1977) found only 'essentially zero' correlations between measures of maternal and home stimulation and the results of Piagetian testing for Zambian infants. She commented that

> this is consistent with previous work with Pagietian scales showing no difference in sensorimotor development attribut-able to home environment as indicated by social class (Corman and Escalona, 1969; Golden and Birns, 1968). Wachs, Uzgiris and Hunt (1971) found social class differences in sensorimotor performances, but these appeared primarily in the case of eliciting responses and number of trials needed to achieve the required number of success.

When this is contrasted with class differences in cognitive measures which, although clearest in later childhood (Hess, 1970), begin to appear before age one year (Kagan et al., 1978) there is a strong indication that, despite the potential advantages of specificity, the Piagetian tests are concerned with competencies for which certain social experiences may be less important than for others.

This does not mean that we find no correlations between experiences and test performances (see, for example, Agiobu-Kemmer, Chapter 4), but it does mean that the lack of cross-cultural test differences says little about the significance of the differences in experience. On the other hand, we cannot fly in the face of the data and say the latter definitely do matter; to know this requires the construction of assessment procedures more comprehensive than either the Piagetian or traditional IQ tests.

The extent of the differences in Figure 3.10 and likely consequences predicted by the literature reviewed would cer-tainly argue for doing this, and for extending the investigation of educational experiences to later ages.

If such research confirmed what we hypothesise – that in the respects covered particularly by MODIFY INTERACTION, traditional child-rearing has inadequacies when it comes to preparing children for education and for a quickly changing and expanding technological culture – then another of our findings may be referred to in relation to any future pattern of pre-school educational intervention. Before discussing this, it must be re-emphasised that our research indicates that certain patterns of traditional child-rearing continue to be valuable, and quite apart from this, there can normally be little justification for imposing cultural change on people who do not welcome it. However, our own interviews showed that (in so far as we can generalise from our samples) Nigerian parents today want a good education for their children and are prepared to invest a good deal in the pursuance of the betterment this can achieve. It is in this context we discuss 'intervention'.

Normally this involves educational intervention by professionals or the involvement of the mother, and one of the 'rules of success' quoted by Bruner (1971) is this latter. For Nigerian readers it will hardly seem a novel 'finding' that child caretakers were responsible for much of the care of the infants in our sample. The description of children's involvement in infant care in Kenya given by Leiderman and Leiderman (1974) might as well have been for Nigeria, and informal sources indicate that it is very widespread, perhaps particularly in parts of Africa and Asia. In this context it is interesting that our data show in addition that these children exhibited CREATE POSSIBILITY behaviour which only in the case of COMFORT fell at a lower frequency to that of the mother.

Now against this CREATE POSSIBILITY behaviour of the children, we may juxtapose the child-to-child programme originated by D. Morley and developed by an international team (Aarons and Hawes, 1979). This was developed primarily as a health programme, and as its title suggests a central concept was the education of children in health care and their subsequent involvement in using and transmitting their knowledge to friends and siblings, as in detecting malnutrition or recording immunisations. However, there is a section on educational play and the manufacture of accompanying play-objects from cheap or free local materials. The potential success of these ideas is supported not merely by the fact that in playing with their infant siblings the children we observed did almost as much CREATE POSSIBILITY behaviour as their mothers. More than this, they actually performed REVEAL OBJECT PROPER-

TIES at a higher rate, much of this involving showing the infant FUNCTIONAL PROPERTIES – that is, given an object with certain properties, what can be *done* with it, both conventionally and unconventionally. And, as in CREATE DISCOVERY ENVIRONMENT, in several categories the children's behaviour changed through time like the mothers', apparently in a manner appropriate to the infants' development. In these ways the children are pre-adapted for introducing modifications in infants' educational environments where needed, and this together with the readiness to try new behaviour characteristic of childhood (in contrast to parenthood as mentioned earlier), the accessibility of children in school, and their future parental role, combine to make this approach well worth putting to the test in Nigeria.

Table 3.1   *Eluama sample background characteristics based on interviews with twenty-five mothers in Eluama*

Education	Mother	Father
none	6	5
some primary	12	2
primary	6	12
some secondary	0	1
secondary	1	2
teacher	0	1

Occupations of fathers:		
trader	7	
labourer	12	
businessman	1	
teacher	4	

Religion:	Christian	22
	Pagan	3

Marriage:	Monogamous	24
	Polygamous	1

Family size:	1 child	3
	2 children	4
	3 children	4
	4 children	4
	5 children	1
	6 children	1
	7 children	2
	8 children	6

Table 3.2 *Eruwa sample background characteristics based on interviews with mothers of the twenty-four infants*

	Group I (6-9½ months)	Group II (8½-12 months)	Group III (11-14½ months)
Infant's sex: male	4	5	5
female	4	3	3
Birth order:			
median (range)	3 (1-7)	3.5 (1-7)	3 (2-6)
Mean age of:			
mother	27.5	26.5	28.3
father	33.4	33.9	34.0
Mean age at marriage			
of: mother	20.6	20.0	20.7
father	27.4	26.5	27.7
Religion: Christian	6	7	6
Moslem	2	1	2
Marriage:			
Monogamous	6	5	5
Polygamous	2	3	3
Number of siblings:			
0	3	1	0
1	0	1	4
2	2	2	1
3	2	3	3
> 3	1	1	0
Education of mother (father):			
none	3 (3)	2 (3)	5 (2)
some primary	0 (0)	2 (0)	0 (0)
primary	2 (2)	0 (0)	1 (3)
some secondary	1 (1)	2 (3)	1 (0)
secondary	1 (1)	0 (0)	0 (0)
teacher	1 (0)	2 (0)	1 (3)
graduate	0 (1)	0 (1)	0 (0)
Occupation of mother (father):			
farmer	0 (2)	0 (3)	1 (2)
trader	5 (2)	4 (0)	3 (3)
hairdresser	0 (0)	1 (0)	0 (0)
needlework	0 (0)	1 (0)	2 (0)
soldier	0 (1)	0 (2)	0 (1)
student	0 (0)	0 (2)	0 (0)
teacher	2 (0)	2 (0)	2 (2)
other	1 (3)	0 (1)	0 (0)

Appendix: definitions of categories of CREATE POSSIBILITY referred to in this chapter (see Figures 3.6-3.10)

Inter-observer reliabilities and the number of instances on which these were based are given for levels 1-3

Code	Category Name	Definition
M1000	CREATE POSSIBILITY (95% n = 643)	M's behaviour creates the potential enhancement of B's cognitive development through play with objects.
M2000	SUPPORT INTERACTION (95% n = 370)	M's behaviour makes it more likely that B will play with objects but does not *influence what* B may learn. *What* B learns depend only on the powers of B and the properties of the objects.
M2001	MODIFY INTERACTION (95% n = 273)	M goes beyond simply increasing the likelihood of B interacting with objects and *what* B may learn with respect to any given object is potentially *further influenced* by M's behaviour.
M3000	PROVIDE STABLE BASE (97% n = 186)	M's behaviour is likely to maintain B in a state which allows the possibility that he will play with objects, but will not influence *what* B may learn.
M3001	SUPPORT MANIPULATION (93% n = 184)	The potential in M's behaviour goes beyond *maintaining* B's state to *promoting* interaction with particular objects, without further influencing what he may learn from this. (She may enhance the probability that B will be able to manipulate where he would otherwise be incompetent, or that he will be motivated to do so, or both. This

distinction between competence and motivation was not made a high-level one in the hierarchy because

(i) SUPPORT B, PROVIDE OBJECTS and SUPPORT LOCOMOTION clearly provide support with respect to B's incompetence, but in so doing they might also provide motivation, and

(ii) while the main function of LURE TO OBJECTS might be thought of as motivation, SIGNAL ATTENTION might also provide support with respect to incompetence in visual search. Thus although the distinction is potentially a major conceptual one, it presents problems for objective application.)

M3020	ASSIST (94% n = 16)	M's behaviour may help B to achieve his own goal, which he is, or had been, unable to do competently. (Thus M neither initiates B's interaction with objects nor changes their direction from that intended by B. The information input is low in that the mother is making minor interjections while B proceeds with his own task, or (as in PROVIDE SOLUTION) doing a part for him: it does not include demonstration or teaching which are major categories in their own right.)
M3022	REVEAL OBJECT PROPERTIES (95% n = 140)	M provides B with information about object properties, other than in the service of assistance.

M3024	CREATE DISCOVERY ENVIRONMENT (98% n = 115)	M provides an environment which may influence what B learns, but she does not provide information on how he should perform or on object properties: B will learn by discovery only through behaving in this environment.
M3027	DEMONSTRATE	M provides B with information which clarifies how to perform a particular act.
M3028	TEACH (100% n = 2)	M provides B with information on how to perform an act and supports his attempt to perform it.
M4000	ELIMINATE UNDESIRABLE BEHAVIOUR	M's behaviour may terminate B behaviour which detracts from B's attention to objects he may learn from.
M4001	BACKGROUND PARTICIPATION	M's behaviour involves minimal interaction which may nevertheless maintain B's motivational state which is allowing play to continue (examples so far do not involve object manipulation).
M4010	SUPPORT CONTACT	M's behaviour may facilitate B's contact with objects in reach.
M4011	SUPPORT APPROACH	B is out of reach of objects and M's behaviour may facilitate his making contact with them.
M5000	MAINTAIN IN FIELD	M's behaviour may counteract B's attempt to leave the field of play.
M5001	COMFORT	M comforts B, who is fussing or crying.

M5002	RESTORE ATTENTION	M's behaviour may restore B's attention to the field of play.
M5010B	RECEIVER	M accepts objects offered to her by B.
M5011	MAINTAIN PROXIMITY	M comes or stays within reach of B and makes him aware of her physical proximity.
M5012B	ONLOOK	M just watches B playing.
M5013	COMMENT	M says something relevant to B's play, which could indicate to B that she is attending to what she is doing.
M5050	SUPPORT BABY	M helps B into a bodily posture which could facilitate contact with toys.
M5051	PROVIDE OBJECT	M's behaviour may facilitate contact by acting with respect to the environment rather than on B directly.
M5060	SUPPORT LOCOMOTION	M's behaviour may physically support B's locomotion to objects.
M5061	LURE TO OBJECTS	M's behaviour may lure B towards objects.
M6000	RESTRICT LOCOMOTION	M restrains B's attempts to move away from the field of play.
M6001	GET BACK TO FIELD	M prevents B permanently leaving the field of play by acting on him when he has moved away.
M6010	SOOTHE BY PHYSICAL CONTACT	M expresses affect by physical contact with B.

M6011	SOOTHE WITH TOYS	M comforts B by providing him with toys.
M6012	SOOTHE BY NOISES	M comforts B by talking or making other noises.
M6020	PREVENT COMPETING STIMULI	M directly prohibits B's interest in competing objects.
M6021	DISTRACT	M's behaviour may divert B's interest away from competing objects or activities.
M6053B	POSITION B	M sets B down by objects which could be manipulated.
M6054B	ORIENT B	M carries, lifts or leans B into a position where he could manipulate objects.
M6060	OBTAIN ATTENTION	M's behaviour may attract B's attention to an object but not to any of its particular properties.
M6061B	OFFER OBJECT	M presents B with an object so he can take it.
M6062B	STABILISE	M holds objects steady so B can manipulate.
M6063B	BRING NEAR	M brings objects near to B, making them more accessible.
M6064B	LAY OUT OPTIONS	M spreads out toys in front of B.
M6065B	ENCOURAGE TO OBTAIN	M's behaviour may motivate B to obtain an object which is in view.
M6066B	MAKE OBJECT AVAILABLE	M makes an object available for B (as in removing an object from a container which B could not open).
M6067B	PUT IN HAND	M puts an object into B's hand.

M6080	SIGNAL ATTENTION	M6060 in the service of luring.
M6081	ENCOURAGE TO OBTAIN OBJECTS	M's behaviour may motivate B to obtain objects.
M7020	CHANGE B'S POSITION	M changes B's position other than cuddling or rocking.
M7021B	RHYTHMIC BEHAVIOUR	M rocks B rhythmically.
M7022B	CUDDLE	M holds B close to her chest, encircled by one or both arms.
M7030	DISTRACT WITH TOY	M presents objects which may distract B.
M7031B	VARY	M performs various actions with objects which may distract B.

Acknowledgments

This research was supported by the Boise Fund, Oxford, the Social Science Research Council, London, and the March of Dimes Birth Defects Foundation, New York.

We are grateful to the University of Lagos and the Nigerian Government for permission to conduct fieldwork in Nigeria and to Professor A.C. Mundy-Castle and Dr R. Bundy of the Psychology Department, University of Lagos, for their support. We also wish to thank the District Officer and Assistant District Officer of Orlu, Chief O.V.E. Emeneha II of Owerri Ebeiri, the Rev. J.A. Ajani and Mr and Mrs C. Ibeh and J. Ibeh for their help in arranging local fieldwork, and the staff of Orlu Child Welfare Clinic, Eruwa General Hospital, Adamson Hospital, Cupar and St Andrews Child Welfare Clinics for their co-operation.

For their assistance in parts of the research reported here we thank I. Agiobu-Kemmer, A. Ibeh, H. Kennedy, J. Moseley, M. Sutherland and S. Whiten. Finally, we wish to record a special note of thanks to the parents involved in our studies.

References

Aarons, A. and Hawes, H. (1979), *Child-to-Child*, Macmillan, London.

Ainsworth, M.D.S., Bell, S.M. and Stayton, D.J. (1971), 'Individual differences in strange situation behaviour of one-year-olds', in H.R. Schaffer (ed.), *The Origins of Human Social Relations*, Academic Press, London.

Bell, S.M. (1970), 'The development of the concept of object as related to infant-mother attachment', *Child Development*, 41, pp. 291-312.

Bell, S.M. (1972), 'Infant crying and maternal responsiveness', *Child Development*, 43, pp. 1171-90.

Bell, S.M. and Ainsworth, M.D. (1972), 'Infant crying and maternal responsiveness', *Child Development*, 43, pp. 1171-90.

Biesheuvel (1959), *Race, Culture and Personality*, South African Institute of Race Relations.

Blurton-Jones, N. (1972), 'Characteristics of ethological studies of human behaviour', in N. Blurton-Jones (ed.), *Ethological Studies of Child Behaviour*, Cambridge University Press.

Bronfenbrenner, U. (1976), 'Is early intervention effective? Facts and principles of early intervention: a summary', in A.M. Clarke and A.D.B. Clarke (eds), *Early Experience: Myth and Evidence*, Open Books, London.

Bruner, J.S. (1971), *The Relevance of Education*, Allen & Unwin, London.

Bruner, J.S. (1975), 'Poverty and childhood', in J. Sants and H.J. Butcher (eds), *Developmental Psychology*, Penguin, Harmondsworth.

Carew, J.V. (1977), 'Social class, experience and intelligence in young children', in H. McGurk (ed.), *Ecological Factors in Human Development*, North-Holland, Amsterdam.

Carothers, J.C. (1953), *The African Mind in Health and Disease*, World Health Organisation.

Clarke, A.M. and Clarke, A.D.B. (1976), in A.M. Clarke and A.D.B. Clarke (eds), *Early Experience: Myth and Evidence*, Open Books, London.

Corman, H.H. and Escalona, S.K. (1969), 'Stages of sensorimotor development: a replication study', *Merrill-Palmer Quarterly*, 15, pp. 351-62.

Douglas, J.W.B. (1964), *The Home and the School*, McGibbon & Kee, London.

Douglas, J.W.B., Ross, J.M. and Simpson, H.R. (1968), *All Our Futures*, Davies, London.

Draper, P. (1976), 'Social and economic constraints on child life among the !Kung', in R.B. Lee and I. De Vore (eds), *Kalahari Hunter-Gatherers*, Harvard University Press, Cambridge, Mass.

Dunn, J. (1976), 'How far do early differences in mother-child relations affect later development?' in P.P.G. Bateson and R.A. Hinde (eds), *Growing Points in Ethology*, Cambridge University Press.

Dunn, J. (1977), *Distress and Comfort*, Open Books, London.

Durojaiye, M.O.A. (1976), *A New Introduction to Educational Psychology*, Evans Brothers, London.

Goldberg, S. (1977), 'Infant development and mother-infant interaction in urban Zambia', in P.H. Leiderman, S.R. Tulkin and A. Rosenfeld (eds), *Culture and Infancy*, Academic, London.

Golden, M. and Birns, B. (1968), 'Social class and cognitive development in infancy', *Merrill-Palmer Quarterly*, 14, pp. 137-49.

Hess, R.D. (1970), 'Social class and ethnic influences on socialisation', in P.H. Mussen (ed.), *Carmichael's Manual of Child Psychology*, Wiley, London.

Kagan, J., Kearsley, R.B. and Zelazo, P.R. (1978), *Infancy*, Harvard University Press, Cambridge, Mass.

Kellaghan, T. (1977), *The Evaluation of an Intervention Programme for Disadvantaged Children*, NFER, Windsor.

Konner, M. (1977), 'Infancy among the Kalahari Desert San', in P.H. Leiderman, S.R. Tulkin and A. Rosenfeld (eds), *Culture and Infancy*, Academic, London.

Lambo, T.A. (1969), 'The child and the mother-child relationship in major cultures of Africa', *Assignment Children*, 10, pp. 61-71.

Leiderman, P.H. and Leiderman, G.F. (1974), 'Affective and cognitive consequences of polymatric care in the East African highlands', in A.D. Pick (ed.), *Minnesota Symposia on Child Psychology*, 8, pp. 81-110.

Leiderman, P.H., Tulkin, S.R. and Rosenfeld, A. (1977), 'Over-view of cultural influences in infancy', in P.H. Leiderman, S.R. Tulkin and A. Rosenfeld (eds), *Culture and Infancy*, Academic, London.

Le Vine, R.A. (1970), 'Cross-cultural study in child psychology', in P.H. Mussen (ed.), *Carmichael's Manual of Child Psychology*, Wiley, London.

Lewis, M. (1976) 'What do we mean when we say "infant intelligence scores"? A socio-political question', in M. Lewis (ed.), *The Origins of Intelligence: Infancy and Early Childhood*, Plenum, London.

Lewis, M. and Coates, B. (1976), 'Mother-infant interaction and infant cognitive performance', paper presented at the Sixth Annual Meeting of the International Primatological Society, Cambridge, England.

Lindsay, P.H. and Norman, D.M. (1977), *Human Information Processing*, Academic, London.

Newson, J. and Newson, E. (1963), *Infant Care in an Urban Community*, Penguin, Harmondsworth.

Tizard, B. and Rees, J. (1974) 'A comparison of the effects of adoption, restoration to the natural mother and continued institutionalisation on the cognitive development of four year old children', *Child Development*, 45, pp. 92-9.

Uzgiris, I.C. and Hunt, J.McV. (1975), *Assessment in Infancy*, University of Illinois.

Vernon, P.E. (1969), *Intelligence and Cultural Environment*, Methuen, London.

Wachs, T., Uzgiris, I.C. and Hunt, J. McV. (1971), 'Cognitive development in infants of different age levels and from different environmental backgrounds', *Merrill-Palmer Quarterly*, 17, pp. 283-318.

White, B.L., Watts, J.C., Barnett, I., Kaban, B.T., Marmor, J.R. and Shapiro, B.B. (1973), *Experience and Environment, Vol. I*, Prentice-Hall, Englewood Cliffs, NJ.

White, B.L., Kaban, B., Attanucci, J. and Shapiro, B.B. (1978), *Experience and Environment, Vol. II*, Prentice-Hall, Englewood Cliffs, NJ.

White, B.L., Kaban, B.T. and Attanucci, J.S. (1979), *The Origins of Human Competence*, Lexington Books, Lexington, Mass.

Whiten, A. (1977), 'Assessing the effects of perinatal events on the success of the mother-infant relationship', in H.R. Schaffer (ed.), *Studies in Mother-Infant Interaction*, Academic Press, New York.

Whiten, A., Milner, P., Moseley, J. and Agiobu-Kemmer, I. (1979), 'Infant Education in Britain and Nigeria', Ms presented at BPS Developmental Psychology Conference, Southampton.

Whiten, A., Whiten, S. and Ibeh, A.E. (1980), 'Human infancy in Britain and Nigeria', *The Nigerian Field*, 45(1), pp. 21-6.

Whiten, A., Moseley, J. and Milner, P. (in prep.), Describing the educational environment of infants.

4 Cognitive and affective aspects of infant development

Ibinabo Agiobu-Kemmer

Introduction

This chapter focuses on the experiences of infants in their home environment and discusses how some aspects of these experiences might influence the cognitive development of the infants. The main argument is that greater consideration should be given to the interaction of cognitive and affective factors in development, and the suggestion is made that affective factors may be more important than cognitive factors for the development of intelligence during the period of infancy.

DEFINITIONS

It is helpful to begin any discussion by an attempt at definition of the most important concepts which in this instance are the terms 'cognitive' and 'affective'. Their meanings might seem obvious as the related words 'cognition' and 'affection' are in very popular use. However, as is often the case in psychology and the other social sciences, when we attempt to define such concepts whose meanings we take for granted, we run into problems and find to our dismay that we cannot really pin them down in any comprehensive definitions. Flavell (1977), in his Introduction to the book *Cognitive Development*, suggests that it is probably a good thing that our favourite concepts have this elusive quality and complexity which he says some might prefer to call creativity and richness. He goes on to advise that we do not spend too much of our time and energy attempting to fix them in formal definitions. Definitions are probably necessary because they help us to be clear in our minds about the particular aspects of behaviour on which we wish to focus our research interest and this in turn might suggest possible methods and techniques which may be employed in their investigation.

The term 'cognitive' usually refers to the acquisition of knowledge about the objective world and the higher mental processes such as thinking and problem-solving, while 'affective' refers to relationships with people and the emotions and feelings that often accompany such relationships. It is useful to bear in mind, however, that the 'objective world' includes people as well as things and it is not only for people that one can have emotions: we can have very strong feelings for particular objects or ideas. Therefore, rather than think in terms of a dichotomy, it might be more appropriate to consider a progression along which behaviour varies from being more affective to becoming more cognitive.

THEORETICAL APPROACHES TO CHILD DEVELOPMENT

This idea of a progression along which behaviour varies from being more affective to being more cognitive is useful in conceptualising human intellectual development. The development of intelligence in early infancy is characterised by a high degree of emotionality and is to a very great extent determined by social factors in that people are the primary objects that the infant interacts with and they also mediate his first interactions with the non-social environment. As the infant grows older, the variety and stimulation provided by his physical non-social environment assume increasing importance in determining the level of his intellectual development.

Various theories of development have described the growth of the intellect as proceeding from being very context-bound to increasing degrees of abstraction. Piaget (1953, 1954) describes a progression from sensorimotor activity to concrete operations and formal operations; Bruner (1964) speaks of enacting, iconic representation and symbolic activity; Werner and Kaplan (1963) make distinctions between sensorimotor, perceptual and symbolic activity, and Freud (1953) speaks of the impulsive id preceding the rational ego and the superego. These theories describe the stages of development in the life-span of the

individual. That a similar pattern can be seen in the development of the human species has been suggested by Humphrey
(1976) who suggests that highly technical modern civilisation is
the 'offspring' of the 'social intelligence of primitive man'.

The point that is being made here, however, is that affective
relationships with people appear to be more important for
development in infancy as opposed to interactions with objects.
Some might wish to make the point that infants at an early age
probably do not distinguish between inanimate objects and
people because very often we observe infants smiling and
talking to objects and occasionally becoming angry with an
'unco-operative' toy just as they would with persons. While these
observations may be taken as further illustrations of the high
emotionality that is characteristic of infancy, we do have
evidence to show that babies respond differently to people and
objects (e.g. Brazelton *et al.* 1974; Trevarthen, 1979). They seem
to be pre-programmed to respond to people and learn through
the help of caretakers to obtain desired consequences from the
natural non-social environment.

There are very few studies of African infants. Most of what
appears in the literature is comparative reports in which
African infants are compared against developmental norms
already established for Western middle-class children who are
often the subjects for any psychological investigation of what
constitutes 'normality' in development. Thus African infants
who live in materially deprived environments are found to be
quite advanced in their development when compared with
Western children who usually have a variety of toys and other
stimulating objects in their environment (e.g. Geber, 1958;
Ainsworth, 1963, 1967; Goldberg, 1972; Lusk and Lewis, 1972).
This precocity of the African infant has been attributed to the
highly responsive social environment into which the African
child is born. There are a few studies that seem to contradict the
evidence of precocity of the African infant as Warren (1972) in
his review has pointed out. What seems interesting, however, is
that these infants are not found to suffer disadvantages from the
reported lack of toys or play objects in their environment. The
highly stimulating social environment seems to be adequate for
their intellectual development at this early age; it is what might
be called the 'environment of adaptiveness' (Bowlby, 1969) for
human intelligence during this period of infancy.

The most popular theories of development have originated from the West and as such have been influenced to different extents by Western philosophical thought which, in contrast to African approaches, tends to divide man up into his component parts. This analytical approach has encouraged scientific enterprise and the development of technological societies (Mundy-Castle, 1968). It has also led to theories of development in which the child is seen either (a) in terms of his genetic component on the one hand or his reactions to environmental stimuli on the other, or (b) from the point of view of the 'cognitive' aspects of his experiences as opposed to the 'affective' aspects of his relationships with the environment. It made better sense when psychologists stopped talking about which one of either heredity or environment determined development and instead began to ask the question of *how* one or other or both factors influenced development. Thus the interactionist theorists went a step further when they considered that development was a product of the individual's interactions with his environment rather than just being dependent on one to the exclusion of the other.

Thomas (1979) gives a comprehensive review and critique of the most popular theories of development and each one is described in some detail. Jonas Langer (1969), in *Theories of Development*, found it more useful to classify contemporary theories into three major perspectives on development and these he called the psychoanalytic, the mechanical mirror and the organic lamp theories. The psychoanalytic perspective is that represented by Freud (1953); the mechanical mirror is behaviourism represented mainly by J.B. Watson (1924, 1928) and B.F. Skinner (1953); the organic lamp viewpoint is largely represented by Piaget (1954). In focusing on particular aspects of development these theories have tended to neglect or exclude other aspects. It makes better sense that an attempt should be made at synthesis in theory-building to obtain a more comprehensive picture of development.

THEORETICAL FRAMEWORK OF THE PROJECT

The theoretical approach adopted is basically interactionist deriving a great deal from the cognitive developmental theory of Jean Piaget (1954) but also embracing some of the ideas of the psychoanalytic and behaviourist perspectives. More than any other theorist, Piaget sees the infant as an active agent who makes demands upon his environment while at the same time accommodating a variety of information from his environment. Our view of the infant is no longer that of a passive recipient of 'handouts' from the racial gene pool or the circumstantial environment. Rather, the image which emerges from recent data demonstrates that the infant is quite competent at initiating and maintaining interactions and takes a great deal of pleasure in his own capacity to achieve desired environmental effects. The concept of 'interaction' suggests mutual influence between the parties involved in a relationship. Thus there is an increasing emphasis on what the *infant* does in the interactive relationship rather than just on what caretakers do *to* him. Interactionism should also emphasise the co-operation of the various factors involved and how their interplay influences the course of development.

Behaviourism generally conceptualised the infant as being very passive, an empty slate for experience to write on (said John Locke), or as a lump of clay that can be shaped at will by environmental influences (Watson, 1924, 1928). However, B.F. Skinner, in a slightly different position, has put forward the theory of operant conditioning to account for the way in which new behaviours are acquired by the organism (Skinner, 1953). An animal sometimes emits an unlearned response which operates upon the environment to generate consequences which, if favourable, will lead to a reinforcing of the behaviour that generated them or to its extinction if the consequences evoked are aversive. A key concept of the operant learning theory is contingency. This emphasises the importance of responsiveness in the environment and maintains that for environmental events to achieve their full impact on behaviour, they must occur in close temporal relationship to the behaviour that produced them. For instance, if every time an infant cries the mother appears immediately, say within ten seconds, to attend to him, then he soon learns that he can have an effect on his environment provided that his memory span is not much shorter than ten seconds. On the other hand, if the mother comes only after about five minutes have elapsed, the infant may not be able to connect that the mother's coming was a result of his crying. Operant theory is not concerned with the inner representation of contingent events and what this might mean to the infant. Such a dimension was given special emphasis by Rotter (1954) in his expectancy theory and also Watson (1966) and Lewis and Goldberg (1969). They suggest that the young infant develops an expectation that he can have an effect on his environment through his experiences with responsive people and objects around him.

Against this theoretical background, the present project aimed at fulfilling three objectives:
(1) to describe the experiences of infants in relation to their physical and social environment;
(2) to investigate possible relationships amongst aspects of infant-environment interaction and infant performance on Piagetian tests of infant intelligence;
(3) to strengthen the evidence obtained in fulfilling the first two objectives by a replication study and comparison of findings using a different sample.

The project

The research project was based on two short-term longitudinal studies of Nigerian and British infants. The Nigerian study was carried out during the period of August 1978 to February 1979 and the study of British infants about a year later, September 1979 to March 1980.

THE ERUWA SAMPLE

The sample was a group of twenty-four infants whose parents lived and worked in Eruwa, a town in Oyo State of Western Nigeria. These twenty-four infants were chosen on the basis of their age and sex from a list of 66 likely subjects who had been selected at random from hospital birth records by two family health visitors associated with these families. All families were very enthusiastic about participation in the study and many excuses had to be made to others who could not be included for practical reasons.

There were fourteen males and ten females in the sample and their ages ranged from $5\frac{1}{2}$ to $11\frac{1}{2}$ months when they were first visited. Four of the infants were first-borns and twins were not included in the sample. There were six polygamous families and in two of them we had one infant each from both wives in the marriage so that there were twenty-two families (fathers) in the sample, twenty-four infants and twenty-four mothers. One third of the infants had fathers with no formal education, about a quarter had full primary education (six years of schooling) or less, another 25 per cent had full secondary education, possibly including some teacher training (eleven years of schooling). Only two of the fathers were university graduates. Their occupations ranged from farmers and blacksmiths, to army corporal and businessman. Most of the mothers in the sample were also engaged in some paid employment which sometimes took them away from home and the infant was then left in the care of the housemaid, grandmother or neighbour. Six of the mothers were in formal employment as primary school teachers. More details about the background characteristics of all infants are given in Table 4.1.

Households were shared by two or more families who might or might not be related. The houses were all built to a similar design: adjacent rooms on two sides with doors opening on to a central corridor where most social interactions took place during the day. There was also a front verandah where people sat in the cool of the evenings occasionally calling out to friends as they passed by. Cooking and washing were usually done in a shed at the rear of the house. Most families had some farmland where they grew crops for domestic use or for commercial purposes if they were full-scale farmers. All such farms were some distance away from the dwelling-houses, that is on the outskirts of town.

THE FIFE SAMPLE

The 24 infants that made up the Fife sample were selected from a list of forty-nine whose mothers had indicated their willingness to participate in the study by filling a 'request for volunteers' form at the local hospital or child-welfare clinic. Twins and infants of non-British parents were excluded from the sample. Ten of the infants were first-borns. Infants were selected on the basis of their age and sex and matched as far as possible with the Nigerian infants on these two variables. One infant had to be dropped from the final sample because he was often ill and it was not possible to test him or take any meaningful observations several weeks after the study was already in progress.

Table 4.1 Background characteristics of the Nigerian sample

		Name	Sex	Birth order	Number of siblings (full, living)	Age at beginning (months)	Age at end (months)	Marital status of mother	Father Education (years of schooling)	Father Present occupation	Mother Education (years of schooling)	Mother Present occupation
Group 1	1	Adigun	M	5	4	6	9½	Monogamous	0	Driver	0	Food seller
	2	Ahmed	M	4	3	6½	9½	Monogamous	6	Corporal	6	Trader
	3	Bolaji	M	1	0	6	8	Monogamous	11	Clerk	11	Teacher
	4	Kunle	M	3	2	6	10½	Monogamous	6	Trader	6	Trader
	5	Bunmi	F	1	0	6	10	Polygamous	0	Farmer	0	Trader
	6	Bukola	F	3	2	6	9	Monogamous	17	Businessman	12	Teacher
	7	Funmilayo	F	1	0	6	9	Polygamous	6	Electrician	6	Photographer
	8	Rashida	F	7	3	6	7½	Monogamous	0	Farmer	0	Trader
Group 2	9	Joseph	M	5	4	8	11	Monogamous	9	Corporal	3	None
	10	Oludele	M	7	2	9½	12	Polygamous	0	Farmer	0	Trader
	11	Oluyemi	M	3	2	9	12	Monogamous	10	Corporal	8	Trader
	12	Opeyemi	M	1	0	8½	12	Monogamous	9	Student	9	None
	13	Sanya	M	2	1	8½	12	Monogamous	14	Agric. superinten.	12	Teacher
	14	Bolanle	F	4	2	8½	12½	Monogamous	16	National Service	12	Teacher
	15	Bose	F	3	1	8	11	Polygamous	0	Farmer	3	Farmer
	16	Rafatu	F	4	3	8½	12½	Polygamous	0	Farmer	0	Food seller
Group 3	17	Ezekiel	M	4	3	11	14½	Monogamous	6	Blacksmith	0	Embroiderer
	18	Gbenga	M	2	1	11½	14½	Monogamous	12	Teacher	9	Teacher
	19	Joachim	M	3	2	11	14½	Polygamous	12	Corporal	6	Weaver
	20	Mose	M	6	3	11	14½	Polygamous	0	Farmer	0	Farmer
	21	Ramoni	M	3	1	11½	14½	Monogamous	6	Baker	0	Trader
	22	Bukola	F	4	3	11	14	Monogamous	12	Teacher	12	Teacher
	23	Funmilola	F	2	1	11½	14½	Polygamous	6	Electrician	0	Embroiderer
	24	Muti	F	2	1	11	14	Monogamous	0	Farmer	0	Food seller

The parents of these infants were resident in five towns in the Fife region on the east coast of Scotland. Their socio-economic background and level of education were generally higher than those of the parents of the Eruwa infants. None of the fathers or mothers in this sample had less than secondary education and a few of the fathers held doctorate degrees. Fathers' occupations ranged from lecturers and garage owners to journalists and paper-makers. All the mothers had left full-time employment on the arrival of the baby and only four had a part-time job while the study was in progress. They were alone with the infant and possibly one older sibling for most of the day, in self-contained houses, while the fathers were away at work. The presence of another adult seemed most welcome even when this was a researcher who just sat there observing and saying nothing. Only one family expressed some reluctance to go on with participation in the study having volunteered. They were anxious that the infant's identity should be properly concealed in any publications of the findings. They were quite willing to continue, however, once this assurance was given. Table 4.2 gives more background details of all the infants who have been identified by fictitious names.

GENERAL PROCEDURE

The infants in each sample were divided into three groups of eight on the basis of the age at which they entered the project. Group one infants were first visited when they became six months old, group two infants when they were about eight to nine months old, and group three infants after they were eleven months. Each infant was observed once every fortnight, at home or wherever he happened to be, over a period of three months. During such visits, which lasted for one and a half hours, the caretakers were told to carry on with whatever they would be doing normally and that we were interested in what usually happened to the infant in his day-to-day interactions.

The Uzgiris-Hunt scales of infant intelligence, based on Piaget's theory of cognitive development, were administered to the infants at the beginning and at the end of the three-month observation period.

Table 4.2 Background characteristics of the British sample

	Name	Sex	Birth order	Number of siblings (full, living)	Age at beginning (months)	Age at end (months)	Marital status of mother	Father Education (years of schooling)	Father Present occupation	Mother Education (years of schooling)	Mother Present occupation
Group 1	1 James	M	2	1	6	9	Married	10		14	Housewife
	2 Alan	M	2	1	6	9	Married		Joiner		P/T Health visitor
	3 Jack	M	2	1	6	9	Married	16	Forrester	13	P/T Nurse
	4 Lena	F	5	3	6½	10	Married	17	Bank manager	18	Housewife
	5 Angela	F	2	1	6	9	Married	15	Engineer	11	Housewife
	6 Rosie	F	1	0	5½	9	Married	20	Lecturer	16	P/T Research assis.
	7 Mabel	F	1	0	6	9	Married				Housewife
Group 2	8 Colin	M	2	1	8½	11½	Married	12	Technician	12	Housewife
	9 Bob	M	3	2	8	11	Married	12	Printer	12	Housewife
	10 Sean	M	1	0	9	12	Married	14	Police constable	12	Housewife
	11 David	M	1	0	9½	12	Married	12	Teacher	12	Housewife
	12 Brian	M	2	1	9½	11½	Remarried	14	Service manager	16	P/T Social worker
Group 3	13 Peter	M	3	2	8	11	Married	20	Lecturer		Housewife
	14 Heather	F	3	2	7	11	Remarried	10	Driller	14	Housewife
	15 Elsie	F	1	0	9½	13	Married	14	Journalist	13	Housewife
	16 James	M	1	0	11½	14½	Married	14	Naval officer	14	Housewife
	17 Andy	M	1	0	11½	15	Married	14	Business manager	14	Housewife
	18 Chris	M	2	1	11	15	Married	11	Taxi operator	11	Housewife
	19 Doug	M	2	1	11	15	Married	13	Air Force	13	Housewife
	20 Alvan	M	1	0	13½	14	Married	20	Lecturer	16	Housewife
	21 Jenny	F	1	0	12	14	Married	12	Papermaker	13	Housewife
	22 Susie	F	1	0	11	14½	Married	14	Farmer	12	Housewife
	23 Kathy	F	2	1	11	14½	Married	13	Storekeeper	13	Housewife

CHECKSHEET DESIGN

The infant's interactions with people and objects in his natural environment were recorded on checksheets using symbols to represent selected behaviour categories and a time-marking instrument ('bleeper') which delivered a bleep to an earpiece every ten second and two bleeps to signal the end of a minute. Thus it was possible to record the sequence of behaviours, their duration and the contingency of one behaviour in relation to another. The design of the checksheets is illustrated in Figure 4.1.

Each sheet is divided into six ten-second columns and one column at the end for comments on the nature of the interactions that may have taken place during the minute. There are ten horizontal divisions, the right end of each row signalling the end of a minute. Thus each checksheet that was used contained ten minutes of interactions and nine of these were necessary for each of the 90 minute observational visits. The behaviour of the mother or some other caretaker was recorded in the top horizontal half of each one-minute segment (M) and that of the infant in the bottom half (C). Any actions of a third interactant that may have had a bearing on the on-going interaction was recorded in further subdivisions of this segment (dotted horizontal lines).

DESCRIPTION OF BEHAVIOUR CATEGORIES AND SYMBOLS

There were seven major categories of behaviour which were selected because of their theoretical interest. Each major category was represented by an alphabetical symbol and its subclasses by a numerical suffix. For example, one class of behaviour is body contact represented by 'B'; its subclass, say, 'carrying baby on hip', is given by the symbol 'B1' and 'carrying baby on lap' is 'B4'. In addition, behavioural 'adverbs' were used to further characterise certain actions and these were written in the form of accents on the symbols. Locomotory behaviour, for instance, is symbolised as 'L' which ordinarily would mean 'approach' but L̄ with an accent meant approach at a fast pace or 'run' (the accent denoting a high degree of intensity). The use of suffixes and qualifiers not only gave more information on the

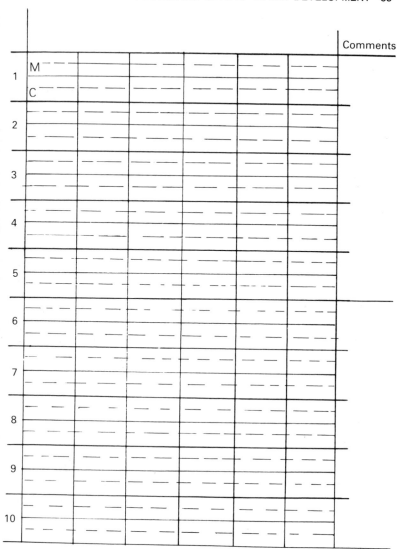

Figure 4.1 *Checksheet design*

nature of the actions of the interactants, but also provided for the economic use of symbols. It was also very easy to incorporate any new unanticipated behaviour into the system by a combination of two categories, one of which is written as a suffix. For example, 'V' symbolises vocalisation and 'D' is the symbol for rhythmic pleasurable activity such as dancing; thus 'V^d' could be used to symbolise singing, nursery rhymes, and so on.

THE INFANT SCALES

Three scales out of the six described by Uzgiris and Hunt (1975) for infant assessment were administered to the infants at the beginning and at the end of the three-month observation period. These were scale I on Visual Pursuit and the Permanence of Objects, scale IV on the Development of Operational Causality, and scale V on the Construction of Object Relations in Space. The author administered the scales to the Nigerian infants and the scoring was done by P. Milner who was working on a parallel project. Miss Milner also did the first testing for the British infants while the author did the scoring; however, she was not available at the end to do the second testing and this was done for all these infants by J. Moseley. It took about 45 minutes on average to administer the scales to each infant. Understandably the amount of co-operation received varied from one infant to another.

BRIEF DESCRIPTION OF THE SCALES

Scale I on Visual Pursuit and the Permanence of Objects focuses on Piaget's (1953) concept of the construction of objects of independent existence. According to Piaget, infants believe that an object that disappears behind a screen no longer exists, that is 'out of sight, out of mind'. They begin to develop a sense of object permanence only after about six months of age. The construction of the object takes place in stages beginning from visual following to more complicated retrieval of the object after a series of displacements at the latter stages. Development along this sequence according to the test's authors implies 'increasing persistence of representative central processes, increasing differ-entiation of central processes allowing for separation of the construction of objects from first the action and then the spatial contexts in which they are embedded, and increasing mobility of central processes leading up to representational thought ...' (Uzgiris and Hunt, 1975, p. 108).

Scale IV measures the development in the infant of an appreciation of causal relationships. Infants will shake their legs or wave their arms in anticipation that this will make the adult repeat an interesting spectacle because such limb movements or 'procedures' (Piaget, 1953, ch. 3) 'presumably feedback to the infant's feelings of effort which become associated in time with obtaining such interesting inputs as the movement of a stationary object' (Uzgiris and Hunt, p. 117). At this level of development, the infant's sense of causality is egocentric and it is only later that he begins to show an appreciation of centres of causality outside himself. At this later stage the infant would act directly on a mechanical object to produce some interesting effect or else he would make a clear request for any attending adult to do so, thus showing an appreciation of objective centres of causality.

The third scale used was scale V for the Construction of Object Relations in Space. This measures the infant's ability to recognise that objects differ in their positions and relationships to each other in space. Rudimentary appreciation of this construct is demonstrated at an early age by slow alternate glancing at two objects, then later the infant is able to show by his actions that he is aware of the effects that the forces of gravity and equilibrium have on objects and their spatial relationships to each other.

The infants were scored according to the highest step they had reached on the scales as indicated by their performance in the test situations.

PROBLEMS OF TESTING

Besides the usual problems of testing infants such as difficulties in retaining their attention and co-operation for a considerable period, and any problems that may be inherent in the scales themselves, two problems need special mention as they may have been peculiar to our situation. Initially, we had some misconceptions about what the ideal testing conditions should be for the Nigerian infants. The authors of the scales had advised that testing should be done in a quiet room with few distractions and only the mother present. These conditions were all right for Western infants; in Nigeria, however, infants normally played outdoors surrounded by the noise and activity of family and friends. Thus we had created a strange situation and this affected the performance and scores of some of the infants before we became wise to our mistake. The second problem was that it was not possible to test some of the oldest infants at the end of the observation period because they seemed to have developed acute stranger anxiety at about 15 months. Despite repeated visits to their homes, we could not get their co-operation. Similarly, two of the youngest infants had moved away before the end of the project and it was not possible to make further contacts. These problems were taken into account in the analyses of the results.

ANALYSIS OF THE DATA

Three classes of infant-environment interaction were selected for statistical analysis on the basis of their theoretical interest. These were:

   I   playful interactions with objects and people;
  II body contact and kinaesthetic stimulation; and
 III distress and comfort.

   The measures computed under these classes of interaction are defined in the appendix.

Results and comments

A   INFANTS' EXPERIENCES WITH THEIR SOCIAL AND NON-SOCIAL ENVIRONMENTS

1   Playful interactions

Figure 4.2 shows the amount of time spent in playful interactions in minutes per hour of observation for all three age groups. In both cultures infants spent more time playing alone, exploring and manipulating objects in their environment (i.e. technical play), than they did playing with people. Similar findings were also obtained by White (1972). The amount of time spent in such technical play increased significantly with age (p < .01). The Nigerian sample showed a steady increase in the amount of technical interaction from six to fourteen months. The British infants spent significantly more time in technical play than the Nigerian babies at every age (F = 16.68, p < .01).

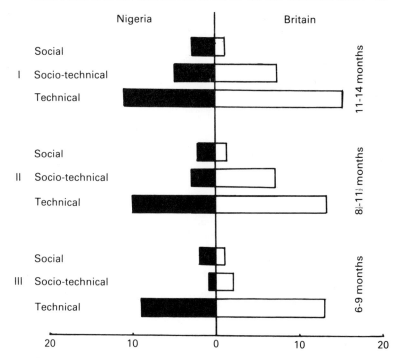

Figure 4.2 *Amount of time spent in playful interactions (minutes per hour)*

Generally more time was spent in play involving objects and people (socio-technical) than in purely social play. This was found to be true in every age group studied in both cultures with one exception: the youngest Nigerian infants (6-9 months) spent more time in social play than they did in socio-technical. The amount of time spent in socio-technical interaction increased significantly with age in the two samples, the British infants spending significantly more time in this type of interaction in every age group (F = 4.86, p < .05).

Whereas the patterns of the findings for technical and socio-technical interactions were more or less similar in that the British infants spent more time in these forms of play than the Nigerian infants, the data for social playful interaction showed a reversal in trend: the Nigerian infants at every age group studied spent significantly more time in purely social play than did the British infants ($F = 4.29$, $p < .05$). While the amount of time spent in social interaction increased with age for the Nigerian sample, the data for the British showed a decrease with age.

INFANTS' INITIATIVE IN INTERACTIONS

The proportion of social and socio-technical interactions initiated by the infants increased as the infants grew older and this was found to be true in both cultural samples (see Figure 4.3). The British infants initiated proportionately more of both social and socio-technical play than the Nigerian infants at all ages except the 11-14 months group where they were initiating social interactions less frequently than the Nigerian group of the same age.

Infants at all ages in both cultures initiated more social interactions than socio-technical. The only exception to this general trend were the oldest British infants who at 11-14 months were initiating far more interactions with people using objects than purely social games which did not include objects.

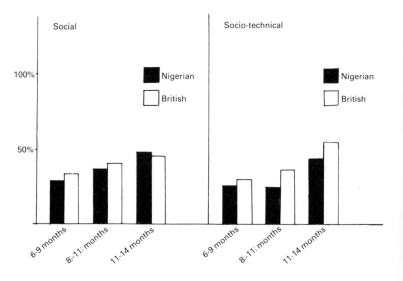

Figure 4.3   *Proportion of playful interactions initiated by infants*

INFANTS' GAMES

Infants frequently played games with their caretakers. The most popular social game among infants and caretakers in the two cultures studied was 'facial-vocal'. This was a kind of 'look/-laugh' game in which the caretaker made a face at the infant accompanied by vocalisation and this would evoke a smile or laughter in the infant. As the infants grew older they were able to initiate this game themselves by, for example, screwing up the nose and sniffing at the caretaker. The second most frequently occurring class of social games was dancing, clapping and singing for the Nigerian sample, while for the British tickling was the next most frequent form of social play. The percentage frequencies of occurrence of all social games are shown in Figure 4.4.

Figure 4.5 shows the percentage frequencies of socio-technical games for the different age-groups of the two cultural samples. Caretakers were more likely to engage in object-oriented interaction with the infant if there was a socially recognised play object available, i.e. a toy. Thus in Nigeria the most frequently occurring category of socio-technical interaction was 'demonstrate/comply' in which the caretaker performed the conventional use of the toy (e.g. shake a rattle, wind up a mechanical car), and the infant in turn waved his arms in appreciation or attempted to have a go if he was old enough to do so. Infants in both cultures at six to nine months were very fond of the 'drop and pick' game in which they dropped objects repeatedly for reluctant caretakers to pick up. This was more frequent among Nigerian infants who often played this game while being carried on the back or on the lap of the caretaker. In Britain it occurred sometimes while the baby was carried on the lap but more often babies sat in their baby chairs and took special delight in sweeping toys down to the floor as frequently as their mothers were willing to pick them up.

Nigerian mothers and other caretakers frequently stimulated their six- to nine-month-old infants to crawl by luring them with play objects. There was very little of this 'locopromotion' among British mothers. British mothers, however, played a greater variety of object-oriented games with their infants (as shown in Figure 4.5) probably because they had a wider and more interesting range of toys to play with.

'Give and take' games were common in both samples and

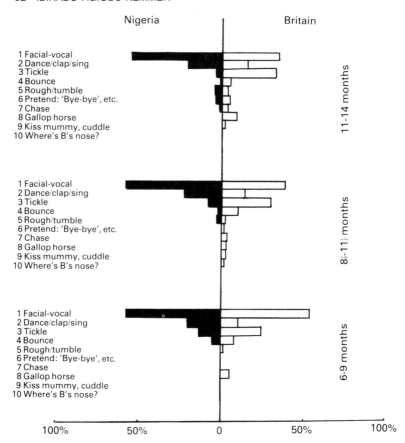

Figure 4.4 *Percentage frequency of social games*

particularly so at the oldest ages, 11-14 months, when they were quite often initiated by the infants. Another form of socio-technical interaction which occurred most frequently with the oldest infants was the 'domestic' category. Older infants in both cultures were often quite keen to join the adult in some task that he or she was doing around the house such as repairing a bicycle, washing the dishes or hoovering the carpet. Older infants seemed to get a lot of fun out of these adult activities and gadgets, sometimes in preference to their own toys. Adults in

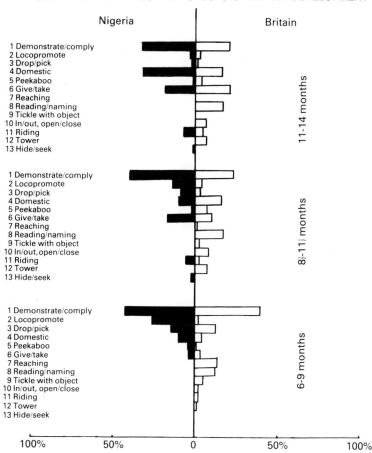

Figure 4.5   *Percentage frequency of socio-technical games*

both cultures were quite indulgent and would welcome the infant's participation until he became a nuisance.

One very conspicuous difference between the two samples was the absence among the Nigerian subjects of joint reading of a book with a caretaker which occurred frequently at all ages in the British sample. (One recalls from the social background data that very few of the Nigerian mothers in the sample had had any experience of formal education beyond the primary school level.) Naming and pointing were also included in the reading category because they were observed to be closely associated. These experiences were conspicuously absent among the Nigerian subjects studied.

2 Body contact and kinaesthetic stimulation

Figure 4.6 shows the data for the amount of time spent in body contact for all age groups in the two cultures. Nigerian infants spent twice as much time in physical contact as British infants of the same age. A similar finding was obtained by Whiten *et al.* (1980). The amount of time infants spent in contact decreased as they grew older. Younger infants in both cultures were in contact for much longer than older ones. Most of the infants in our British sample were not kept in a pram all day although this was the experience of two of them.

Nigerian infants experienced more posture changes during an hour of observation than the British infants of the same age. However, for every minute in contact the British infant was twice as likely to have his posture changed as the Nigerian infant of the same age. British infants did not seem to be content

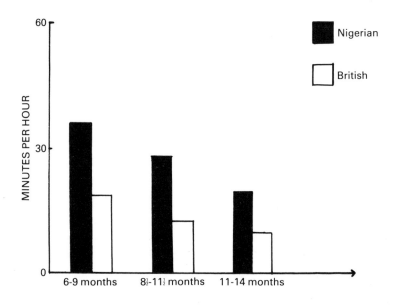

Figure 4.6 *Amount of time spent in body contact (minutes per hour)*

to stay in contact for very long and were always very eager to reach out or get down to play with the attractive toys and objects in their environment. Nigerian infants on the other hand remained on the back or lap of the caretaker for quite long periods; only as they grew older did their demand to get down and explore increase.

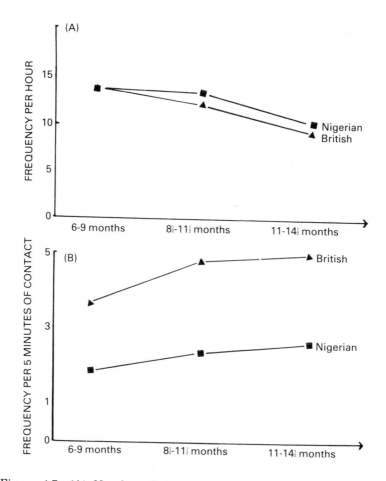

Figure 4.7 *(A) Number of times infant's position was changed per hour (B) Number of times infant's position was changed per every five minutes of contact*

3 Distress and comfort

CRYING AND FUSSING

Infants in both cultures generally cried less frequently as they grew older (see Figure 4.8b). British infants cried more often than Nigerian infants of the same age although the differences were not significant. The frequency of fussing decreased slightly with age among British babies whereas for the Nigerian sample it tended to increase (Figure 4.8a). British infants fussed more frequently than Nigerian infants ($F = 5.44$, $p < .05$).

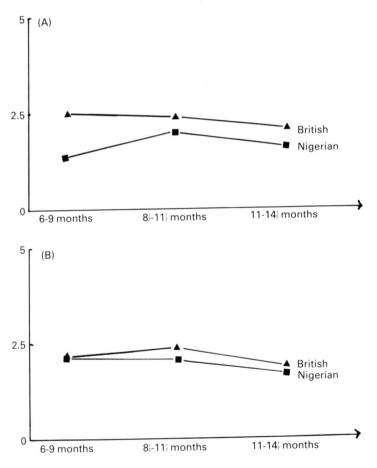

Figure 4.8 *(A) Frequency of fussing per one hour of observation   (B) Frequency of crying per one hour of observation*

RESPONSIVENESS TO THE INFANT'S CRY

The cry of an infant was generally given very prompt attention and the younger the infant, the more immediate was the response to his distress (Figure 4.9a). As infants grew older caretakers tended to ignore them more and the infants in turn became more capable of calming themselves.

The first response to infant crying generally occurred within a latency of ten to twenty seconds for both samples. Whiten *et al.* (1980) also found that the initial response to distress in their Oxford and Eluama samples occurred within a latency of fifteen seconds. The infant's distress was usually calmed within a minute of its onset (Figure 4.9b). As infants grew older caretakers became more understanding of their needs and the infants too were better able to communicate their wants. Thus the latency of the effective response to crying (see Appendix for definition of measures) decreased significantly with increasing age of the infants ($F = 7.45$, $p < .01$). The latencies of the initial and effective responses to crying were shorter for British infants ($p < .01$). This finding was unexpected given other evidence in the literature (e.g. Whiten *et al.* 1980). More comments will be made on this later on when the findings on responses to crying are reported. The first response to crying as well as the response that was effective in calming the infant depended on what was the cause of the infant's distress.

WHY DID THE BABIES CRY?

Babies in the two cultural samples cried for different reasons: in Nigeria the most frequent cause of the infant's distress (the derivation of this measure is described in the Appendix) was the departure of his caregiver. Hunger and need for contact and attention were also quite frequent causes of infant crying. Figure 4.10 shows per cent frequencies of the various reasons why infants cried in the two samples. The pattern is very similar within samples regardless of the age of the infant although quite different when the two cultures are compared.

The crying need of British infants up to twelve months was mainly for physical contact. After the first year infant crying in Britain was most often caused by injury which was the result of their trying to 'get into everything' or from fights with older siblings over a desired toy. British infants also cried quite often because they were prevented from playing with household

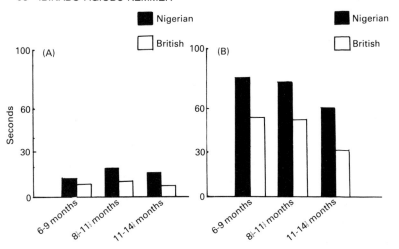

Figure 4.9   *(A) Initial latency of response to infant's cry in seconds   (B) Effective latency of response to infant's cry in seconds*

equipment or other unsafe objects which caretakers kept out of their reach.

RESPONSES TO CRYING

British mothers talked quite often to their babies and this was their most frequent first response to infant crying (Figure 4.11a, over 60 per cent of the time). A similar finding was obtained by Whiten *et al.* (1980). In Nigeria since the departure of the caretaker and loss of contact were frequently the main causes of crying, the caregiver's first response was to try to get back to the infant as quickly as she could calling to him as she approached. Thus vocalisation and approach were combined as one category because they often occurred simultaneously (Figures 4.11a and 4.11b). However, in Britain, where the mother was quite often in the same room with the infant, her first response was to talk to him when he cried. The breast was rarely given as the initial response to crying in either sample.

Nigerian mothers tended to ignore the crying of their babies more often than the British sample did especially if the infant was older. Many of them were busy much of the time, attending

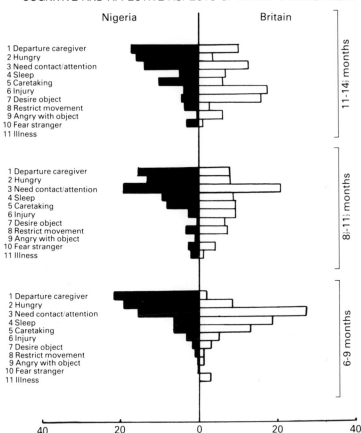

Figure 4.10 *Percentage frequency of causes of infant's distress*

to customers at a foodstall, preparing the midday meal or supervising several other older siblings who also demanded attention. In contrast, almost all the British mothers in our sample were full-time housewives having given up their jobs on the arrival of the baby who, five times out of ten, was their first and only child (see Tables 4.1 and 4.2). First-time mothers are perhaps more anxious about the infant's distress than a mother who has already had three or four and therefore knows from experience that not all infant crying is a genuine cause for alarm.

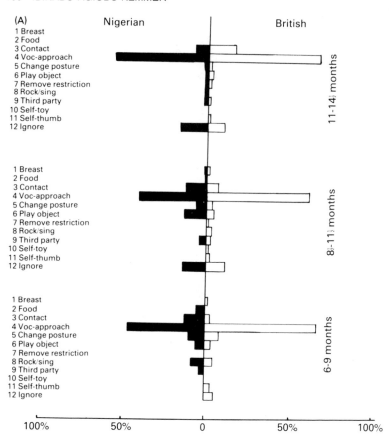

Figure 4.11 *(A) Percentage frequency of first responses to infant's distress (B) Percentage frequencies of responses effective in calming infant's distress*

Contact with the caretaker was the most frequent effective response to the baby's cry in the Nigerian sample except for the oldest infants who were sufficiently calmed by the sight or sound of the approaching caretaker if their distress had been caused by her departure. Contact was also the most frequent effective response to crying for the British infants except for the youngest babies who, although their behaviour indicated that they wanted physical contact with the caretaker, did not always get it. Thus

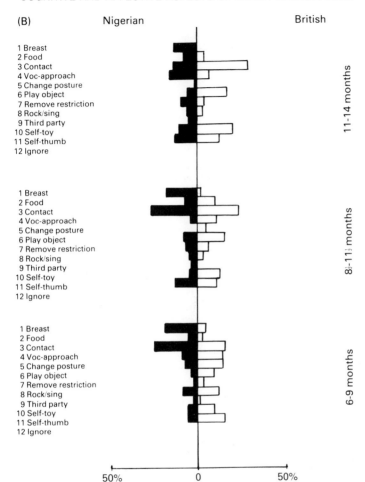

(B)   Nigerian   British

1 Breast
2 Food
3 Contact
4 Voc-approach
5 Change posture
6 Play object
7 Remove restriction
8 Rock/sing
9 Third party
10 Self-toy
11 Self-thumb
12 Ignore

11-14 months

1 Breast
2 Food
3 Contact
4 Voc-approach
5 Change posture
6 Play object
7 Remove restriction
8 Rock/sing
9 Third party
10 Self-toy
11 Self-thumb
12 Ignore

8½-11½ months

1 Breast
2 Food
3 Contact
4 Voc-approach
5 Change posture
6 Play object
7 Remove restriction
8 Rock/sing
9 Third party
10 Self-toy
11 Self-thumb
12 Ignore

6-9 months

50%   0   50%

thumbsucking was often their self-initiated response to calm themselves. About half of all the infants that made up the British sample were thumbsuckers compared with only two among the Nigerian subjects.

Infants sometimes stopped crying on their own either by becoming interested in a toy, sucking their thumbs or they just stopped for no obvious reason. These self-initiated calming responses became more frequent as the infants grew older. The oldest of the British infants, more than any other group, quite often picked up some other interesting toy from their rich supply especially when the cause of their crying had been the desire for a prohibited object. Figure 4.11b shows the per cent frequencies of the responses which were effective in calming infants at the different age groups studied for both cultures.

B PERFORMANCE ON THE INFANT ASSESSMENT SCALES

The analyses in this section were based on the test scores obtained at the end of the observation period when the mean ages of the infants were $9^{1}2$, 12 and 15 months respectively for the three groups in both samples. Some of the infants were dropped from these analyses because they could not be assessed for various reasons such as their getting into a temper every time the object was hidden, becoming scared of a mechanical object, or simply refusing to perform. This meant that we were left with very small numbers for the within-group comparisons, thus limiting the scope for variation.

Overall comparisons between cultural samples

Object permanence: generally there were no significant differences between the two samples. However, trends were that the Nigerian infants were ahead of the British at nine months, at twelve months the mean performance was the same for both samples on this scale, and at fifteen months the British infants had overtaken the Nigerian subjects by a slightly better performance (see Table 4.3).

Operational causality: the Nigerian infants generally performed better than the British subjects at every age studied, although these differences were slight and insignificant.

Object relations in space: there was a significant difference between the two cultural samples in performance on this scale: the Nigerian infants scored higher than the British at nine and fifteen months (T = 13, p < .01).

Correlations of test scores with aspects of interaction

The highest steps reached by the infants on the scales were correlated with selected aspects of their interaction with their

Table 4.3 *Mean test scores for Nigerian and British groups*

Scales	9½ months Nigerian	British	12 months Nigerian	British	15 months Nigerian	British	p
1 Object permanence	26.0	22.1	28.5	28.0	34.7	35.5	
2 Operational causality	11.7	11.3	17.6	16.5	22.8	22.4	
3 Object relations in space	22.0	14.7	27.9	24.4	29.5	28.9	<.01
	N = 6	N = 7	N = 8	N = 8	N = 6	N = 8	

Table 4.4 *Correlations between aspects of interaction and performance on object permanence*

Aspects of interaction	9½ months Nigerian	British	12 months Nigerian	British	15 months Nigerian	British
Technical	0.83	—	—	—	—	—
Socio-technical	—	—	—	- -	—	—
Social	—	—	—	—	—	—
Initial latency	—	0.53	—	—	—	—
Effective latency	0.63	—	—	—	—	—
Changes of posture	—	—	—	—	—	—

Note: dashes represent correlation < .50.

caretakers and with the physical environment. Because the number of infants within groups is small there was very little variation among the infants in certain aspects of interaction which may be one reason for the low correlations obtained with those aspects.

Also in using the scales it was found that some scales were more discriminating among infants of a particular age than others. This could mean that the distances between scale steps were too large for some scales, or perhaps there just was not much change in psychological development along that branch measured by the scale at the ages in question. Thus, for example, the object permanence scale was found to be the most differentiating among infants below nine months of age, while between nine and twelve months most of the infants appeared to be fixated on the same step (8) of the scale. It was therefore not possible to obtain any meaningful correlations using this scale for the nine to twelve months age group. Similar reasons account for the absence of data under some of the other scales in the table.

Significant correlations

Nine months: only the object permanence scale was found to differentiate among infants of this age in the two cultures. None of the correlations of infants' performance on this scale with aspects of infant-environment interaction were found to be significant. However, there was a very high positive relationship between the amount of time the Nigerian infants spent in technical interaction and the level of performance on the object permanence scale. There was also a moderate relationship between performance on the same scale and the initial latency of response to crying in the British group, and the effective latency in the Nigerian group.

Twelve months: only scale V on the development of object relations in space was found to give differences among the Nigerian infants of this age, while scale IV on operational causality was the most differentiating among British infants of the same age.

The amount of time spent in socio-technical interaction was found to be significantly correlated with the development of operational causality among British infants ($p < .05$), and the construction of object relations in space among the Nigerian group ($p < .05$). The amount of time spent in social games was also found to be highly correlated with the development of causality in the British infants, while among the Nigerian sample a very strong relationship was found between prompt response to the infant's distress and his level of development on the construction of spatial relationships among objects ($p < .01$).

Fifteen months: the amount of time the infant spent playing alone with objects as well as immediate and effective response to his crying were found to be significantly correlated with the level of performance on the operational causality scale for Nigerian infants at fifteen months ($p < .05$).

Table 4.5 *Correlations between aspects of interaction and performance on operational causality*

Aspects of interaction	9½ months Nigerian	British	12 months Nigerian	British	15 months Nigerian	British
Technical	—	---	—	—	0.95*	—
Socio-technical	—	—	—	0.70*	—	—
Social	—	—	—	0.59	—	—
Initial latency	—	—	—	—	—	—
Effective latency	—	—	—	--	0.95*	--
Changes of posture	---	---	—	—	—	—

Note: dashes represent correlation < .50.
* p < .05

Table 4.6 *Correlations between aspects of interaction and performance on object relations in space*

Aspects of interaction	9½ months Nigerian	British	12 months Nigerian	British	15 months Nigerian	British
Technical	—	—	—	—	—	—
Socio-technical	—	---	0.71*	—	—	---
Social	—	—	—	—	--	—
Initial latency	—	—	0.83**	—	—	--
Effective latency	—	—	—	—	—	--
Changes of posture	—	---	—	—	—	—

Note: dashes represent correlation < .50.
* p < .05
** p < .01

Summary of findings

INFANTS' PLAY

1 Infants in both cultures spent more time playing alone, exploring and manipulating objects, than they did playing with people.

2 The amount of time spent in play, as well as the proportion of playful interactions initiated by the infants, increased significantly with age in both cultures.

3 There were significant differences between the two samples in the amount of time spent in the different forms of playful interaction. British infants spent more time in technical and

socio-technical play than the Nigerian infants who in turn spent significantly more time in social play than the British sample.

4 There were differences between the samples in the kinds of social games that were played but caretakers in both cultures frequently played facial-vocal games with infants in order to amuse them. Dancing, clapping and singing were quite frequent among the Nigerian subjects whereas tickling games were preferred by the British sample.

5 Object-oriented games were common to both cultures; there were differences, however, in the type and variety of object-games that were played. British mothers played a wider range of socio-technical games with their babies which included reading/naming and pointing at objects, and construction games such as tower-building. These activities were absent among the Nigerian subjects. Nigerian mothers on the other hand frequently played 'locopromotion' games with their six- to nine-month old infants in order to stimulate crawling. The British mothers did not do this.

CONTACT WITH CARETAKERS

At every age studied the Nigerian infants spent considerably more time in contact with their caretakers than the British sample. Their posture was also more often changed during a visit, although British infants tended to have more frequent posture changes for every minute in contact.

DISTRESS AND COMFORT

1 Younger infants in both cultures cried more often than older ones.

2 British infants cried and fussed more frequently than Nigerian babies of the same age.

3 Very prompt attention was given to the cry of an infant by caretakers in both cultures. However, there was a tendency to ignore older infants particularly among Nigerian mothers.

4 British mothers gave more prompt attention to their distressed infants than their Nigerian counterparts in our sample.

5 Caretakers' effectiveness in calming their crying infants increased as the babies grew older for both samples.

6 Self-initiated responses to calm distress, i.e. thumbsucking or

picking up a distracting play object, occurred more frequently among British subjects.

7 Infants in the two cultural samples cried for different reasons. In Nigeria the major cause of infant distress was the departure of the caretaker, whereas in Britain the desire for physical contact was the most frequent cause.

TEST PERFORMANCE AND CORRELATIONS
WITH INTERACTIVE ASPECTS

1 There were no significant differences between the two cultural samples on the object permanence and causality scales; however, the Nigerian sample gave better performance on these scales particularly at the youngest ages.

2 Nigerian infants performed significantly better than the British babies on the construction of object relations in space scale.

3 Both cognitive and affective aspects of infants' experiences with their environment were found to be significantly correlated with performance on the assessment scales.

4 The amount of time spent in socio-technical interaction was found to correlate significantly with the development of operational causality among 12-month-old British infants, and with the construction of object relations in space among Nigerian infants of the same age.

5 Immediate response to the infant's cry also correlated significantly with construction of object relations in space among 12-month-old Nigerian infants.

6 The amount of time spent in technical interaction and immediate and effective response to infant crying were found to correlate significantly with the development of operational causality in 15-month-old Nigerian infants.

DISCUSSION

In this project we have obtained descriptive data on various aspects of the home experiences of infants, aged six to fifteen months, in both Nigeria and Britain. We have also found that both cognitive and affective factors are significantly correlated with the development of intelligence in infancy. Given the limitations of space in this chapter, it is not possible to discuss all aspects of our findings in detail. Reference will be made, however, to some salient findings, especially as they relate to our argument that more emphasis should be given to the influence of affective relationships on cognitive development during infancy.

Why did the British infants not do significantly better than the Nigerian subjects on any of the scales, even though they spent more time in play involving numerous toys and objects around their homes? Their performance was worse than that of the Nigerian babies particularly at the youngest ages, and especially on the construction of object relations in space. However, they were closing the gap as they grew older and at fifteen months their performance on the object permanence scale had overtaken that of the Nigerian infants of the same age.

This finding supports earlier ones of precocious development of African infants (e.g. Geber, 1958; Ainsworth, 1963, 1967; Goldberg, 1972; Lusk and Lewis, 1972). Such precocity has been attributed to accelerated motor development due to the child-rearing practice of carrying the infant on the back for long periods, a highly stimulating social environment, prenatal and perinatal attitudes and practices, and some have even suggested the possibility of genetic factors (e.g. Freedman, 1974).

We have found that the Nigerian mothers in our sample, besides providing contact stimulation, actively encouraged crawling in their 6-month-old babies. However, when asked in an interview whether they had tried to stimulate motor development in any way, all the mothers (100 per cent) said they had not (Dodsworth, 1980), but they believed it was important for a child to develop his motor skills as quickly as possible. British mothers, on the other hand, said they had tried to encourage motor development although they did not believe that it mattered very much if a child was a bit slow (*ibid.*). Apart from putting their 7- or 8-month-old infants in a walking pen, British mothers were not observed to engage in any 'locopromotion' games with their babies. Nigerian babies sat and crawled earlier than the British infants in our sample but there was no significant difference in the age at which infants in both cultures walked (Kennedy and Whiten, personal communication).

Object permanence

The early motor advantage of the Nigerian infants facilitated greater exploration and manipulation of objects in their environment. This limited amount of technical interaction was adequate for object concept development at the early stages. Coupled with this was the fact that they had a lot of social play with significant others. Piaget (1954), though he focused mainly on interactions with inanimate objects, suggested the concept of persons as permanent objects as a homologous but more accelerated process of development. This acceleration takes place because a baby finds people the most interesting of objects and they are also the ones with whom he first interacts. They stimulate many of his senses simultaneously and give prompt responses to his signals.

Consequently Piaget concluded that while developing in parallel with the concept of object, the concept of person permanence begins and is completed first. This is an example of what he called 'horizontal décalage'. The term refers to a child's ability to perform, with varying degrees of success, tasks involving the same basic mental operations although presented in different contexts.

Nigerian infants may achieve the concept of persons as permanent objects earlier than the British babies due to their experience of greater social stimulation. Once the concept of permanence is in their competence system (Flavell and Wohlwill, 1969) they can 'generalize or transfer it to all tasks for which it is an effective solution procedure' (ibid.). Any limitations in their ability to perform in the given task would depend on the amount of relevant experience they have had, given that the competence required has been demonstrated in another context. Thus the Nigerian babies demonstrated a cognitive head start in the development of object permanence at the early ages, but their more limited experience with objects was not sufficient to maintain this advantage at the more complex stages.

An alternative explanation would be to consider that the different experiences which the Nigerian infants were having in other forms of play were not geared towards success at the higher levels of the object permanence scale. Success at these higher levels depended on the ability to allow a series of displacements of the object in the face of confusing visual cues. It could be that the Nigerian babies at this early age were already beginning to demonstrate a different 'sensotype' (Wober, 1966) from that emphasised by the culture on which the scale was based. Sensotype, according to Wober (1966), refers to the 'pattern of relative importance of the different senses by which a child learns to perceive the world and in which pattern he develops his abilities'. The pattern may be predominantly visual in one culture, while in another auditory or proprioceptive senses may be of greater relative importance. Western cultures are thought to emphasise the visual sense while African cultures emphasise the proprioceptive sense.

Object relations in space

There was a remarkable difference between the two samples in performance on this scale. The superior performance of the Nigerian infants can be attributed to two factors: early crawling and being carried on back or lap for long periods. Being able to crawl earlier than the British infants they could make a detour around furniture to obtain a toy before the British babies were able to do this. Similarly, while they were carried on the back or on the lap, they had a lot of opportunities for engaging in 'drop and pick' games with reluctant caretakers, thus experiencing the effect of gravity on objects. Both these tasks, making a detour and dropping objects systematically, were at the top of the scale. The Nigerian infants, consequently, were placed at the 'ceiling' quite early even though they might not have been able to 'build a tower', a task which was lower down in the scale. Most of the British infants performed the tasks in the expected sequence but the performance of the Nigerian subjects does throw some question on their assumed logical ordering.

It is interesting to find that the infants' performance of the various tasks reflected their different environmental experiences. Nigerian babies showed an early understanding of the effect of gravity on objects, while British infants demonstrated a better appreciation of the effect of equilibrium forces derived, no doubt, from their experiences in 'tower building' games with their mothers.

The practice of carrying the infant on the back or lap for long periods not only provided much needed physical contact. It also gave the Nigerian babies the added advantage of stimulating their motor devlopment, and providing a 'scaffold' from which they could experience various perspectives of objects in space and the effect of gravitational forces acting upon them. The ability to understand the impact of gravity supersedes an appreciation of the effect of equilibrium forces according to the logical ordering of the steps of this scale (Uzgiris and Hunt, 1975). However, the authors did suggest that 'the circumstances encountered by infants can alter the order' in which certain steps in the sequence appeared (*ibid.*, p. 121).

Operational causality

A number of investigators (Lewis and Goldberg, 1969; Bell, 1970; Ainsworth and Bell, 1974; Bronson, 1971; Yarrow *et al.*, 1975) have reported that a relationship exists between an infant's experience of consistent contingent responding by caretakers to his signals, and the growth of his intellectual competence. The finding, in group three of the Nigerian sample, of a significant relationship between the level of performance of the infants on the operational causality scale and short latencies of effective responding to their distress, lends further support to this hypothesis. Level of performance on this scale was also found to be significantly related to the amount of time the same group of infants spent playing alone with responsive objects, and with the amount of time group two British infants spent in socio-technical interaction.

Since the British infants as a group had shorter latencies of responses to their crying than the Nigerian babies, and also had more opportunities to initiate playful interactions, it was expected that their overall performance on the operational causality scale should be better than that of the Nigerian infants. This was not the case, however. The mean performance of the two samples at all the ages tested were about the same.

An appreciation of external causality – that is, that there are causal centres outside the self in other persons and in inanimate objects – depends on the development of an understanding of the fact that animate and inanimate objects have an independent existence of their own. Thus if the Nigerian babies are developing the concept of object faster than the British infants for the reasons already stated (see section on object permanence), their objectification of causal sources would also be accelerated. This presumably would balance out the effects of any advantage that the British infants may have had as a consequence of their more frequent experiences of contingent caretaking. There may be other explanations for these findings and it would be interesting to further test the hypothesis that there is a relationship between the development of operational causality and contingent effective responding to the infant's distress.

CONCLUSION

The practice of carrying the infant for long periods on the back or lap as well as frequent social play with the infant appear to be the most outstanding factors which may account for the precocious development of the Nigerian babies studied. The ways in which these experiences may have contributed to the cognitive development of the babies have been explained. Towards the end of the first year, the Nigerian infants begin to lose their cognitive advantage indicating that the kinds of experiences they were having were no longer appropriate to maintain and continue their precocious development.

Carothers (1953) advised that the African practice in dealing with babies in the first months of life should be adopted by everyone. We agree with him. Some Western mothers who read the latest baby books are already adopting these practices although not widely as yet.

Many Nigerian mothers, like the ones in our sample, do not have the advantages of literacy and education. They do what they do because it is traditional practice and has been found to be convenient. They are not aware of the positive effects of their early child-rearing practices on development, and therefore stand in danger of abandoning them in the modernisation process which in Nigeria and other African countries often means adopting *all* Western attitudes. These parents need to be informed, perhaps by medical experts and social workers, of the necessity of retaining their own ways of doing things – ways which have been found to be of psychological advantage to the infants.

At the same time, the Nigerian mothers must be told that it is important for them to play object-games with their older infants. The Nigerian mothers in our sample when interviewed said they did not think that play affected the infant's development in any way, but the British mothers did (Dodsworth, 1980). These differences in attitudes were reflected in actual practice.

The more toys there were available the more frequently adults tended to engage in object play with infants. There is a need for the provision of inexpensive toys for infants in Nigeria, inexpensive educational toys. Since the Nigerian government is currently laying great emphasis on the development of technical skills, investing in the toy industry would be one way of securing the foundations of this development and ensuring its future growth.

Acknowledgments

I am grateful to the University of Lagos for sponsorship of the research on which this paper is based, and to the University of St Andrews for the use of their facilities. Very special thanks are due to Dr A. Whiten for his able supervision of the research and helpful comments and criticisms of the manuscript. The assistance of P. Milner and J. Moseley on the testing of infants is also gratefully acknowledged.

The Eruwa study could not have been possible without the generous hospitality and friendship of the Rev. (Chief) J.A. Ajani, his daughter, Mrs J.A. Esisi, and other members of their family, to all of whom I am greatly indebted. I am also grateful to the staff of the Child Welfare clinics at Eruwa in Nigeria, and Cupar and St Andrews, both in Scotland.

To all the mothers and babies, in Nigeria and Britain, who have been the focus of my research interest, I give my warmest and biggest thanks for the opportunity to enter into their home experiences.

Appendix

DEFINITION OF MEASURES

I *Playful interactions.* There were three subdivisions of this class of interactions and they were defined as follows:
(i) Social – the amount of time spent by an infant in playful interactions with people, not involving any object or toy;
(ii) Technical – the amount of time an infant spent playing alone with object(s) without the co-operation of others who may be present or absent from the field of observation;
(iii) Socio-technical – the amount of time spent in playful

interactions with people involving the use of objects or toys.

Infants' initiative in interactions The proportion of social and socio-technical play initiated by the infant was measured. How did the observer know that an infant is initiating play with his caretaker? Infants initiated play in a variety of ways. Obviously for the sequence to go through, the caretaker must be attentive and responsive to the infant's initiating signals, and interpret them correctly as an invitation for play. An infant might initiate play by a direct smiling gaze at the partner sometimes accompanied by vocalisation. Such vocalisation might develop into a loud fuss or cry if the caretaker refused to give attention because she was too busy with other commitments. Sometimes a playful posture is assumed by the infant or he might make a playful face at the caretaker by screwing up his nose or smacking his lips and this begins the sequence for a social game. Alternatively the infant might give a toy to his mother to operate, or he might go behind a door or curtain and peep out several times at the caretaker saying 'boo' or just smiling at her until she took the hint.

Infant's games A game consisted of repeated sequences which were quite often reciprocal in nature and usually accompanied by obvious signs of pleasure in the partners involved. Social games involved the infant and other people (person-person); socio-technical games included the infant and other people as well as objects (person-person-object(s)). The name ascribed to a game was based on what appeared to be the main element or repetitive event and was thus largely dictated by the data obtained in each culture.

II *Body contact and kinaesthetic stimulation* There were three measures computed in this class and they were defined thus:

(i) Body contact – the amount of time the infant was in physical contact with someone else during the visit;

(ii) Kinaesthetic stimulation – frequency count of the number of times the infant's posture was changed during the visit;

(iii) Demandingness for varied stimulation – the infant's posture was quite often changed by the caretaker in response to his restlessness. This measure was derived from the first two and was defined as how frequently the infant's posture was changed in every five minutes of being in contact:

$$\frac{\text{number of posture changes per visit}}{\text{total time in body contact}} \times 5$$

III *Distress and comfort* This class of interactions was concerned with the infant's distress signals and the promptness and nature of the attention that he received to calm his distress.

(i) Crying and fussing – a cry was distinguished from a fuss by the fact that it was louder and more prolonged; also the infant's face when crying was usually greatly contorted. It sometimes happened that an infant's fusses developed into a full-blown cry. The frequencies of crying and fussing were recorded for each observation visit.

(ii) Latency of the initial response – this is the amount of time in seconds, measured by the distance in seconds on the checksheet, between the onset of crying and the first response to cry, the checksheets having been divided into ten-second blocks.

(iii) Latency of the effective response – the amount of time in seconds, measured by the distance in seconds on the checksheets, between the onset of crying and the response that was effective in calming the infant.

(iv) Forms of response – there were twelve categories to describe the initial and effective responses to the infant's cry and their selection was dictated by the data. The per cent frequency of occurrence of each category was measured for each sample.

(v) Cause of distress – the cause of the infant's distress was determined by the event(s) that immediately preceded the cry and the response that was *finally* effective in terminating it, taking into account non-effective intermediate responses. The comments of caretakers about the state of the infant were also taken into consideration. There were eleven categories to describe the causes of infant distress and their selection was also dictated by the data. The per cent frequency of occurrence of each of these categories was computed for both samples.

References

Ainsworth, M.D.S. (1963), 'The development of infant-mother interaction among the Ganda', in B.M. Foss (ed.), *Determinants of Infant Behaviour II*, Methuen, London.

Ainsworth, M.D.S. (1967), *Infancy in Uganda: Infant-care and the Growth of Love*, Johns Hopkins University Press, Baltimore.

Ainsworth, M.D.S. and Bell, S.M.V. (1974), 'Mother-infant interaction and the development of competence', in K. Connolly and J. Bruner (eds), *The Growth of Competence*, Academic Press, London.

Bell, S.M. (1970), 'The development of the concept of object as related to infant-mother attachment', *Child Development*, 41, pp. 291-311.

Bowlby, J. (1969), *Attachment and Loss, Vol I: Attachment*, Hogarth Press, London.

Brazelton, T.B., Koslowski, B. and Main, M. (1974), 'The origins of reciprocity', in M. Lewis and L.H. Rosenblum (eds), *The Effects of the Infant on its Caregiver*, Wiley, New York.

Bronson, W.C. (1971), 'The growth of competence: issues of conceptualization and measurement', in H.R. Schaffer (ed.), *The Origins of Human Social Relations*, Academic Press, London.

Bruner, J.S. (1964), 'The course of cognitive growth', *American Psychologist*, 19, pp. 1-15.

Carothers, J.C. (1953), *The African mind in health and disease*, World Health Organization.

Dodsworth, H. (1980), 'A Study of the Social Aspects of Infant Development in Two Cultures – Britain and Nigeria', unpublished undergraduate thesis, University of St Andrews.

Flavell, J.H. (1977), *Cognitive Development*, Prentice-Hall, Englewood Cliffs, New Jersey.

Flavell, J.H. and Wohlwill, J.E. (1969), 'Formal and functional aspects of cognitive development', in D. Elkind and J.H. Flavell (eds), *Studies in Cognitive Development: Essays in Honor of Jean Piaget*, Oxford University Press, New York, pp. 67-120.

Freedman, D.G. (1974), *Human Infancy: An Evolutionary Perspective*, John Wiley, New York.

Freud, S. (1953), 'Three essays on the theory of sexuality', *Standard Edition* of the *Complete Psychological Works of Sigmund Freud*, vol. 7, Hogarth, London, pp. 73-102.

Geber, M. (1958), 'The psychomotor development of African children in the first year and the influence of maternal behaviour', *Journal of Social Psychology*, 47, pp. 185-95.

Goldberg, S. (1972), 'Infant care and growth in urban Zambia', *Human Development*, 15, pp. 77-89.

Humphrey, N.K. (1976), 'The social function of intellect', in P.P.G. Bateson and R.A. Hinde (eds), *Growing Points in Ethology*, Cambridge University Press, London, pp. 303-17.

Langer, J. (1969), *Theories of Development*, Holt, Rinehart & Winston, New York.

Lewis, M. and Goldberg, S. (1969), 'Perceptual-cognitive development in infancy: a generalized expectancy model as a function of the mother-infant interaction', *Merrill-Palmer Quarterly*, 15, pp. 81-100.

Lusk, D. and Lewis, M. (1972), 'Mother-infant interaction and infant development among the Wolof of Senegal', *Human Development*, 15, pp. 58-69.

Mundy-Castle, A.C. (1968), Paper presented at the Center for Cognitive Studies, Harvard University.

Piaget, J. (1953), *The Origins of Intelligence in the Child*, International Universities Press, New York.

Piaget, J. (1954), *The Construction of Reality in the Child*, Basic Books, New York.

Rotter, J.B. (1954), *Social Learning and Clinical Psychology*, Prentice-Hall, New York.

Skinner, B.F. (1953), *Science and Human Behavior*, Macmillan, New York.

Thomas, R.M. (1979), *Comparing Theories of Child Development*, Wadsworth, California.

Trevarthen, C. (1979), 'Communication and cooperation in early infancy: a description of primary intersubjectivity', in M. Bullowa (ed.), *Before Speech: The Beginnings of Human Communication*, Cambridge University Press, London.

Uzgiris, I.C. and Hunt, J.McV. (1975), *Assessment in Infancy: Ordinal Scales of Psychological Development*, University of Illinois Press, Chicago.

Warren, N. (1972), 'African infant precocity', *Psychological Bulletin*, vol. 78, 5, pp. 353-67.

Watson, J.B. (1924), *Behaviorism*, University of Chicago Press.

Watson, J.B. (1928), *Psychological Care of the Infant and Child*, Norton, New York.

Watson, J.S. (1966), 'The development and generalization of contingency awareness in early infancy: some hypotheses', *Merrill-Palmer Quarterly*, 12, pp. 123-35.

Werner, H. and Kaplan, B. (1963), *Symbol Formation*, John Wiley, New York.

White, B.L. (1972), 'Fundamental early environmental influences on the development of competencies', in M.E. Meyer (ed.), *Third Symposium on Learning: Cognitive Learning*, Washington State College Press, pp. 79-105.

Whiten, A., Whiten, S. and Ibeh, A. (1980), 'Human infancy in Britain and Nigeria', *The Nigerian Field*, vol. 45, 1, pp. 21-6.

Wober, M. (1966), 'Sensotypes', *Journal of Social Psychology*, 70, pp. 181-89.

Yarrow, L.J., Rubenstein, J.L. and Pedesen, F.A. (1975), *Infant and Environment: Early Cognitive and Motivational Development*, Halsted, New York.

5 Developmental perspectives on memory

H. Valerie Curran

Introduction

How do our memories change as we grow from babies into adults? Do they somehow 'grow' like our bodies – from smaller to bigger – so that there is increasingly more room to store all that we have learned over the years? Is that why adults seem to remember more efficiently than children? Or is it that as we grow older we learn more sophisticated ways of using our memories – how to squeeze more into a limited capacity? And is that partly because, as adults, we are more aware than children of our own limitations – of how we often forget things? Does this make us deliberately plan our learning to accommodate the constraints of our memories?

One reason why it is important to ask these questions about the development of memory is that memory is a very wide-ranging ability. It is involved in almost everything we do. We use memory whenever we recognise faces, pictures, smells, places or music; whenever we tell jokes or stories; whenever we hold a conversation, solve problems, read a book, sit examinations, ride a bicycle or cook a meal. In fact, only rarely do we not use our memory of previous experiences to help us interpret a situation and act accordingly. Memory not only affects what we do – our overt, observable behaviour. It also influences our covert behaviour – like our perceptions, thoughts and dreams. And in turn, memory itself is affected by all our behaviour. Memory is therefore an intrinsic part of most of our social, emotional and intellectual activities.

In this chapter I shall be reporting a study of the memory

development of 6–12-year-old Nigerian children. These children were attending state primary schools in Ibadan. The importance of memory abilities for the school child is clear. School learning involves remembering large amounts of information and further, the child's learning is usually assessed in terms of what he remembers at a later date. Before describing the study itself, I shall give a brief introduction to how memory can be studied and then an outline of the three perspectives (metamemory, memory strategies and meaning in memory) which I used.

STUDYING MEMORY

How do we study the development of memory? How can we identify the crucial changes in memory as children grow to maturity? Unfortunately, there is no direct keyhole through which we can look at memory, so we cannot just watch how it changes over the years. For the most part, we must make inferences about memory development from children's actual behaviour.

We could, for example, do a simple experiment. We could ask a child to try and remember something – a list of words, perhaps. After he has had time to study the list, we could remove it and ask him to tell us all the words he could remember. If we asked quite a lot of children of different ages to do the same thing, we could then look at the words they actually remembered in several ways: the number of words recalled by children of different ages; which words in the list were most often recalled (e.g. those at the beginning or end); the order in which words were recalled (e.g. were words which had something in common with each other recalled together in clusters?) and so on. On that basis, we might find that older children not only recalled more words but also clustered similar words together more than younger children. We might infer from this that when the older children were asked to study the word list, they looked for associations between words to a greater extent than the younger children. And we might therefore conclude that, with increasing age, children increasingly organise information for memory.

There are clearly many variations on this basic approach. There are a limitless number of different things we could ask them to remember – pictures, stories, faces, positions of objects, etc. Instead of asking for verbal recall, we could ask them to write answers down, draw pictures, recognise items they had previously been shown from a mixture of old and new ones. We could test their memories immediately after they had studied material, or two days later or two years later. We could vary the instructions we give to a child, asking her to do something other than deliberate memorising. Clearly, the variations are endless and several variations would usually be used together. This allows inferences to be drawn from differences in children's performance under different memory conditions.

MEMORY STRATEGIES, MEANING IN MEMORY AND METAMEMORY

This kind of approach to studying memory is classified in several ways, according to whether it focuses on recognition or recall; on memory for visual or verbal materials; on factors affecting storage or retrieval of information; on memory over short time intervals or long-term memory and so on. It is also classified according to whether it is concerned with *memory strategies* or with *meaning in memory*.

Memory strategies refer to a repertoire of techniques we may use to help us remember. In our hypothetical experiment with the word list, one example of a strategy would be to categorise the words into groups so that the recall of one group name would prompt recall of all the items in that group. Another example of a strategy is verbal rehearsal, whereby a child would repeat the words on the list several times over to himself. Other strategies would be to elaborate the list of words either verbally (e.g. making up sentences or stories containing the words) or visually (e.g. picturing in one's head a scene containing the things named in the list). Typical research findings in the West are that, as a child grows older, he not only broadens his repertoire of memory strategies but also becomes increasingly efficient in using any one strategy (cf. Kail and Hagen, 1977; Kail, 1979).

Memory strategies are generally used deliberately to remember the kinds of information which do not have much meaning beyond the particular task at hand. This distinguishes them from memory for meaningful material whereby the intrinsic relevance or interest of the information (like a story, a personal experience, or knowledge one uses regularly) is generally enough to ensure its retention in some form or other. As a child grows older, he acquires more sophisticated ways of understanding and this means he is able to extract more meaning from this kind of material (e.g. Harris, 1978). This in turn appears to result in his remembering it more accurately. Memory in this sense is closely dependent on the child's general level of intellectual operations at any stage in his development (cf. Piaget and Inhelder, 1973).

There is a third and very different area of research on memory development, which involves asking children questions about their own memories. This approach is concerned with the child's *metamemory* – his subjective awareness of his own memory: his knowledge of what affects how and how much he remembers, his understanding of what, when and why he forgets. Metamemory is a relatively new research area in memory development. What studies have indicated so far is that even young (4- or 5-year-old) children express considerable awareness of their memories and this increases greatly as the child grows older (e.g. Flavell and Wellman, 1977).

In the rest of this chapter, I report a study of memory development which used all three perspectives of metamemory, memory strategies and meaning in memory. This has the advantages of both giving a broad picture of memory development and allowing one to look for possible interactions between the three aspects of memory.

It is not my task to review all the relevant literature on memory development here (Kail (1979) provides a concise introduction to the subject). Most of it is based on studies with Western children so one cannot assume it provides any developmental prototypes to which Nigerian or any other children will necessarily conform. If, as many psychologists would argue, the growing child acquires new skills mainly through applying them to different problems in different contexts, then as problems and contexts vary across cultures, so too may the application of those skills vary (cf. Curran, 1980). Cultural universals probably exist in the various component processes of memory, like categorising, rehearsing, elaborating, structuring meaning and so on. But, as Cole and Scribner (1974) argue, cultural differences may well emerge in how children use those component processes for any particular memory task.

We can take this argument a step further. It is clearly

possible that some cultures provide certain 'special' contexts which allow culture-specific skills to be developed. One such possibility, which I discuss later in this chapter, is suggested by the fact that Yoruba is a tone language. Does this mean that Yoruba speakers may use tone as an organising principle in memory?

I have written the rest of this chapter in five sections. Section 1 gives a broad outline of the designs and methods of the study as a whole. Specific experiments on metamemory, memory strategies and meaning in memory are described in sections 2, 3 and 4 respectively. In section 5 I draw together my main findings and present an overview of memory development during the primary school years.

1   The study

The study involved children from primary grades I, III and VI which generally correspond to age groups 6–7, 8–9 and 11–12 years. Those age groups were selected partly to scan development during primary schooling, but more importantly, those ages are thought to parallel major developmental stages in the acquisition and use of memory strategies (e.g. Kail, 1979). Research has largely been restricted to Western children, but typical findings are that the 5- or 6-year-old is unlikely to use memory strategies spontaneously (sometimes termed 'pre-strategic'). Children between about six and nine years of age are 'transitional', firstly, in that they use some kinds of strategies (e.g. verbal rehearsal) and not others (e.g. categorisation), and, secondly, in that the strategies they do use are employed in relatively unsophisticated ways. At around ten years, a child has developed an adult level of expertise in verbal rehearsal and is starting to use categorisation and other sophisticated mnemonics spontaneously.

I could obviously not attempt any global investigations of the many aspects of memory development. And in taking the three perspectives on memory, I inevitably sacrificed the depth of a single viewpoint for the breadth of three. Therefore, our research area had to be limited. This was done first by focusing on factors affecting how information is stored in memory, rather than directly investigating retrieval variables. Secondly, the number and variety of different tasks presented had to be restricted according to practical constraints both of time and non-disruption of school activities.

The study reported here was a major part of a memory development project involving over 500 children from seven state primary schools in Ibadan. Selection of subjects was always at random from class lists which were previously obtained from school registers. Apart from excluding the small 'elite' group who attend fee-paying schools, the children represented a broad cross-section of Yorubas. For example, their fathers' occupations spanned a manual to professional spectrum and the vast majority of their mothers were described as different sorts of traders.

For the whole study – whether an experiment or structured interview was involved – each child took part on his or her own in the quietest place the school had available at the time. Seldom were we able to find an empty classroom. More often, the sessions were held outside in a courtyard with a bench, a table and whatever shade and shelter construction we could improvise. Although the best that circumstances allowed, such arrangements did not preclude occasional interruptions from curious passers-by or even the odd goat. This meant that a fair number of sessions had to be abandoned and subjects dropped from the analyses of results.

Communication always took place entirely in Yoruba, including the initial 'chat' where the experimenter tried to put the child at her ease and obtained biographical details. The experimenters were bilinguals with Yoruba as their first and English as their second language. They were each given a detailed training for the separate experiments and interviews, and training always finished with practice sessions with the three age groups of children in the schools. Special emphasis was placed, first, on helping the children to feel relaxed – that they were playing 'games' not being tested – and second on observing the child during experiments and noting any overt behaviour.

A major preparatory effort was directed towards ensuring that all aspects of the materials, instructions and procedures used could be understood by the youngest children. Yoruba psychologists advised on cultural and linguistic issues. Interview questions, word lists, stories and instructions were all translated into Yoruba and then back-translated into English until an agreeable format was found. Where the children's own responses were complex, as in their story recall, or ambiguous in any way, they were translated into English separately by two different people (the experimenters themselves or post-graduate education students) and any non-trivial differences were jointly discussed.

2   The individual and social aspects of remembering: metamemory

We shall look firstly at the study of metamemory – the children's awareness of their own memories. A structured interview was used in which the child was asked a series of 42 questions designed to assess his awareness of his own memory and of the social or cultural context of remembering. A free recall task was also given so that the relation between metamemory and memory could be explored. The questions focused on the following five topics:

(a) *General evaluation of memory abilities.* Examples include: 'Do you sometimes forget things?' 'Which kinds of things do you forget?' 'Is your memory better than your friend's, or is it the same, or is it worse?' 'How do you know it is better/same/worse?'

(b) *The social context of memory.* Examples include: 'Do you know of any Yoruba people who have to remember many things?' 'Which people?' 'What must they remember?' 'Does your mother ever insist that you remember certain things?' 'Which things?'

(c) *Information storage and retrieval.* Examples include: 'Suppose that your teacher has asked you to bring a special book to school tomorrow. Your teacher says it is very important that you remember to bring it. What would you do to help you remember to bring it?' 'What other things could you do to be sure you don't forget it?' 'Look at these pictures. How would you try to remember them?' 'What else could you do?' 'Suppose you have lost your pen at school. What would you do to try to find it? What else could you do?'

(d) *Variables affecting memory.* Examples include: 'Yesterday I showed these pictures to two children I know. I asked them how long they would need to remember the names of all the things in the pictures. One child said one minute. The other child said five minutes. Why do you think that the other child wanted more time?' 'I took the pictures away and asked each child to tell me the names of all the things they could remember. Which child do you think remembered most?' 'Why?' 'Suppose your mother has told you an important message to tell your aunt. Would it make any difference if you stopped to play on your way to your aunt's house instead of going straight there?' 'Why?' 'Which do you think is easier for you to remember – a story or a song?' 'Why?' (e) *Metamemory and free recall*. A free recall task was given during the interview so that the relations between memory awareness and actual memory performance could be looked at.

Sixty children were interviewed but interruptions led to two first and two sixth graders being dropped from the analyses. The results of the study will be looked at for each of the five topics in turn.

GENERAL EVALUATION OF MEMORY ABILITIES

Even the youngest group of children interviewed showed considerable knowledge about how they remember. All age groups were aware that their memories were not infallible. They all said that they sometimes forgot things and that they were more likely to forget some things than others.

The younger children, however, were less articulate in describing which kinds of information were easier to remember: one third of grade I children did not know, eight cited particular school subjects and a further three mentioned actions (e.g. washing, cleaning the house, reading their school books). Fifty per cent of grade III and 28 per cent of grade VI children also mentioned school subjects and actions but the rest of these older children gave more generalised responses. For instance, one third grader and five sixth graders talked about dates or songs. Most interesting was the fairly large proportion of older children who said that things were easier to remember in Yoruba than in the English language (40 per cent grade III, 44 per cent grade VI). That no first graders cited language may reflect their relative lack of contact with English at that stage in school.

When asked what they tended to forget, most children quoted specific school subjects (100 per cent grade I, 70 per cent grade III, 67 per cent grade VI). The remaining, older children again gave more generalised answers like: 'When I don't write something down'; 'when I have too many things to remember at the same time'; 'when I have other things to do in the meantime'.

These apparent age differences in the generality of the children's answers were not reflected in their replies to a series of questions asking them to evaluate their own memory abilities. Indeed the three groups of children were nearly unanimous in assessing their memories in terms of their intellectual performance at school. Typical replies to 'How do you know your memory is better than your friend's?' were: 'because she cheats from me in class'; 'because I answer the teacher's questions and he cannot'; 'I am more brilliant in the exams.' On the one hand, this may reflect the school's emphasis on the retention of large amounts of information. On the other hand, it may reflect the children's awareness of the intimate relation between memory and the intelligence as a whole.

THE SOCIAL CONTEXT OF MEMORY

Questions on the role of memory in Yoruba culture released a wealth of information from the sixth graders and a lot of blank expressions from the youngest children. Answers to: 'What things are important for a Yoruba child to remember?' are summarised in Table 5.1. The older children listed several aspects of verbal tradition (greetings, songs, proverbs, riddles, stories) and various kinds of festivals and ceremonies (e.g. naming, marriage, masquerade, Muslim festivals and fasting times). Several children simply said that a Yoruba child must remember the Yoruba culture and its customs.

Table 5.1   *What should a Yoruba child remember?*

| | Grade | | |
	I	III	VI
Verbal tradition	1	6	10
Festivals/ceremonies	1	0	9
Religion	1	3	9
Yoruba culture	0	5	5
Actions (dance, forbidden acts)	0	0	3
To respect elders	0	1	0
To work/behave well	2	3	0
Don't know	13	7	0

Table 5.2   *Who in Yorubaland must remember many things?*

	Grade		
	I	III	VI
Ifa priests	0	0	6
Babalawos	0	2	2
Our seniors/elders	11	4	4
Obas	0	4	2
Military, schoolteachers, doctors	2	7	4
Parents	2	2	0
School pupils	2	3	3
Don't know	3	1	0

The older children were also aware that traditionally, certain Yoruba people had special memory responsibilities (see Table 5.2). Fifty-five per cent of sixth graders and 30 per cent of third graders specifically mentioned Ifa priests, Babalawos or Obas. A majority of grade I children did reply that 'older people' had greater memory loads – that, in one sense, the old people are a culture's memory. Many third graders gave less traditional roles as requiring special memory effort such as schoolteachers.

When subsequently asked what those people had to remember, the younger children were less articulate than the older groups. Only three of the first graders who had cited seniors gave any reply. Most of the older children gave some details but only two sixth graders who had cited the priests of Ifa knew of the vast numbers of poems they had to be able to recall.

To find out about the child's own mnemonic responsibilities, she was asked in turn whether her mother and father told her to remember particular things. No age or sex differences were found in the children's replies. Boys and girls in all age groups said that both parents stressed domestic chores (50 per cent mother, 46 per cent father) and school-related activities (27 per cent both parents) but few children mentioned trading or farming. Fourteen per cent of all the children said their mothers emphasised 'moral' issues. For instance: 'My mother says I should remember that I must not look forward to my father's heritage'; 'My mother tells me to respect my elders.' Only one child said his father stressed such things.

INFORMATION STORAGE AND RETRIEVAL

Even the youngest children were aware that verbal rehearsal improves memory performance. When asked about delivering a spoken message, 83 per cent of first graders and all the older children said they would repeat it over to themselves (either thinking of it, singing it, or saying it) as they were going along.

Similarly, all age groups were aware that longer times for storage led to better retention. So, for instance, nearly all the children said they themselves would want to study a set of pictures for five minutes rather than one minute in order to remember the names of the items. And most of them (78 per cent I, 85 per cent III, 24 per cent VI) generalised this to say that other people would also remember more pictures if they had had the longer study time.

Developmental differences emerged in the numbers of ways of storing information which were articulated by the children. Table 5.3 summarises the replies to questions on how each child would try to remember to bring a particular book to school the next day. As Kreutzer *et al.* (1975) found with North Americans, the older children expressed more distinct ways of storing information than the younger children ($chi^2(2) = 7.5$, $p<0.05$). However, unlike the North Americans, there were also qualitative age differences between the children in this study in the types of storage strategies reported. Table 5.3 (b) shows these results using Kreutzer *et al.*'s distinction between *external* and *internal* memory devices. Internal mnemonics include all self-based strategies like verbal rehearsal (e.g. 'I would say the name

Table 5.3   *Percentages of children citing the different numbers and types of strategies for remembering to bring a book to school*

Grade	(a) Number of strategies		(b) First strategy given		(c) Whether internal strategy cited at all	
	One	Two or more	Internal	External	Yes	No
I	61	39	50	50	50	50
III	25	75	15	85	20	80
VI	22	78	0	100	17	83

of the book over in my head'; 'I would remember it by heart'). External mnemonics cover non self-based strategies like writing down the name of the book, or putting the book in a particular place ('in my metal box', 'by my bed') or asking other people to remind one.

Older children relied more on external and less on internal devices than the younger children. Only a small proportion of third and sixth graders cited internal strategies at all (Table 5.3) and significantly fewer older children gave them as a first strategy $(chi^2(2) = 14.1, p<0.01)$. *Thus older children are not only aware of having more strategies at their disposal than younger children, but are also likely to rely less on their own heads and more on external cues to ensure retrieval.*

Explicit questions on object retrieval (e.g. 'a pen lost at school') revealed no clear developmental differences. Fifty per cent of first, 75 per cent of third and 78 per cent of sixth graders cited two or more distinct search strategies. Nearly all the children suggested recruiting other people in some way (to help search; to announce the loss publicly; to be asked if they had taken it). Rather more first graders (50 per cent) than third (25 per cent) or sixth (33 per cent) graders suggested an exhaustive search of the school. Twenty per cent of all grades suggested looking in certain 'likely places' and only five children in all mentioned retracing where one had been since last seeing the pen. However, as we noted in section 1, the main focus of our study was on storage rather than retrieval variables and few explicit questions were asked about retrieval problems. More detailed and varied questioning may well have revealed developmental differences in retrieval plans akin to those found with storage plans.

EFFECTS OF TASK VARIABLES ON MEMORY PERFORMANCE

When asked about strategies for storing information – a verbal message or to bring a book to school – many of the older children spontaneously stressed *time* factors in their responses: 'I would go home and put the book in my special box *straight away*'; 'I would write it down *immediately*'; 'I would *run quickly* to my aunt's house and tell her.' Seventy per cent of grade III and 72 per cent of grade VI compared with only 33 per cent of grade I children spontaneously mentioned time factors when giving strategies for remembering the book (comparing numbers of children in each grade who did and did not cite time factors, chi^2 = 7.1, p<0.05).

As we noted in the last section, there were no grade differences in the children's awareness that longer study times led to better retention. Questions elaborating this theme, however, produced some interesting replies. For instance, when asked why one child wanted five minutes and the other wanted one minute to study a displayed set of pictures many first and third graders said it was because the first child was relatively limited in his intellectual *abilities*. For example, 'he is less brilliant than the other'; 'he cannot quickly understand all the things'. Table 5.4 shows the numbers of children giving such reasons initially and (numbers in parentheses) eventually. The two groups of younger children initially gave ability reasons as opposed to any other kinds of reasons more than the sixth graders (chi^2(2) = 6.3, p<0.05). The other main grade difference was in the numbers of children citing *task factors*, such as: 'there are too many pictures to learn quickly' or 'he will remember more if he studies for a long time'. The sixth graders gave task as opposed to any other sorts of reasons more than the third or first graders respectively (chi^2(2) = 10.0, p<0.01 for 'eventually' given reasons). There were no grade differences in the numbers of children citing the different motivations of the learner (e.g. 'he wants to remember them very well'; 'she has the patience to study hard'). Thus although all three groups gave equal weight to motivational factors, the younger children emphasised the intellectual constraints of the person remembering while the

Table 5.4   *Numbers of children giving different categories of reasons for a person wanting longer study time*

| Grade | Category of reason | | | |
	Task factors	Motivation of learner	Abilities of learner	Don't know
I	0 (0)	6 (6)	9 (9)	3
III	3 (5)	9 (9)	7 (10)	1
VI	8 (8)	8 (10)	2 (4)	0

oldest children stressed the constraints of the particular memory task.

When told that the child who studied for the longer period had actually remembered more items than the other child, subjects were again asked why this was so. Seventy-eight per cent of the sixth graders explicitly said it was because he had a longer study period compared with only 40 per cent of grade III and 33 per cent of grade I ($chi^2(2) = 8.4$, $p<0.02$). Some children said it was because he had looked harder or more closely (28 per cent I, 15 per cent III, 11 per cent VI), while the remaining children either did not know (four grade I, two grade III and one grade VI) or again attributed the difference to one child's greater abilities or 'brilliance'.

A similar stress by older children on task factors and by younger children on personal/ability factors was found in responses to several other questions aimed to assess their awareness of task variables. For example, a series of questions was asked about the relative difficulties of remembering pictures, songs, stories and poems (comparing each pair successively). For each comparison, the child was also asked to explain why one was easier to remember than the other. Reasons were categorised according to whether the child cited: (1) aspects of the material itself (e.g. 'you can see pictures'; 'tunes are hard to forget'; 'stories teach you important lessons'; 'you can tell stories again and again'); or (2) aspects of the person remembering (e.g. 'I like stories more'; 'I sing every day'; 'I can understand stories but not poems'; 'I am happy when I can sing'). Between 20 and 40 per cent of the two older groups gave both sorts of reasons on the various comparisons (cf. 0–11 per cent grade I). The most notable difference, however, was that the first graders tended to give exclusively personal reasons. Indeed, less than 20 per cent mentioned aspects of the material itself on any comparison, whereas between 40 and 60 per cent of grade III and 50–72 per cent of grade VI did so on every comparison. Within the two broad categories of person- and task-related reasons, actual responses were very varied and no meaningful sub-categorisations could be found. There were, however, several sophisticated replies by the oldest children. For instance, one sixth grade girl explained that stories were easier to remember than pictures: 'because pictures are many separate things but a story is only one thing and I can learn it all at once'.

One further result of this sequence of questions is relevant. If the responses of individual subjects are examined across the various two-way comparisons of materials, there can be cases of inconsistency whereby, for example, a story is said to be easier to remember than a song, and a song easier than pictures but then pictures are said to be easier than stories. Such inconsistencies were found in the responses of a third of the first grade children but no others. This may again reflect the first graders' (as opposed to the sixth graders') approach to remembering as being not so firmly based on an understanding of the different kinds of task factors but more (in this case) a question of spontaneous personal preferences.

METAMEMORY AND PERFORMANCE IN A FREE RECALL TASK

During the interview sessions, each child was shown an array of twenty-five pictures which were of five items from each of five categories: transport, food, clothes, animals and cooking utensils. These were the same pictures as used in Experiment 1 (see section 3). The child was first asked about what they could do to help them remember the names of all the things in the pictures. Secondly, they were told to try and remember them so that when the experimenter removed them the child could tell him all their names. A three-minute study interval was given and the child was then asked for immediate verbal recall.

One surprising result was the fairly narrow range of study plans articulated by even the oldest children. No child suggested a classificatory strategy, despite the pictures being from familiar categories. This result contrasts with the clear increase with age in category-based study plans expressed by North American children in Kreutzer et al.'s study. In fact, none of the Yoruba children interviewed suggested using any kinds of association *between* the pictures as an aid to remembering them.

The study plans reported were categorised as either *visual study* (e.g. 'I would look at them very closely') or *labelling* (e.g. 'I would call out their names'; 'I would read the pictures to myself'). A more general category, *learning*, included responses which did not cite any distinct strategies such as: 'I would learn them by heart'; 'I would think about them very hard.' An additional, *sequential* category included instances where the child had also specified that the pictures would be learnt in some order – 'one by one', 'taking each in turn'. Because no reply referred explicitly to names being repeated in any way, no verbal rehearsal category was scored. Table 5.5 shows the number of children giving responses in each category initially and (numbers in parentheses) eventually. Apart from the predominance of visual study plans by the two younger groups and the tendency of grade VI to specify sequence, the results are interesting only in showing an overall *lack* of developmental differences in reported study plans.

About half the children were observed 'doing something' during the study interval. Of those children, over 75 per cent in each age group were heard saying the names of the items depicted. Taken with the fact that few children articulated labelling study plans, this implies a gap between what a child says he will do and what he actually does when it comes to remembering things. Only seven of the twenty children who were observed labelling had proposed it in their study plans.

This apparent gap between the articulation and use of a study plan was further implicated when attempts were made to relate the children's recall to various aspects of their interview replies. No relation was found between the type or number of study plans proposed and levels of recall or clustering (see section 3 for recall results). Nor did performance relate to the type or number of strategies articulated in replies to questions on more everyday memory tasks – remembering to bring a book to school; finding a lost pen; delivering a spoken message. This result means we cannot assume any direct correspondence between meta-memorial knowledge and memory performance (cf. Hagen *et al.*, 1975; Kail, 1979).

Table 5.5 *Numbers of children suggesting each type of study plan*

Grade	Visual study	Labelling	Learning	None	Sequence specified
I	12 (13)	3 (4)	2 (5)	1	0
III	14 (16)	3 (5)	3 (6)	0	2
VI	8 (9)	7 (7)	3 (3)	0	8

METAMEMORY: A KEY TO MEMORY?

At this point, we can usefully summarise our findings on metamemory. Even the youngest children interviewed were aware of certain important aspects of their memories. They all said that they sometimes forgot things and some things more often than others. And all age groups were aware that verbal rehearsal aids retention of a verbal message, and that the longer one studied material, the more of it one would remember.

Developmental *differences* in metamemory were mainly in terms of the emphasis placed on: (1) constraints of the *person* remembering as opposed to constraints of the memory *task*; (2) reliance on one's own *internal* memory processes as opposed to a variety of *external* aids to remembering. The oldest children expressed a greater awareness of the effects of task variables such as the time between storage and recall and the actual materials being remembered. In contrast, the youngest children stressed that the main determinants of memory efficiency were the intellectual abilities and preferences of the person remembering. The third graders appeared 'transitional' between those extremes in generally stressing the person remembering but sometimes also articulating factors involved in the task itself.

One can relate the first graders' emphasis on the person remembering to their expressed reliance on the person's 'in-the-head' strategies as memory aids. This contrasts with the two older groups of children who articulated not only *more* strategies but also put more reliance on *external* devices like making notes, telling people to remind them and putting retrieval cues in likely places.

It would be interesting to see if age differences in how the children said they remembered in everyday kinds of situations were reflected in their actual memory performance in similar situations. Certainly, it was not reflected in their performance in an artificial, experimental task of recalling the pictures. There, what children *said* they would do bore no discernable relation to what they *did* do. Metamemory was no key to memory functioning in the free recall task. What children actually do when they remember things is the topic of the next section.

3 The use of memory strategies

THE ROLE OF CATEGORISATION IN MEMORY DEVELOPMENT

Experiment 1

My starting point for looking at memory strategies was one unexpected finding of the metamemory questions. When asked what they might do to help them remember a set of twenty-five categorisable pictures, no child suggested using categorisation or any other kinds of associations *between* the various items. This differs from findings with Western children which generally show an increase with age both in the articulation (e.g. Kreutzer *et al.*, 1975) and use (e.g. Moely, Olson, Halwes and Flavell, 1969) of categorisation as a mnemonic. Clearly, just because no child *said* he would use categorisation does not mean that no child would use categorisation when it came to actually remembering. To look at how the child might *use* categorisation, I gave children those same twenty-five pictures in a free recall task.

Before describing this experiment, we must make one further distinction. That no child articulated categorisation as a study plan may have been because the categories in the material were not noticed. The use of categorisation as a mnemonic depends on the extent to which the existing categories are both *perceived* and *used* in aiding memory. To investigate the role of categorisation we have to look at both the children's perception of categories and how they use them in memory. We can do this by combining a 'sorting' or categorisation task with a memory task (cf. Mandler and Pearlstone, 1966). In this way we examine how the children categorise the pictures separately from how they use that categorisation in recalling them. Such a sorting-recall procedure was one basis for Experiment 1.

SUBJECTS AND PROCEDURES

Ninety children were allocated randomly to one of three experimental groups. All the children were initially asked to name the twenty-five items in the pictures (shoe, hat, agbada (gown), trousers, belt; onion, groundnut, banana, orange, pineapple; cow, cat, dog, goat, monkey; knife, spoon, cup, plate, kettle; car, lorry, motorbike, aeroplane, boat). Subsequent instructions varied for each experimental group. Group A were simply told to try and remember all the items so that when the experimenter removed the pictures they could tell him all their names. Group B were not asked to remember but told to categorise the pictures – 'putting together the ones which belong together in some way'. Group C were instructed to perform a task which was comparatively 'irrelevant' to memory – arranging the pictures in various shapes (triangle, circle, square) on the table and counting them. All three groups were subsequently asked to recall the names of the items.

Thus group A were given an *intentional* memory task whereby, in their deliberate effort to remember, they were free to choose from their available repertoire of strategies whichever they felt was most appropriate to the task at hand. Groups B and C were *incidental* memory conditions whereby no deliberate effort to remember was made. Their recall had therefore to be based on a prescribed strategy of the particular (non-mnemonic) activity they were asked to do – either categorisation or spatial arrangement.

After the first recall trial, all the children were instructed to try to remember the items for two subsequent trials. Trials 2 and 3 were therefore intentional memory conditions. Following trial 3, groups B and C were asked to categorise the pictures.

RESULTS AND DISCUSSION

When sorting the pictures before recall, the sixth graders used fewer categories ($\bar{x} = 6.2$) than the third ($\bar{x} = 10.0$) or first graders ($\bar{x} = 9.8$). There were no such differences in groups B and C who sorted after the recall task. Most of those children sorted the five defined categories. This has two implications. Firstly, a familiarity effect for the younger children whereby doing other things with the pictures had facilitated their subsequent categorisation (cf. Curran, 1979). Secondly, the children could clearly perceive category associations between the pictures when asked to sort them. So the absence of associative study plans in the interview was not due to any inability to perceive the categories.

Results in terms of the percentage of items recalled on the first trial are shown in Figure 5.1. Analysis of variance showed both the main effects ($p < 0.001$) and the two-way interaction of

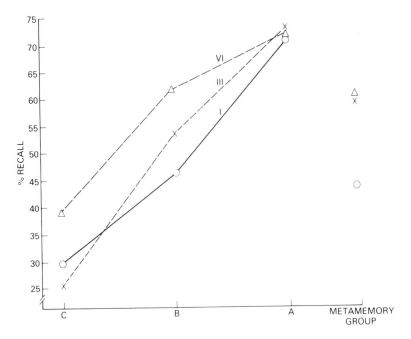

Figure 5.1 *Percentage of items recalled by each grade and experimental group*

grade and experimental group ($p < 0.05$) were significant. Thus age differences depended on the type of instructions the children had been given. All three grades recalled equally highly when simply instructed to remember the items; grade VI recalled more than grades III and I respectively after categorising; and the sixth graders recalled more than either younger group after the memory-irrelevant task.

To the extent that all the age groups recalled more after categorising than after spatially arranging the pictures, they could all use categorisation as a mnemonic. Similarly, to the extent that all the groups recalled more when instructed to remember the pictures than when asked to categorise them allows us to infer that they used their self-selected strategy more efficiently than the imposed categorising strategy. This difference between the recall levels of groups A and B decreased with age, implying that the older children were more efficient in using categorisation as a mnemonic. This was very noticeable over trials, where only the sixth graders in group B increased their recall levels. The two younger groups actually remembered less on trial 2 than on trial 1, almost as if they were starting afresh in studying the pictures for recall.

I could find few clear patterns as to the kinds of organisation that children were imposing on the items, despite various detailed analyses of order of recall. Even in group A, clustering in terms of the defined categories was at chance levels (Bousfield and Bousfield, 1966). Analysis of subjective organisation (based on the inter-trial consistency in the order items were recalled) showed generally higher levels of clustering by the sixth graders than the younger children. Further, in group B only the sixth graders had clustering levels which were above chance and which increased over trials, again indicating their more efficient use of categorisation than the younger children.

The recall levels of the 56 children who were asked to remember the pictures during the metamemory interview are also displayed in Figure 5.1. Like group A, theirs was an intentional memory task. We clearly cannot compare the two groups directly, as a different experimenter carried out the interview and study times were not equivalent. But what are interesting are the different *patterns* of group differences. Why should the recall levels of the first graders be lower than the other children's in the interview group but not group A? There were two main differences in procedure. Firstly, unlike group A, the interview children were asked to articulate a study plan prior to the study period. Presumably, this may have been detrimental to the first graders' subsequent recall performance and not the third or sixth graders', but this seems unlikely especially in that the study plans given by the first and third graders were nearly identical (cf. Table 5.3). The second difference was that, unlike the interview group, group A children were all asked to name the items in pictures at the outset of the experiment. Children in the interview group would therefore have been at a disadvantage if they did not label the items spontaneously. This would imply that even though they were instructed to remember the names of the items in the pictures, the first graders did not spontaneously label them as much as the older children.

To summarise, the role of categorisation in the development

of the children's memories is not a central one. Categorisation was not used spontaneously by any age group. At the same time, however, the children had no problem in organising the material into categories, especially after they were familiar with the pictures. And the children could all use category association as a basis for recalling the items. Grade differences were in the extent to which they did so efficiently. With increasing age, the children used categorisation efficiently, approaching their levels of recall in intentional memory. What remains an intriguing result of this experiment is that the performance of all three grades of children was equal and best when they were simply asked to remember the items. And this leaves the question of what strategies the children had used to produce such high recall. As Scribner (1974) complains, available methods of analysis make it easier to characterise what children don't do, rather than what they do, when they remember things. We know that the children did not use categorisation in intentional memory, but what did they use?

THE ROLE OF TONE AND VERBAL REHEARSAL IN MEMORY DEVELOPMENT

Experiment 2

To characterise the strategies which might have been used by the children, we have to use different types of materials and procedures which allow for analyses of forms of organisation other than taxonomic categorisation. Experiment 2 used word lists which were verbally presented and could therefore allow us to examine verbal rehearsal as indicated by serial position effects. The word lists used were so constructed as to allow another possible strategy to be looked at – that of tone categorisation.

Tone categorisation appeared a suitable candidate for a culture- or language-specific mnemonic. The Yoruba language has three tones: low (L), medium (M) and high (H). Words with the same written appearance differ radically in meaning according to the tones of the syllables. To give a few examples, *agbon* (MH) means wasp and *agbon* (ML) means basket; *ogun* (MM) means war, *ogun* (ML) means medicine, *ogun* (MH) means inheritance and *Ogun* (LH) is the god of iron. Despite the fact that a majority of the world's languages are tone languages, almost nothing is known of them from a psychological or developmental viewpoint (for a linguistic account, see Fromkin, 1978). It therefore seemed especially valuable to explore possible uses of tone structure in memory development.

Two word lists, given in Table 5.6, were drawn up. List 1 consisted of sixteen three-syllable words which were categorisable by tone patterns into four groups. List 2 consisted of sixteen three-syllable words, no two of which shared the same tone pattern. Ninety-six children were subjects, half of them heard list 1 and the other half heard list 2. Each list was read at a rate of about one word every three seconds and the child was then asked to repeat all the words she could remember.

When parallel experiments are performed using taxonomically categorisable and uncategorisable lists, it is generally found that children who use categorisation as a strategy recall more items from the categorisable than the uncategorisable list. So in Experiment 2, one would expect that list 1 would be recalled better than list 2 if children had used tone categories as an organising principle in recall.

Table 5.6 *Clusterable and unclusterable word lists*

| *1 Clusterable List* | | | *2 Unclusterable List* | | |
Meaning	Word	Tones	Meaning	Word	Tones
box	*apoti*	LHH	type of cloth	*adire*	LLM
port	*ebute*	LHH	broom	*igbale*	LHL
squirrel	*okere*	LHH	plant	*eweko*	MHM
melon seed			cooked maize	*agbado*	LMM
soup	*egusi*	LHH	alligator		
child	*omode*	MMH	pepe	*atare*	MMM
bucket	*koroba*	MMH	cat	*ologbo*	MHL
pigeon	*eyele*	MMH	key	*kokoro*	HHH
fellow wife	*orogun*	MMH	elder	*alagba*	MLL
pot	*ikoko*	LLL	rice	*iresi*	LML
beads	*ileke*	LLL	stone	*okuta*	LHM
ladder	*akaba*	LLL	beads	*ileke*	LLL
banana	*ogede*	LLL	gown	*agbada*	MHH
gown	*agbada*	MHH	box	*apoti*	LHH
air	*afefe*	MHH	bible	*bibeli*	HHL
knee	*orunkun*	MHH	table	*tabili*	MML
bitter kola	*orogbo*	MHH	bucket	*koroba*	MMH

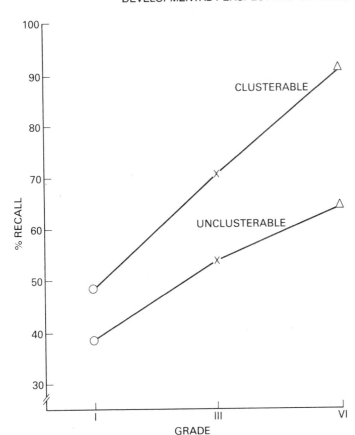

Figure 5.2 *Percentage of words recalled by each grade – clusterable and unclusterable lists*

As Figure 5.2 shows, this was indeed the case. Analysis of variance showed significant list (p<0.001) differences. Grade differences were also significant (p<0.001) and interacted with list effects (p<0.002) whereby older children were more susceptible to list differences than younger children. I infer first that tone patterns can provide an effective organising principle in memory. Second, older children use tone categories as mnemonics more than younger children.

Several subsequent analyses did not reveal a pattern of age differences directly in terms of differences in levels of clustering together same-tone words. Qualitative analyses showed clustering mainly of same-tone words on list 1 and of consecutively presented words on list 2 as well as few 'semantic' clusters (e.g. box–beads, rice–cooked maize).

Serial position curves were drawn up for each list and are shown in Figure 5.3. If the children were using verbal rehearsal strategies, one would expect to find a 'primacy' effect where words at the beginning of a list have a higher probability of being recalled than words in the middle of the list. No grade showed primacy on the categorisable list; grade I showed primacy on the uncategorisable list. This indicates that something other than serial organisation was being used by all the groups for list 1, and that grade I children were verbally rehearsing list 2.

Another short experiment is relevant here because it also focused on tone and memory. Essentially, it used a proactive interference paradigm (cf. Wickens, 1970). This paradigm has been used to determine which aspects of materials are encoded in memory. Forty-eight children were asked to remember words presented in threes over seven trials. After each group of words was presented, the child performed an interfering task of counting backwards in ones from a number given by the experimenter. She was then asked to recall the three words. After a practice task, the first three trials involved three three-word groups where all nine words had the same tone pattern (LH). The next three trials used nine words with another tone pattern (LL). The seventh trial presented three longer words (three syllables instead of two).

As would be expected from Wickens's findings, release from proactive interference was found for all three grades on trial seven, showing that word length is encoded in short-term memory. However, the same release was only found for grade VI on trial 4. This implies, like the recall experiment, that the oldest children do encode tone in memory and more so than the younger children. Also interesting was the pattern of errors. A fairly large number of words which the children recalled in this experiment were not actually presented. Group totals were 34, 17 and 14 for grades I, III and VI respectively. For each grade, about 25 per cent of such words were intrusions from previous trials. However, age differences were apparent in the extent to which semantic and tonal factors could account for most of the

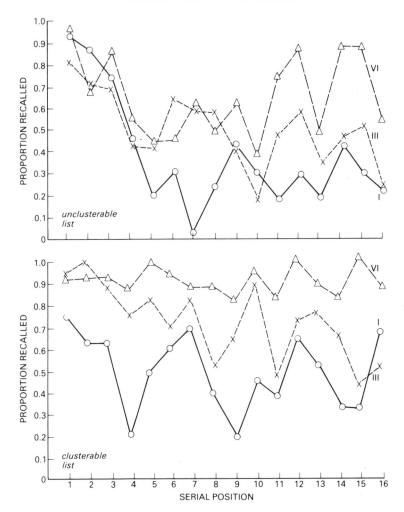

Figure 5.3 *Proportion of words recalled according to their position in the presentation lists for (i) unclusterable and (ii) clusterable words*

remaining words recalled but not presented. Semantic variations on words from present or previous trials accounted for 41 per cent grade I, 23 per cent grade III and 14 per cent grade VI words. And a further 17 per cent grade I, 23 per cent grade III and 35 per cent grade VI words were apparent tonal variations – words not presented but which had the same tones as those which were. This incidental finding again suggests that tone is a more relevant feature in the older than the younger children's memory strategies.

The findings on the use of tone in memory by the older children need further experimental support and clarification. Lacking the intuitions of a native speaker of a tone language, I can only speculate on how tone categorisation might function as a mnemonic strategy. A reasonable guess is that perhaps like other aspects of verbal material such as rhyme or word length, tone operates mainly as a selection principle at retrieval, checking recalled words against presented words (cf. Anderson and Bower, 1972).

Why should tone be used mnemonically more by the older than the younger children? Again, the lack of psycholinguistic research on tone means we can only give speculative answers. But one likely candidate for linking age differences in performance with tone language is *literacy*. For the literate child, tone is more salient in that it distinguishes the meaning of words with the same spelling. *Agbon* (MH) meaning wasp sounds quite different from *agbon* (ML) meaning basket and, compared with the literate child, the pre-literate child would not think the two words had that much in common. The nearest analogy I can think of in English is words like bough, enough, though and through where the 'ough' ending sounds quite different even though it is written identically. It would follow from this that tone may assume greater saliency as the child acquires higher levels of literacy during primary schooling. One way of testing this explanation would be to compare older literate and non-literate speakers of a tone language. If literacy is the crucial variable, then literate speakers of the language would use tone in memory more than non-literate speakers regardless of their age.

How have our findings on tone and memory illuminated the results of Experiment 1? The first experiment showed that, unlike typical Western findings, there was no developmental trend in the three age groups towards spontaneously using categorisation as a mnemonic. At the same time, however, another unusual and intriguing finding was that all age groups performed equally and best when simply asked to remember the pre-labelled pictures. What strategies were the children using to achieve this? Experiment 2 found evidence that one strategy available to Yoruba speakers is to use tone categories. However, we found that older children use such categories more than younger children. Verbal rehearsal appears to be one strategy used by younger children for word lists. If that is their main and preferred strategy, it may explain why the first graders who did not label the pictures (i.e., the interview group) performed relatively worse than those who did (i.e. group A), as labelling is clearly a pre-requisite to verbal rehearsal.

We shall cut short our discussion of memory strategies at this point and must leave unanswered questions on the nature of the use of tone in memory. We shall turn instead to look at memory for meaningful material. When investigating memory strategies, the use of picture sets and word lists are an attempt to control for developmental differences in the meaning children of different ages derive from the materials. However, such developmental differences are themselves important in memory, as a child's understanding of things clearly affects how she remembers them.

4 Meaningful memory

In the course of normal events, things are remembered because their natural contexts are organised in ways that matter to the individual and make sense in terms of his social experience. (Cole and Scribner, 1974, p. 139)

What Cole and Scribner are pointing out here is simply that most of what we remember does not require any special effort. This is a sharp contrast to the picture presented in the last section where very deliberate efforts had to be made to remember lists of items which had little meaning for the children beyond the immediate, experimental situation.

In the last decade, researchers have increasingly tried to find ways of looking at memory for meaningful information. And what they have found so far is that even the young child's memory is much more planful and organised than we were led to believe from experimental studies of strategies.

One approach, which is particularly suitable for research with children, has been to look at their recall of stories. It is also an ideal method for cross-cultural studies in that every culture 'tells its stories' and so each culture provides it own kind of readily available material.

In this section I shall report an experiment looking at how the same three groups of children understand and remember a story. A story was invented to fulfill three criteria: (1) it should make sense as a story to the children; (2) it should contain explicit kinds of factual, numerical and sequential information; (3) it should contain implicit kinds of information which depend on logical inferences being made between events and facts given in the story. Here is a back-translation of the story:

> This is a story about Taiwo Adeyemi. One day, Mrs Adeyemi said: 'Taiwo, today our family will eat well. You must go and buy the food. Buy 4 cups of rice, 5 kobo salt, 10 kobo pepe, 20 kobo tomatoes and 2 fish. Here is 2 Naira to pay.'
>
> Taiwo walked for about 10 minutes and then she saw a trader selling doughnuts. Taiwo said: 'I have money today, so I will buy a big doughnut.' She walked away, eating the doughnut.
>
> When she arrived, she bought the rice, the salt, the pepe and the tomatoes. She then saw her friend Aderonke, and greeted her. Aderonke said: 'I am hungry, Taiwo, and you have money. Please buy 10 kobo groundnuts for me to eat.' Taiwo pitied her friend and bought the groundnuts.
>
> Then Taiwo had a shock. She had only 15 kobo left of her mother's money. So that night, Taiwo's family had no fish to eat in their soup.

The story was read slowly and clearly to each of 96 children. Half the children were then asked simply to tell the story to the experimenter (*immediate recall*). Two or three days later, those same children were again asked to tell Taiwo's story (*long-term recall*). The other 48 children, after hearing the story, were asked a series of 20 questions about it. The questions required both factual recall (e.g. 'What did Mrs Adeyemi ask Taiwo to buy?' 'How much money did she give her?') and making inferences (e.g. 'What did Taiwo not buy?' 'Why didn't she buy fish?') After answering the questions, the child was asked to tell the story to the experimenter (*post-question recall*). The children's story recall was tape recorded under all three conditions and later transcribed and double-translated.

Story recall varied not only in the amount and types of information remembered but also in how that information was structured within the framework of the story. This is illustrated clearly in the following two examples of children's recall:

ABIMBOLA, GRADE III, IMMEDIATE RECALL

Taiwo, Taiwo, she said . . . everybody, she said . . . she said she should buy 10 kobo groundnut for her. She bought 10 kobo groundnut. She was shocked that only 15 kobo was left out of her money. She said she should go and buy salt, fish and pepe so all of them will eat. Taiwo and her friend reached the market. She saw the person that was selling at the market and bought fish, pepe and groundnut from her. She took out her money. She bought everything and she ate them with her mother.

IDOWU, GRADE I, LONG-TERM RECALL

One day in the morning, Taiwo's mother said that all of them will eat delicious food. She said that they should buy fish. She saw her friend. Taiwo's mother gave Taiwo 2 pounds. She used 5 kobo to buy groundnuts for her friend. She did not buy fish. Taiwo went to buy pepe. She bought the fish. She bought the fish, and then she sold it. After buying the fish, they ate it that night. The story ends.

To examine memory for both information and structure, story recall was analysed, first in terms of eight events which, in sequence, formed a framework for the story. The events were: (1) *Mrs Adeyemi asked Taiwo (to buy things)*; (2) *she gave her a list of items*; (3) *Taiwo bought a doughnut*; (4) *Taiwo bought some of the items asked for*; (5) *Taiwo met a friend*; (6) *Taiwo bought her some groundnuts*; (7) *Taiwo had little money (15 kobo) left*; (8) *Taiwo's family did not eat fish*. Recall was scored if an event was mentioned in any way. For example, 'Taiwo's mother told her to buy ingredients for the soup,' scores 1 and 2; 'she bought groundnuts for her friend,' scores 5 and 6.

Table 5.7 shows the results in terms of children recalling all or some of the eight events and whether or not those events were sequenced correctly. (Two of seventeen first graders were

Table 5.7   *Children's recall and sequencing of 8 events in Taiwo's story*

	Time of recall								
	Immediate			Post-question			Long-term		
GRADE	I	III	VI	I	III	VI	I	III	VI
Correct Sequence									
total recall	0	2	8	2	8	11	2	3	7
partial recall	4	9	6	7	5	5	6	9	6
Incorrect Sequence									
total recall	1	0	2	0	1	0	2	1	3
partial recall	11	5	0	6	2	0	6	1	0

dropped from the analysis after the twenty questions, one because of a bad tape recording and the other because he did not want to tell the story. Two third graders were absent for the long-term recall session.) Developmental differences were clear in all three recall conditions. With increasing age, the children not only recalled more events but were more likely to structure those events correctly within the story framework.

Age differences were greater for immediate recall than long-term or post-question recall. The oldest children's performance was near optimum anyway and varied little, but the younger children did better after the questions or after 2–3 days. One would clearly expect them to do better after the questions which were in themselves practice at retrieving the events in sequence. But one would normally expect some forgetting, rather than an improvement in performance, over a two- or three-day delay.

This long-term increase in event recall was, however, paralleled by a decrease in the recall of details from the story. The average number of items asked for and bought was reduced. And fewer young children recalled details like the money given to Taiwo, the name of her friend, that Aderonke was hungry or that Taiwo pitied her, or that Taiwo was shocked about the money. This suggests that the improvement in recalling major events had been at the expense of forgetting minor details. Or, to put it another way, the children had consolidated the basic framework or theme of the story over time and discarded the 'frills'.

Age differences were also found in the recall of quantitative or numerical information. When asked how much money Taiwo was given, 59 per cent of first graders compared with 94 per cent of third and sixth graders remembered the 2 Naira. Only two grade I children (five grade III, thirteen grade VI) mentioned the quantities of any item on the 'shopping list' in their immediate recall. No first graders ever mentioned the amount of money Taiwo had left whereas nine third and all the sixth graders immediately recalled this.

One explanation of the age difference in recalling and sequencing events might be that the younger children did not understand the story as fully as the older children. That is, in as much as memory is a by-product of meaning, the younger children may have extracted less meaning from the story. We can assess this possibility by looking at the children's answers to questions needing implicit inferences. Such inferences require making logical connections between events in the story and therefore reflect a child's comprehension.

One implicit theme of the story was that *because* Taiwo had spent some of the given money on a doughnut and the groundnuts, she did not have enough left for the fish. However, only six of the seventeen first graders (cf. eleven of sixteen third and twelve of sixteen sixth graders) inferred that Taiwo did not buy the fish ($chi^2(2) = 6.29$, $p<0.05$). And when asked why she did not buy fish, only eight of those grade I children (cf. thirteen grade III and fifteen grade VI) inferred that this was because she did not have enough money or that she had spent the money ($chi^2(2) = 9.93$, $p<0.01$).

Developmental differences in comprehension and recall are reflected in which particular events were most frequently omitted by the children when they told the story. For the first graders, the most frequent omission was 'Taiwo had little money left' (nine children omitted this on immediate and ten on long-term recall). This event is clearly more logically important to the story than the third graders' most common omission – 'Taiwo bought some of the items asked for' (ten immediate, nine long-term omissions).

The relation between making inferences and recalling information can also be seen by looking at the children's responses to inference questions in terms of their responses to factual recall questions. Recall levels (for eighteen items asked for) are plotted against the number of inferences made in Figure 5.4. As Paris and Upton (1976) found with North Americans, the relationship is a positive one. Children who made more correct inferences also recalled more information.

A final test of the relation between understanding and remembering the story would be if children who made more correct inferences are more likely to correctly sequence their subsequent story recall. Only six first and three third graders made sequencing errors after the twenty questions, and their average inference scores were 1.0 and 2.7 respectively. This compares with scores of 2.8 and 3.2 respectively for the other children whose recall was correctly sequenced. Thus children who draw inferences are more likely not only to recall more information but also to correctly sequence the events within the story.

5   Conclusions

These findings present a very clear picture of developmental change in 'meaningful memory'. Growing older is not simply a question of remembering more. Rather, *quantitative* differences in retention appear to depend on *qualitative* differences in the

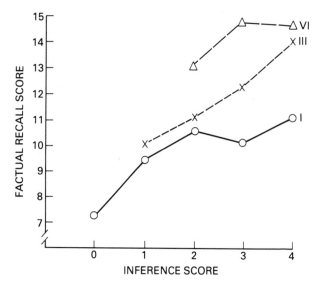

Figure 5.4 *Average number of facts recalled as a function of each grade's average inference scores*

meaning derived from a story. Children who infer the logical links between the events in a story also tend to subsequently structure their recall around that logic and thereby recall more information. In this way, more meaning means more memory. I cannot draw such a clear picture of development from the experiments with relatively 'meaningless memory' for picture sets and word lists. Unlike research with Western children, this study did not find that taxonomic categorisation plays a central role in memory development. Although the children had no problems in organising the materials into categories and, with increasing age, could use those category associations more efficiently as a basis for recall, they did not do either spontaneously.

The findings of the experiments on memory strategies suggested that categorisation by tone patterns, rather than taxonomic associations, may be a culture-specific mnemonic and one which is used more by older than younger children. Differences in levels of literacy were suggested as a factor which might account for such age differences in the use of tone. Before the findings on tone can be viewed as anything more than suggestive, we will clearly need more empirical research as well as a far greater psycholinguistic understanding of tone languagues.

Unlike most of our everyday remembering, the experiments on memory strategies not only involved fairly meaningless material but also forced the child to rely on *internal* memory devices. However, the metamemory study suggested that a central feature of memory development is a *decreasing* dependence on such internal mnemonics and a corresponding *increase* in the use of a wide range of *external* memory cues. By concentrating on situations where only internal devices can be used, we therefore risk ignoring a major source of age differences in memory.

In using the three perspectives of metamemory, memory strategies and meaning in memory, the study has generated three 'pictures' of the child's memory development. As I warned in section 1, each picture is only a thumb-nail sketch, and each requires more detail and integration. But at the same time, I can use the breadth of the study to try to overview the different aspects of memory development during the primary school years.

In drawing together the findings from the three perspectives, one central theme emerges and that it is the *meaning* a child derives from a memory task. This theme emerges in two related ways: first in terms of the implicit meaning of what is being remembered, such as a list of known words as compared with a new story; second, in terms of the context in which the task is set – whether, for example, it is part of a formal experiment or about one of the child's more everyday activities.

With relatively meaningless materials like the set of pictures, the children's metamemorial knowledge (to the extent it was articulated in the interview) appeared very limited. No child suggested using any kinds of association between the items to help him remember them. And this was true even though a similar group of children had no problems in sorting those same pictures and then basing their recall on the categories sorted.

This apparent gap between what children do when they actually remember and what they say they would do beforehand in an interview is not surprising if one considers both the meaning of the tasks and the situations in which they took place. First, the experimental situation itself is hardly an everyday experience. To be asked to remember something for no apparently better reason than to please the experimenter or even to get back to class as soon as possible is not a common reason for memorising. This combines with the fact that what they were asked to remember was also artificial. It was nothing new or 'educational' but simply a series of pictures of things they had seen many times before. For those reasons, it would have been more surprising if the children had been eloquent in suggesting ways of handling such information. Rather than being a prerequisite, metamemorial knowledge of memory strategies probably cannot develop without the child's actually having used those strategies in similar situations. And for those same reasons, it was hardly surprising that no relation was found between the children's interview responses and their performance in recalling the pictures. As Luria (1928) warned long ago, by testing a child only in artificial, experimental situations, we are apt to create a distorted and narrow view of his developing memory.

With more meaningful material like stories, the picture was one of the developing child increasingly extracting the essential meaning or theme and using this as a basis for increasingly more efficient remembering. Unfortunately, I did not broaden the study to include a direct examination of the relation between meaning in memory and metamemory. But when interviewed about ways of remembering in meaningful, familiar situations, the children's metamemorial knowledge was far greater than that implied by their replies to questions on how they might remember picture sets. They suggested a wide variety of memory plans when they were asked questions which made sense in terms of their everyday experiences, like bringing a book to school or delivering a message. It seems likely that there would be a greater correspondence between metamemory and memory performance in these situations. One way of testing this would be to interview the children about, and then observe them doing, some Yoruba equivalent of games like hunt-the-thimble or hide-and-seek.

In summary, just as memory itself cannot be separated from the complex of cognitive processes of which it is part, nor can memory be isolated from the contexts in which it is used. A child's memory at different points in her development will depend primarily on the meaning she derives both from what she is trying to remember and from the context in which she is doing it.

Finally, what are the implications of this study for the primary school child? If educationalists are concerned about improving the young child's retention of school subject matter, then my conclusions have two relevant and important implications. Firstly, the educationalist should direct his attention primarily to the child's understanding of materials, rather than attempt any broadening of memory 'capacity'. As we have seen, the older child does not just remember more than the younger child. She does so because of differences in *how* she remembers. By helping a child to draw out the logical relations between those things she is learning about, a teacher will simultaneously be helping her to remember them. The second and related implication is drawn from the conclusion that the child's understanding will depend on the context in which information is presented for learning. Thus the teacher can also augment the meaning of subject matter by increasing the meaning of the context in which it is presented. Children have many memory devices and skills which they use in their day to day activities outside the classroom. By building on these, by relating subject matter to the child's existing wealth of social as well as intellectual experience, then school learning necessarily becomes more relevant and therefore more meaningful for the child.

References

Anderson, J. and Bower, J.H. (1972), 'Recognition and Retrieval Processes in Free Recall', *Psychological Review*, 79, pp. 97-123.

Bousfield, A.K. and Bousfield, W.A. (1966), 'Measurement of Clustering and of Sequential Constancies in Repeated Free Recall', *Psychological Reports*, 19, pp. 935-42.

Brown, A.L. (1975), 'The Development of Memory: Knowing, Knowing about Knowing and Knowing how to Know', in H.W. Reese (ed.), *Advances in Child Development and Behaviour*, vol. 10, Academic Press, New York.

Cole, M. and Scribner, S. (1974), *Culture and Thought: a Psychological Introduction*, Wiley, New York.

Curran, H.V. (1979), 'Cultural Influences on Learning', PhD thesis, University of London.

Curran, H.V. (1980), 'Cross-cultural Perspectives on Cognition', in G.L. Claxton (ed.) *New Directions in Cognitive Psychology*, Routledge & Kegan Paul, London.

Flavell, J.H. and Wellman, H.M. (1977), 'Metamemory', in R.V. Kailand and J.W. Hagen (eds), *Perspectives on the Development of Memory and Cognition*, Lawrence Erlbaum Associates, Hillsdale, New Jersey.

Fodor, J.A. (1976), *The Language of Thought*, Harvester Press, Hassocks, Sussex.

Fromkin, V.A. (1978), *Tone: A Linguistic Survey*, Academic Press, New York.

Hagen, J.W., Jongeward, R.N. and Kail, R.V. (1975), 'Cognitive Perspectives on the Development of Memory', in H.W. Reese (ed.), *Advances in Child Development and Behaviour*, vol. 10, Academic Press, New York.

Harris, P. (1978), 'Developmental Aspects of Children's Memory', in M.M. Gruneberg and P. Morris (eds), *Aspects of Memory*, Methuen, London.

Kail, B. (1979), *The Development of Memory in Children*, Freeman, San Francisco.

Kail, R. and Hagen, J.W. (eds) (1977), *Perspectives on the Development of Memory and Cognition*, Erlbaum, Hillsdale, New Jersey.

Kreutzer, M.A., Leonard, C. and Flavell, J.H. (1975), 'An Interview Study of Children's Knowledge About Memory', *Monographs of the Society for Research in Child Development*, 40, 1, Serial no. 159.

Luria, A.R. (1928), 'The Problem of the Cultural Behaviour of the Child', *Journal of Genetic Psychology*, 35, pp. 493-505.

Mandler, G. and Pearlstone, Z. (1966), 'Free and Constrained Concept Learning and Subsequent Recall', *Journal of Verbal Learning and Verbal Behaviour*, 5, pp. 126-31.

Moely, B.E., Olson, F.A., Halwes, T.G. and Flavell, J.H. (1969), 'Production Deficiency in Young children's Clustered Recall', *Developmental Psychology*, 1, pp. 26-34.

Paris, S.G. and Upton, L.R. (1976), 'Children's Memory for Inferential Relationships in Prose', *Child Development*, 47, pp. 660-8.

Piaget, J. and Inhelder, B. (1973), *Memory and Intelligence*, Routledge & Kegan Paul, London.

Scribner, S. (1974), 'Developmental Aspects of Categorised Recall in a West African Society', *Cognitive Psychology*, 6, pp. 475-94.

Wickens, D.D. (1970), 'Encoding categories of words: an empirical approach to meaning', *Psychological Review*, 77, pp. 1-15.

6 Home and school: effects of micro-ecology on children's educational achievement

Anya I. Oyewole

Introduction

Free universal primary education was introduced in Nigeria as one of the means of realising the goal of equal educational opportunity (Third National Development Plan 1975–1980). In spite of the federal government's commitment to egalitarianism, it is doubtful whether the free universal primary education scheme can achieve this objective. This is partly because the structure of secondary education continues to perpetuate an elitism which reduces the access of the majority of children to secondary schools (Adeyinka, 1973).

It is also known that because of poor conditions in many public primary schools, the more affluent parents often send their children to fee-paying private schools. It is these children who perform well enough in the common entrance examinations to be admitted into the best secondary schools (Sofenwa, 1976). Hence educational opportunity and attainment in Nigeria, as in some other countries, is very closely tied to parental status and income.

The socio-economic status of a child's parents is not, however, the only factor affecting his chances at school. Psychological studies have indicated many other factors in children's pre-school environments which are associated with their future educational achievement (e.g. Rutter and Madge, 1976). Such factors, and their association with success at school, are the concern of this chapter.

The study I report in this chapter is based on a large-scale project which followed the development of a group of Ibadan

children from one year of age to nineteen years of age. I examine
certain aspects of each child's early 'micro-ecology'. These
include his levels of nutrition, his health and growth as well as
social/psychological factors linked to his home environment. I
investigate how those variables relate to a child's later
achievement in school.

Micro-ecology is the combination of the human and physical
elements in people's immediate home environments, which, in
the early years of life, provide nearly all the care and attention
for a child. Since the human elements are variable, then clearly
children in the same socio-economic stratum may receive very
different nutritional, health and physical care as well as very
different psycho-social stimulation. These may in turn affect
children's physical and psychological development and their
subsequent educational achievements. For example, Hertzig et
al. (1973) found that physical neglect by way of severe
malnutrition significantly reduced IQ scores in children when
such malnourished children were compared in later years with
their sibs and peers on the full WISC scale. Tanner (1969), who
stresses the importance of height as an indicator of long-term
nutritional status, points to the consistent relationship between
height and intelligence. The implications of this relationship to
educational achievement is highlighted by Rutter and Madge
(1976), who made the observation that in all countries,
university students belong to the tallest members of the
population. Hetherington and Martin (1972) claim that
emotional stress caused by severe family disturbance may result
in behavioural and educational problems shown by children.

In Nigeria, it is not known what micro-ecological factors other
than socio-economic status influence educational ability and
success. It is, however, well documented that among the poor
substantial numbers of children experience extreme physical
deprivations as a result of acute and chronic malnutrition,
multiple infections and parasitic infestations leading to bad
general health and stunted growth (Hendrickse 1967, Ransome-
Kuti et al. 1972, Janes 1974). It is less well known that many of
these children are also victims of broken or disrupted homes.
This is probably a result of the disintegration of traditional
social structures and family ties which is created by rapid
industrial development and urbanisation. It is therefore likely
that among the poor in Nigeria, some children, as a result of

negative early micro-ecological experiences, are more 'disadvantaged' than others. This disadvantage is well established before children enter primary schools. It is suggested that free primary education cannot reverse such disadvantage. Rather, it legitimises it as educational achievement is clearly linked to later occupational opportunity and social status.

To assess the effects of negative micro-ecological experiences on educational achievement several negative ecological factors from which many poor Nigerian children are known to suffer are examined. These include acute and chronic malnutrition, poor health status, parental deprivation and family breakdown. Educational opportunity is defined in terms of access to different educational levels while scholastic ability is evaluated by the number of classes repeated in the primary school. To counteract the effects of parental socio-economic status on the intervening micro-ecological variables, the study was carried out among a homogeneous socio-economic and cultural community residing in Ibadan. However, even within a homogeneous community there are slight differences in income and status between families. These differences and their effects on educational achievement are also examined.

Study population

The study population consists of 158 children between the ages of fourteen and nineteen years who are all from a market area called 'Oje' in the centre of Ibadan town. The population in this area is fairly socio-culturally homogeneous and consists mostly of traditional polygynous households. Illiteracy among the people is high and they belong mainly to the lower socio-economic stratum. Their housing and environmental sanitation are poor. In fact, they are the type of people at whom free primary education was directed. The sample was chosen because the children also participated in a study on growth and development carried out at the Institute of Child Health, Ibadan, since 1962. Data obtained from the growth and development study gave the author a unique opportunity of assessing the effects of early physical and psycho-social inputs on later educational opportunity and achievement.

Methods

For the longitudinal study, routine examinations, started during the first year of life, were carried out at the Institute of Child Health at three-monthly intervals up to the age of three years and at six-monthly intervals thereafter. These included an assessment of each child's nutritional, growth and health status as well as detailed recordings of information on social, economic and general family matters. The latter were usually obtained from the mothers or the children's current caretakers in their own homes. For the purpose of this investigation, data evaluating the physical, psycho-social and economic status in the early years were extracted from the records of each child. For physical status these included:

(1)   the presence or absence of signs of protein calorie malnutrition;

(2)   the health status scores;

(3)   the lowest growth in height centile achieved and the height centile at the age of six (calculated from Tanner's standards of 1958).

The period from birth to one year was excluded as many of the children did not join the study until after the age of one year.

Psycho-social and economic status were evaluated by the following factors:

(1)   the child's principal caretaker;

(2)   the incidence of separation of the parents during the time from the child's birth to six years;

(3)   education of the father (education of the mother was ignored since nearly all the mothers were illiterates);

(4)   aggregate family income.

Educational opportunity indicators were chosen for the following reasons:

(1) access or entry into primary school – primary education, although free, was not then compulsory in Nigeria, hence some children may not have been to school;

(2) age of entry into primary school: late entry may be an added educational disadvantage in reducing educational opportunities. For example, in 1978, Oyo State adopted a policy of restricting applications to secondary schools to those under the age of fourteen. This adversely affected late starters.

(3) number of classes repeated in the primary school: since

promotion is by successful examination, this is used as an indication of educational ability;

(4)   admission to secondary schools: secondary education is the avenue to non-manual and higher status jobs as well as to higher education.

Scoring of the variables

1. *Nutrition:* Protein Calorie Malnutrition (PCM) was said to be present if the child had oedema of the face, legs or parotid glands.

2. *Health scores:* these are the means of the scores obtained during the physical examinations. The scores ranged from 1–5: 1 = good or very good health, 2 = fairly good, 3 = fair 4 = fairly poor, 5 = poor.

3. *Height growth centiles:* growth standards of a population are commonly expressed in percentiles or centiles. This is a rank order distribution ranging from 1 to 100 and means that measurements (height or weight) of a large sample of boys or girls (or adult males or females) are ranked in size from the smallest to the largest. Each person is then assigned a percentile that corresponds to his position within the rank order. For example, the middle measurement or median corresponds to the 50th percentile: this means that 50 per cent of the measurements obtained from that population fall at or below the 50th percentile and 50 per cent of the measurements above the 50th percentile. In any population with normal distribution, the heights of half the members of that population can be expected to fall between the 25th and 75th percentiles and 95 per cent will fall between the 3rd and 97th percentile. The remaining 5 per cent, that is, those with scores under the 3rd or above the 97th percentile, are considered the extremes in height or weight in the population.

The Tanner 3rd percentile is considered to be the lowest limit for normal growth in the Western population (Tanner, 1958). Janes (1974) found this to be true also for well-nourished children from elite Yoruba homes in Ibadan. Therefore, anyone scoring below the 3rd percentile must be considered stunted probably as a result of chronic undernutrition. Hence a measurement below the 3rd centile is taken as an indicator of long-term under-nutrition.

4. *Caretaking:* whilst short-term separations between parents and children are fairly common among the 'Oje' families, the children then being cared for by relatives, it was thought that long-term separations from the parents may adversely affect the child's emotional or physical development. For this study, the criterion for separation was for the children to be apart from one or both parents for the period of one year or more. Reasons for long-term separation were most often either the birth of a new baby, or parental discord.

5. *Parental separation:* separation meant that the parents did not live together and conjugal relationships had ceased. The children were then often sent to paternal relatives.

6. *Education of the father:*
(1) No schooling
(2) Some or full primary schooling
(3) Post-primary education

7. *Family income:* The categorisations of poor, fair and fair plus were based on an assessment of the levels of aggregate family income of the 'Oje' population between 1962 and 1973, which was the time of early childhood of our subject population:
(1) Poor = less than £N10.00 per month;
(2) Fair = from £N10.00 – £N30.00 month;
(3) Good = over £N30.00 per month.

Results

It was found that out of the 158 children included in the survey, 157 had started primary school. The only child who did not go to school was a girl who had stayed throughout her life with an old grandmother. Since this girl was the only one and therefore atypical for the population, she was excluded from the analysis.

Table 6.1 shows the educational attainment of the children. Out of the 157 children, 53.5 per cent started school at age six, 28.7 per cent at age seven and 17.8 per cent at age eight or over. In all, 130 children (82.8 per cent) completed six years of primary education and out of these, 81.5 per cent repeated one or more classes. A total of 17.2 per cent dropped out of primary school. Admission into secondary schools was obtained by 49.78 per cent of the children.

Table 6.1   *Educational achievement of children in the study*

Primary school	N = 157	%
Age of entry		
5 or 6 years	84	53.5
7 years	45	28.7
8 years	28	17.8
Obtained six years of schooling	130	82.8
Classes repeated		
0	24	18.5
1	46	35.4
2	34	26.2
3	26	20.0
Drop-outs	27	17.2
Secondary school		
Admitted	78	49.6
Not admitted	79	50.3

Physical inputs and educational achievement

The effects of nutritional status, health status and growth in height during the pre-school years on educational attainment are shown in Table 6.2.

Nutritional status: fifty-five (35.0 per cent) of the children suffered from overt signs of Protein Calorie Malnutrition (PCM) and of these, 29.1 per cent started school at the appropriate age of six. This increased to 66.6 per cent for the 102 children without PCM ($p < 0.001$).

Pre-school nutritional status also affected educational performance especially with regard to non-repetition of classes. Of the malnourished children, just 6.4 per cent were non-repeaters as compared with 25.3 per cent of the well-nourished ones ($p < 0.05$). It was observed that nutritional status did not affect the primary school drop-out rate, but a pre-school history of PCM adversely affected children's admission into secondary schools ($p < 0.001$).

Health status: few children in the study obtained an average score of 1 (good) or 4 (fairly poor) and none scored 5 (poor).

Table 6.2 *Physical inputs and educational achievement*

Primary school	Nutrition		Health scores		Growth in height			
					1-6 years		at age 6	
	PCM	No PCM	1 + 2	3 + 4	-3rd	3rd-97th	-3rd	3rd-97th
Age of entry								
N = 157	N = 55	N = 102	N = 78	N = 79	N = 54	N = 103	N = 32	N = 125
	%	%	%	%	%	%	%	%
5/6	29.1	66.6	66.7	40.5	37.0	62.1	28.1	52.0
7	50.9	16.7	21.8	35.4	38.9	23.3	37.5	26.4
8	20.0	16.7	11.5	24.1	24.1	14.6	34.4	21.6
chi square	x^2=24.26 df = 2		x^2=11.01 df = 2		x^2=8.97 df = 2		x^2=12.12 df = 2	
	$p < 0.001$		$p < 0.01$		$p < 0.05$		$p < 0.01$	
Classes repeated								
N = 130	N = 47	N = 83	N = 66	N = 64	N = 44	N = 86	N = 30	N = 100
	%	%	%	%	%	%	%	%
0	6.4	25.3	24.6	12.5	9.1	23.3	3.3	23.0
1	40.4	32.5	37.9	32.8	34.1	46.0	33.3	36.0
2	36.2	20.5	22.7	29.7	40.9	18.6	43.3	21.0
3+	17.0	21.7	15.6	25.0	15.9	22.1	20.0	20.0
Chi square	x^2=9.52 df = 3		x^2=4.86 df = 3		x^2=9.28 df = 3		x^2=9.28 df = 3	
	$p < 0.05$		$p = $ NS		$p < 0.05$		$p < 0.05$	
Drop-out %	14.5	18.6	15.4	19.2	18.5	16.3	6.3	20.0
Chi square	$p = $ NS		$p = $ NS		$p = $ NS		$p = $ NS	
Secondary school								
N = 157	N = 55	N = 102	N = 78	N = 79	N = 54	N = 103	N = 32	N = 125
	%	%	%	%	%	%	%	%
Admitted	30.9	59.8	61.5	37.9	35.2	57.3	34.4	53.6
Not admitted	69.1	40.2	38.5	62.1	64.8	42.7	65.6	46.4
Chi square	x^2=11.92 df = 1		x^2=8.72 df = 1		x^2=7.63 df = 1		x^2=3.77 df = 1	
	$p < 0.001$		$p < 0.01$		$p < 0.01$		$p = $ NS	

Consequently, children who obtained a score of 1 (good) or 2 (fairly good) are compared with those with a score of 3 (fair) or 4 (fairly poor). Differences in health status affected age of primary school entry to a lesser degree than nutritional status, but was still significantly associated ($p<0.01$). Of the 78 children with a score of 1 or 2, 66.7 per cent started at age six as against 40.5 per cent of the 79 children with a score of 3 or more. Health status scores were not associated with educational performance or school drop-out rate. They did however, influence the admission rate into secondary schools which was 61.5 per cent for children with a score of 1 or 2 and only 37.9 per cent for children with higher scores ($p<0.01$).

Growth in height: fifty-four children (34.4 per cent) fell below the 3rd centile during the pre-school years and 32 (20.3 per cent) still did so at age six. Short stature was significantly associated with late entry into schools since 71.9 per cent of children who, at age six, fell below 3rd centile did not start school at the appropriate time. This dropped to 48 per cent for those children whose height fell within normal limits (i.e. between 3rd – 97th centiles) ($p<0.01$). Short stature did not influence the drop-out rate.

Psycho-social inputs and educational achievement

Table 6.3 shows that 77 children (47.8 per cent) experienced prolonged separation in early childhood from one or both parents and in 67 instances (42.7 per cent) the parents were legally separated. Parental deprivation and family instability was negatively associated with both the age at which children started primary school ($p<0.001$) and whether or not they proceeded to secondary schools ($p<0.01$). It did not relate to children's educational ability (in terms of school performance) or the drop-out rate.

Socio-economic inputs and educational achievement

Table 6.4 shows that paternal education was not related to any of the educational achievement parameters apart from secondary school enrolment. Aggregate family income did not influence educational opportunity at any level.

Multiple disadvantage and educational achievement

The combined effects on educational achievement of the occurrence of PCM, an average health score of 3 or less, a growth in height score below the 3rd centile at any time and at age six, separation from one or both parents and parental divorce are tabulated in Table 6.5. Multiple disadvantage increased the likelihood of late entry into primary schools. It is shown by the fact that only 12 per cent of children without any disadvantage started school late. This increased to 81 per cent for children with five or six disadvantages ($p<0.001$). Multiple disadvantages

Table 6.3 *Psycho-social input and educational achievement*

Primary schl	Caretaker			Marital status of parents	
Age of entry	Parents	Mother	Others	Live together	Separated
N = 157	N = 82	N = 29	N = 46	N = 90	N = 67
	%	%	%	%	%
5/6 years	64.6	51.8	34.8	62.2	41.8
7 years	29.3	24.1	30.4	30.0	26.9
8 years	6.1	24.1	34.8	7.8	31.3
Chi square	x^2=19.3	df = 4		x^2=15.1	df = 2
	p < 0.001			p < 0.001	
Classes repeated					
N = 130	N = 70	N = 25	N = 35	N = 77	N = 53
	%	%	%	%	%
0	28.6	4.0	8.6	24.3	24.5
1	27.1	44.0	45.7	36.4	34.0
2	22.9	32.0	28.6	31.2	18.9
3	21.4	20.0	17.1	18.3	22.6
Chi square	x^2=12.4	df = 6	p = NS	x^2=3.97	df = 3, p = NS
Drop-out rate %	14.6	13.8	23.9	14.4	28.9
Chi square	p = NS			p = NS	
Secondary schl					
N = 157	N = 82	N = 29	N = 46	N = 90	N = 67
	%	%	%	%	%
Admitted	64.6	39.9	30.4	60.0	35.8
Not admitted	35.4	62.1	69.6	40.0	64.2
Chi square	x^2=11.16	df = 2		x^2=9.16	df = 1
	p < 0.01			p < 0.01	

did not influence school performance nor the drop-out rate. On the other hand, the long-term effects of multiple disadvantage on secondary school admissions were important. It was noted that 68 per cent of non-disadvantaged children gained admission compared with an admission rate of 28.5 per cent for children who had been victims of five or more separate disadvantages (p<0.05).

Table 6.4 *Socio-economic inputs and educational achievement*

Primary schl	Education of father			Aggregate family income		
	None	Primary	Post-primary	Poor	Fair	Good
Age of entry						
N = 157	N = 71	N = 75	N = 11	N = 16	N = 69	N = 72
	%	%	%	%	%	%
5/6 years	53.5	52.0	63.6	43.7	55.1	54.2
7 years	31.0	28.0	18.2	43.7	24.6	29.2
8 years	15.5	20.0	18.2	12.6	20.3	16.6
Chi square	x^2=1.004	df = 4		x^2=2.3	df = 4	
	p = NS			p = NS		
Classes repeated						
N = 130	N = 54	N = 65	N = 11	N = 14	N = 56	N = 60
	%	%	%	%	%	%
0	13.0	26.1	—	7.1	21.4	18.3
1	37.0	32.3	45.5	42.9	30.4	38.3
2	29.6	23.1	27.3	42.9	25.0	23.3
3+	20.4	18.5	27.3	7.1	23.2	20.0
Chi square	x^2=6.47	df = 6		x^2=5.16	df = 6	
	p = NS			p = NS		
Drop-out %	23.9	13.3	—	12.5	18.8	16.7
Chi square	p = NS			p = NS		
Secondary school						
N = 157	N = 71	N = 75	N = 11	N = 16	N = 69	N = 72
	%	%	%	%	%	%
Admitted	39.4	56.0	72.7	43.8	49.3	51.4
Not admitted	60.6	44.0	27.3	56.2	50.7	49.6
Chi square	x^2=7.57	df = 2		x^2=0.3	df = 2	
	p < 0.05			p = NS		

Age of entry into primary school and educational achievement

Table 6.6 shows that the age of entry was not related to

Table 6.5 *Accumulative effect of multiple disadvantage on educational achievement*

Educational	No. of disadvantages			
	0	1 or 2	3 or 4	5 or 6
Primary school				
N = 157	N = 25	N = 61	N = 50	N = 21
Age of entry	%	%	%	%
5/6 years	88.0	62.3	40.0	19.0
7 years	8.0	21.3	42.0	42.9
8 years	4.0	16.4	18.0	38.1
Chi square	x^2=29.77	df = 6	p < 0.001	
Classes repeated				
N = 130	N = 22	N = 53	N = 38	N = 17
	%	%	%	%
0	36.4	17.0	15.8	5.9
1	31.8	37.7	34.2	35.3
2	18.2	20.8	28.9	47.1
3+	13.6	24.5	21.2	11.7
Chi square	x^2=10.81	df = 9	p = NS	
Drop-out %	12.0	11.5	24.0	19.1
Chi square	p = NS			
Secondary school				
N = 157	N = 25	N = 61	N = 50	N = 21
	%	%	%	%
Admitted	68.0	54.1	44.0	28.5
Not admitted	32.0	45.9	56.0	71.5
Chi square	x^2=8.22	df = 3	p < 0.05	

educational performance in the primary school. However, late entry increased the risk of school drop-out as indicated by a drop-out rate of 32.1 per cent for children who had entered primary schools at age eight or over, compared with 9.2 per cent for children who started school at age six (p<0.01). Late entry also adversely affected admission into secondary schools with

Table 6.6   *Age of entry into the primary school and educational achievement*

	Age of entry		
	5-6 years	7 years	8 years
Primary school performance: classes repeated			
N = 130	N = 76	N = 35	N = 19
	%	%	%
0	25.0	8.6	10.5
1	28.9	51.4	31.6
2	21.1	28.6	42.1
3+	25.0	11.4	15.8
Chi square	$x^2=11.71$	df = 6	p = NS
Drop-out rate	9.5	22.2	32.1
Chi square	$x^2=9.39$	df = 2	p < 0.01
Secondary school			
N = 157	N = 84	N = 45	N = 28
	%	%	%
Admitted	66.7	42.2	11.5
Not admitted	33.3	57.8	88.5
Chi square	$x^2=26.15$	df = 2	p < 0.001

Table 6.7   *Primary school performance and admission into secondary school*

Secondary school admission	No. of classes repeated			
	0	1	2	3+
N = 130	N = 24	N = 46	N = 34	N = 26
	%	%	%	%
Admitted	75.0	67.4	44.1	53.8
Not admitted	25.0	32.6	55.9	46.2
Chi square	$x^2=7.28$	df = 3	p = NS	

66.7 per cent of the 6-year-old starters continuing their education to the secondary level compared with 11.5 per cent of those who started at eight years or over.

Primary school performance and admission into secondary schools.

In an equitable admissions policy, primary school performance should have been the determining factor in securing secondary school places. From Table 6.7, it can be observed that this was not so for the children of 'Oje'.

Discussion

This study examined the early micro-ecology of poor urban Nigerian children in relation to the educational opportunity brought about by the free primary education scheme. Micro-ecology was defined as a combination of the human and physical elements in children's immediate, familial environments that provide the nutritional, health, physical, psycho-social and socio-economic inputs for children in their early years.

It was noted that less than 16 per cent of the 157 children had not suffered from any of the adverse factors examined. Over one-third of the children were known to have been victims of acute under-nutrition and the same number were physically stunted. Over half of the children had below average health scores. Many children also suffered psycho-social deprivations. Nearly half the children had been without the care of one or both parents for prolonged periods in the early years and over 40 per cent of the children came from broken homes. As is common in the 'Oje' area, half of the fathers of the children were illiterates. Although all the families in the study had low incomes, only 10 per cent were considered poor within the socio-cultural reference group.

The findings show that, except for one child, all the children in the survey started primary school. Thus, one can conclude that free education ensures access of children in the lower income groups to the primary schools. In this respect, the scheme must be considered a success. At the end of the survey, out of the 157 children, 130 had completed their primary school education, while 27 had dropped out before reaching primary class six.

Access to primary school was differentiated by age in that nearly half of the children failed to enter at the correct age. Late entry becomes an handicap if one considers the shortage of secondary school places in the state. To reduce the number of applicants, some states in the Federation, including Oyo State, implemented a policy in 1978 by which children of fourteen years or above were not eligible to sit for the common entrance examinations to secondary schools (*Daily Times* 2 September, 1977, p. 5; 5 November, 1977, p. 3). This policy discriminates against late entrants into primary school since a 6-year-old entrant can remain in primary school for seven years and still sit for the entrance examination. But an 8-year-old entrant will be too old to sit for the examination by the time he completes his six years of his primary education.

Late entry into primary school was associated with early childhood disadvantages such as Protein Calorie Malnutrition (PCM), a below average health status and stunted growth. Although these factors are interrelated, it appears that the height of a child may be a significant factor in the decision on whether or not a child should start school since many parents in 'Oje' do not keep accurate birth records for their children. This was further supported when the author examined the height of the few children who had started school before the age of six and found them to be exceptionally tall compared with their peers.

The psycho-social variables were also associated with late entry. The reason for this may derive from the registration system employed at the time in Oyo State by the Oyo state government where the registration of new pupils to primary schools is done just once a year and only then for one week. The child to be registered is also required to be physically present. Consequently, a child staying with relatives out of town may not have the chance of being registered. In the case of divorced parents, the father usually has the legal custody. A very young infant may be allowed to stay with the mother for physical care until around school age. But then the child is expected to join the paternal household. At the time of registration, the child may not yet be in his permanent home and consequently both parents may have failed to register him.

The generally low performance of the children is likely to be a result of poverty, over-crowding and lack of relevant stimulation in the home which is common to all children in 'Oje'. However, within 'Oje', acute and chronic malnutrition also differentiated the children with regard to scholastic ability. This supports Hertzig's findings that children who are victims of severe malnutrition in the pre-school years have reduced educational ability when compared with their peers (Hertzig *et al.*, 1973). If one considers that one-third of the children in the sample were malnourished, it cannot be overemphasised that education does not start with providing schools, but with proper care and nutrition in early childhood. The drop-out rate was not associated with any of the reviewed micro-ecological disadvantages except late entry. On further examination, it was noted that many drop-outs had shown extremely low educational ability. For example, some of the children who spent six years in school were still in class two before being withdrawn. It was not uncommon to find a 17-year-old (even though looking like a 12-year-old) in class four (Janes, 1975). These findings indicate that the present school system does not cater for children who are below average academically. A universal educational policy should surely make provision for children of different abilities.

Although less than half of all the children proceeded to secondary schools, this was substantially more than Sofenwa's projection of 10 per cent (Sofenwa, 1976). Contrary to expectations, primary school performance had no bearing on secondary school admission while early micro-ecology with regard to physical and psycho-social factors was found to be important. The likelihood of non-admission increased with the number of early childhood disadvantages. The greatest single disadvantage, however, was late entry into the primary schools. As stated earlier, government educational policy since 1978 discriminates against children who start primary schools late. This does not explain, however, why children who should have gone to secondary school before 1978 also failed to continue their education. One likely explanation is that the sort of parenting behaviour which in early childhood resulted in malnutrition, bad general health, stunted growth, emotional stress and delayed primary school admission may also be responsible for parental refusal to make financial contributions towards the secondary education of their children. Consequently chances for upward social mobility, which, in present-day Nigeria, are closely linked with secondary and post-secondary education (Gugler and Flanagan, 1978) are weighted heavily against those who are malnourished, sickly, small for their age and come from unstable family units in the pre-school period as these are the children who enter primary schools late. Such disadvantaged children, despite their average performance in primary school, are between two and five times less likely to enter secondary schools than their peers in the same socio-economic stratum.

In general, the findings highlighted the fact that the pre-school micro-ecology of a child not only affects him during that period of time, but also influences his chances in later life. These findings further suggest that, in Nigeria, like in other cultures, continuous care within a stable parental unit positively influences the physical and emotional well-being of children and enhances their educational opportunities despite parents' low socio-economic status (Bowlby, 1951; Douglas, 1969).

It has been demonstrated that the care of the pre-school child cannot be separated from opportunities in later life. To provide equal opportunities, intervention must start not at the primary school level outside the child's micro-ecology, but at birth and should attempt to improve the quality of care provided within the children's immediate home environment. Such intervention should seek to increase the general standard of living, which, coupled with education, would improve the nutritional and health status of children. However, parents should also be educated on the view that responsible parenthood is more than providing food and money, and that children thrive best within a loving and stable family unit.

In conclusion, the free primary education scheme provides access for all children to the schools. It does not provide equal educational opportunities since such opportunities were shown to be related to early micro-ecological experience rather than educational ability. Obviously, this is not to say that free primary education has failed. Rather, it is a call for better physical and psycho-social care for children from conception and birth onwards. To increase the equalising propensities of education, primary schooling must be made compulsory for all children from age six because late entry itself is a major educational disadvantage. Hopefully, secondary schooling will soon be made free, universal and compulsory. But at the same time as implementing these very necessary improvements in our educational provisions, politicians must not neglect the powerful micro-ecological factors which I have discussed in this chapter. As some countries have found after years of free education at all levels, schools alone cannot iron out the inequalities of society. If that is our ultimate goal, surely our first step must be to improve the health and physical care of children throughout their pre-school years.

References

Adeyinka, Ade A. (1973), 'The Development of Secondary Grammar School Education 18791970: A Historical Analysis', *West African Journal of Education*, XVI (3), pp. 371-82.

Bowlby, J. (1951), *Material Case and Mental Health*, World Health Organisation, Geneva.

Daily Times Editorial, 'Age Limitation and Secondary School Admission', 2 September, 1977, p. 5.

Daily Times, 'Post Primary School: Federal Military Government Urged to Raise Admission Age', 9 November, 1977, p. 3.

Douglas, J.W.B. (1969), *The Home and the School: A Study of Ability and Attainment in the Primary School*, Panther, St. Albans.

Gugler, J. and Flanagan, W.G. (1978), *Urbanisation and Social Changes in West Africa*, Cambridge University Press, London.

Hendrickse, R.G. (1967), 'Social and Economic Factors in the Etiology of Malnutrition in Nigeria', Paper presented at Joint Congress of the Society of Health and Nutrition Society of Nigeria, Zaria, 31 March2 April, 1967.

Hertzig, M.E., Birch, H.G., Richardson, S.A. and Tizard, J. (1973), 'Intellectual Levels of Schoolchildren Severely Malnourished during the First Two Years of Life', *Pediatrics*, 49, pp. 814-24.

Hetherington, E.M. and Martin, B. (1972), 'Family interactions and psychopathology in Children', in H.C. Quarry and J.S. Werry (eds), *Psychotherapy Disorders of Childhood*, John Wiley, New York.

Janes, M.D. (1974), 'Physical Growth of Nigerian Yoruba Children', *Tropical and Geographical Medicine*, 26, pp. 38998.

Janes, M.D. (1975), 'Physical and Psychological Growth and Development', *Environmental Child Health*, Special Issue, 21, pp. 26-30.

Ransome-Kuti, O., Gbajumo, W.O., and Olaniyan, M.O. (1972), 'Some Socio-economic Conditions Predisposing to Malnutrition in Lagos', *Nigerian Medical Journal*, 2, 3, pp. 111-18.

Rutter, M. and Madge, N. (1976), *Cycles of Disadvantage*, Heinemann, London.

Sofenwa, L.A. (1976), 'Observations on Primary School Education in Nigeria in relation to the UPE', *West African Journal of Education*, XX (1), pp. 128-39.

Tanner, J.H. (1958), 'The Evaluation of Physical Growth and Development', in A. Holzel and J.T.M. Tizzard (eds), *Modern Trends in Paediatrics* (Second Series), Butterworth, London, pp. 235-344.

Tanner, J.M. (1969), 'Relation of Body Size, Intelligence scores and social circumstances', in J. Langer and H. Coventon (eds), *Trends and Issues in Developmental Psychology*, Holt, Rinehart & Winston, New York.

Third National Development Plan 1975-80, vol. I, p. 244, paragraph 22.

7 Traditional child-rearing practices of the Oje Market women of Ibadan

Brenda Meldrum

Introduction

In Nigeria, primary and secondary education was instituted in 1976 and, in 1979, free secondary education was incorporated in the manifestos of each of the political parties contesting the October election which ended military rule. However, long before 1979, differences in the scholastic achievement of children of educated ('elite') parents, compared with children of poor, often non-literate, parents, was causing concern among educationists, sociologists and psychologists.[1] All have consistently blamed environmental influences, such as inadequate nutrition, exposure to disease, poor hygiene and lack of cognitive stimulation in the home, for the disparity in performance between the children of the relatively better-off and the poor.

The Institute of Child Health of Ibadan University has carried out a longitudinal study since the 1960s on the physical growth and development of two groups of Nigerian, Yoruba children: an 'elite' group and a poor, 'traditional' group from the Oje Market area of Ibadan. Briefly, the results of this study have shown that the poor group of children compare fairly well with elite Nigerian and European norms of growth and development in the first few months of life; before a year they are lagging, and by two years of age, they have fallen behind on all measures of growth. A model of increasing difference between the two groups seems to have most validity (Janes, 1967; 1970 and 1975). This difference in physical growth and development has also been blamed on environmental influences, leading to a self-perpetuating circular interaction of malnourishment, disease and inadequate hygiene, affecting the health and the growth of the 'traditional' child.

So, both poor physical development and inferior scholastic achievement have been blamed on environmental factors.

Behavioural scientists have understood for some time that variations in nutrition and infection have powerful influences on development. They are major variables to consider in interpreting differences in children's physical development and intellectual achievement. However, in a wide-ranging review of the cross-cultural literature on infant cognitive development, Charles Super (1979) says: 'Except for conditions of minimal stimulation and/or malnutrition, one cannot conclude that infants from a particular culture . . . show more rapid cognitive development in general than infants from another culture.' Although this may be so for infants, it may not be the case for older children. Writing about Yoruba children, Barbara Lloyd, Beatrice Ashem and Margaret Janes Adenle have spoken of a cumulative deficit hypothesis as the most valid in interpreting differences in performance on tests of cognitive development by 'elite' and poor Yoruba children (Lloyd, 1971; Lloyd and Easton, 1977; Ashem and Janes, 1978).

The problem is how to tease out the effects of the different environmental influences on performance. The Oje Market poor children, who were compared with the 'elite' in the studies already discussed, have been called 'traditional'. In the sense used in those studies, 'traditional' implied also that the 'traditional' way of life was a contributory factor in malnourishment, disease and poor hygiene. Since the differences between the two groups of children are manifested physically in infancy, then the way the infant is fed and cared for is of primary importance to his future development. But when we say that a group of mothers is 'traditional', then we imply that they are feeding and caring for their children in a way that is socially acceptable to the traditional culture. The diet of a society is influenced deeply by the cultural values placed on individual foods, which are often unrelated to their nutritional value. The dietary habits affecting growth and development have social as well as economic origins, linked to value systems.[2] Traditional child-rearing has been cited, in these growth and development studies, as a factor contributing to the less than optimal physical growth and development of the poor Oje Market children. On the other hand, several Nigerian writers deeply regret the apparent breakdown of traditional Yoruba family life, where the security and warmth of the extended family sheltered the child both from physical harm and from economic hardship (Asuni 1974, Lambo 1960, Omolulu 1974).

In Chapter 6 of this book, Anya Oyewole reports a disturbing rate of malnutrition among Oje children. It is important, therefore, to examine what the traditional child-rearing patterns are among the Yoruba Oje Market women and how they affect the development of their children. This study was embarked on in order to fill that gap in our knowledge.

What little data there is on infants in traditional Yoruba society has concentrated on ceremonies and taboos surrounding the birth process (Forde, 1950; MacLean, 1966; Lloyd, 1970). Yoruba women stretched and manipulated their babies' limbs and bodies and their faces were marked with incisions (ilà), each family having a different pattern of markings. Both boys and girls were circumcised. In the late 1960s, Barbara Lloyd's research on Yoruba mothers' child-rearing practices included an investigation of these manipulative and marking practices and I decided, in this study, to see if there had been changes in these practices over the ten years.

The data on traditional feeding suggest that Yoruba infants were breast-fed, sometimes until they were four years of age. The traditional weaning food, a maize pap (ogi), consists mainly of water and has almost no nutritional value.[3] Babies were also force fed; the mother held the baby's nose and poured liquid into his mouth. Lloyd studied traditional feeding and I was again interested in whether and how it had changed, particularly in view of the widespread controversy surrounding the use of formula milk in developing countries.

Traditional Yoruba beliefs are that sickness is caused by forces outside the body. It was therefore considered to be extremely important to take medicines regularly, in order to keep healthy. Medicines were either burnt and the ashes rubbed into the body, or drunk, or bathed in. Children needed particular attention, since the infant mortality rate was so high.[4] I wondered whether mothers nowadays give traditional medicines to their infants and what were their attitudes towards (and use of) Western medicines.

A sample of fifty Yoruba women, mothers with unweaned

infants, from the Oje Market area of Ibadan was selected, on the basis that they and their families were willing to participate in the research (cf. Goldberg, 1973). I wanted to concentrate on the mothers, because it is they who are the primary caretakers of breast-fed infants. The three aspects of traditional child-rearing I was looking into were (1) feeding (2) the management of sickness and (3) body manipulation and scarification. Two methods of data collection were used: a semi-structured questionnaire and ethnographic observations. I did not feel that merely to ask the women questions was sufficient. No matter how well the individual items in a questionnaire are piloted, the answers one receives have no context without a personal knowledge of the subject's environment. I was not, of course, being particularly original. Increasingly, cross-cultural psychologists, especially those researching into infancy and child-rearing, are stressing the need for workers to experience the environment of their subjects.[5] I therefore visited the mothers early in the morning, when they fed and bathed their children and when the traditional body stretchings and manipulations were performed. I used two different methods of observation in this study. First was the ethnographical observation and second was an ethological type of observation of breast-feeding, which is not discussed in this chapter.

There are numerous dangers besetting the interpretation of behaviour outside its context. And it is doubly difficult for the cross-cultural psychologist who is trying to describe or interpret behaviour in a culture different from her own. First of all, she must have as wide a knowledge of the culture as she can possibly glean from as many sources as she can find, so that she has a background knowledge both of the ideological and the socio-cultural contexts of her subjects. Leiderman *et al.* (1977) put it this way: 'It is both scientifically and ethically essential that (the investigator) understand the broader cultural contexts within which child-rearing is studied. To ignore them is to risk misinterpreting data and losing sight of essential variables influencing behaviour, to say nothing of alienating the people being studied.' It was for these reasons that I decided not just to ask the women questions, but also to visit them in their homes and to observe, where possible, the behaviours I was investigating.

The study

The first aim of the study was to give a description of the child-rearing practices of the Oje Market women as they apply to infants under weaning age. This descriptive study was seen as hypothesis-generating, as opposed to hypothesis-testing research. Tulkin (1977), writing of cross-cultural research on infancy, says: 'Perhaps, for now we must be satisfied with simply discovering cultural diversity in infant care and generating hypotheses that are suggested by our observations.' It was hoped that my description would throw light on some of the reasons why the Oje Market children do not achieve their growth and development potential, as compared with children of the elite.

The second aim was to see if there was a scale from traditional to modern in child-rearing practices, in order to predict which behaviours would be more amenable to change. This aim was not successfully achieved. However, those aspects more resistant to change were delineated.

The third aim was to compare Lloyd's (1970) findings with this study to see whether and if so how child-rearing practices had changed over the previous decade.

THE SAMPLE

Table 7.1 gives the details of the sample under various social and economic headings, such as education, occupation, marital status and so on. Subjects were fifty Yoruba women from the Oje Market area of Ibadan, with children under weaning age. Weaning was defined as the time when the mother stopped breast-feeding. The fifty mothers were found by the son of the old chief of the Oje Market people. It was not a random sample in the statistical sense, as it consisted of women who were willing to be in the study and whose husbands were in agreement. Goldberg's (1973) Zambian sample was collected in the same way and for the same reason: to receive co-operation. This co-operation might make it easier to go into the homes of the women and observe. Also, it was felt that willing respondents would give more open replies to the questions.

As can be seen from the frequencies in Table 7.1, the average mother in the sample is aged twenty-five and Muslim. She hawks her wares, carrying a pyramid of articles on a large plate

Table 7.1 *The sample: Oje Market women and infants*

Education		Occupation		Mother's age		Infant's age		Marital status	
None	28	Hawker	25	16 - 20 yrs	11	< 34 weeks	12	Only wife	33
Primary	19	Stallholder	15	21 - 30 yrs	31	37 - 68 wks	21	Co-wife	17
Primary +	3	Crafts	6	30+ yrs	8	70 - 92 wks	17		
		Housewife	4						

Religion		Income per month		Years married		Type of marriage		No. of children living with mother	
Muslim	43	Don't know	10	Don't know	5	Common		1 child	24
Christian	7	Housewife	4	1 - 10 yrs	36	consent	43	2 children	14
		₦1 - ₦40	26	> 10 years	9	Muslim rite	7	3+ children	8
		> ₦40	10						

or in an enamel bowl on her head, with her infant on her back, kept closely tied by her wrapper. She earns a small profit each month on her goods; she has been married about four years and has given birth to three children; however, only two live with her; usually, the first child has either died, or is living with relatives. She lives in a monogamous household and her husband is likely to have been to primary school and be literate. The house is owned by her husband's family and she has a room for herself and her children, with the use of a 'parlour'.

METHOD

The 50 mothers were given a semi-structured questionnaire, consisting of 108 items. The questionnaire was translated from English to Yoruba by a fluent Yoruba and English speaker and retranslated into English by a lecturer in Yoruba from the University of Ibadan's Linguistics Department. The items covered background information, mothers' knowledge, beliefs and practices of feeding, health, hygiene and traditional practices. They were also asked about their sources of information concerning baby care. The items were suggested after reviewing the literature on the Yoruba, by discussion with workers in the Institute of Child Health of the University of Ibadan and from observation. Items on traditional practices were taken from Lloyd's (1970) study, relating to scarification, manipulation and feeding. Those relating to children's medicines came from MacLean (1966) and Hendrickse (1965). Pilot studies were carried out in Ibadan and in Oyo. Items concerning traditional practices only are discussed in this chapter (Meldrum, in press). The questionnaire was given in a room at the Institute of Child Health in Ibadan, because of the need for privacy. Several researchers have described how the whole family can become involved when interviews are given in Ibadan (cf. MacLean, 1966). Generally, people are not willing to discuss their personal business, particularly when questions of income arise. Also, it was felt that younger women in the presence of older co-wives would feel constrained in answering questions. The interviewer was a middle-aged Yoruba woman, and the author was present at each interview. The mothers were given a gift of food after the interview.

Forty-eight mothers were visited in their homes when they were bathing and feeding their babies. I went to the houses between 6.30 and 7.00 a.m. when the first breast-feed of the day was given and when the children were bathed. The visits lasted on average an hour. There were three aspects of the ethnographical observations:

(1) observation and description of the physical environment;

(2) observation and description of the social environment;

(3) observation and description of the infant, of feeding, bathing and medicines given.

1 The physical environment

At each house, the building and surroundings were judged on a three-point scale from below average for the area, average for the area and above average for the area. I decided from pilot observations and many previous visits that these were the only three distinctions I could make, because of the relative homogeneity of the population and because the Oje Market area of the old town of Ibadan is fairly uniform. An environmental checklist was filled in at each house and journal notes were made to supplement these data. The checklist included items concerned with the actual surroundings, like drainage, cleanliness, flooring, possessions, cooking area and utensils, toilet facilities, and so on.

2 The social environment

I filled in a social environmental checklist at each visit; this checklist noted how many people were present in the room and their relationship to the mother, who handled the baby, and so on.

3 Observation and description of the infant

The first part of this checklist concerned the infant: whether he looked well or ill; whether his nose was running, or if he had a cough, or a fever; how he was dressed, whether he was clean and so on.

The second part described feeding, bathing, and the medicines given.

These three checklists and full journal notes comprised the ethnographical observations.

Results

TRADITIONAL CHILD-REARING PRACTICES

It is convenient to divide the traditional child-rearing practices into four groups: first, the scarification or marking of the child's face and body; second, the manipulation of the infant's head, hips and limbs; third, the traditional feeding practices of long breast-feeding and force-feeding; and fourth, the giving of traditional 'native' medicine.

The findings of this study will be presented under the following headings:

(a) comparisons with Lloyd's (1970) findings;
(b) children's medicines;
(c) a simple scale from traditional to modern;
(d) the multi-dimensional scaling analysis;
(e) interpretation.

(a) COMPARISONS WITH LLOYD'S FINDINGS

1 Marking and scarification of the infant's body

Table 7.2 gives the percentage of those practising body manipulations, scarifications and force-feeding as reported in 1970 and as found ten years later. From this table, it appears that female circumcision and force-feeding are on the increase. It also seems that there is very little difference in the practice of limb-stretching and the post partum taboo on breast-feeding in ten years. Head moulding and hip moulding appear to have declined in frequency.

In 1970, Lloyd reported that of the thirty Oje Market women in her sample, only three had tribal marks cut on their children's faces. This study found only one. Yet 'Yorubaland', the area where Yorubas live in Nigeria, abounds with adults with their faces scarred with tribal and family marks, as Lloyd (1970) points out. But it is unusual to see a schoolchild with the traditional deep scarifications. Twenty-four mothers did not mark their children's bodies at all; twenty-six mother had put small vertical marks, about two centimetres long, under their children's eyes, and also, at the time of circumcision, had asked the circumciser (olóòlà) to put medicine cuts on the children's bodies. These usually consist of four cuts on the back and front and sometimes also on the back of the hands and feet. When the child is ill, medicine is often burnt and the ashes rubbed into the healed scarifications, which, it is believed, causes the sickness to leave the body through the urine.

Female circumcision, on the other hand, is far from dying out. Lloyd asked the fifteen women in her sample with female children whether they had had their children circumcised: ten said 'yes', five said 'no'. When mothers in this study were asked whether it was necessary for both girls and boys to be circumcised, forty-six said it was necessary and only four said that although it was essential for boys, it was not obligatory for girls. There is, of course, a difference between asking whether a person has carried out an action, and whether it is necessary to carry out the same action. However, comparing Lloyd's data with this study, it was found that there was a significant

Table 7.2 *Traditional practices: comparison with Lloyd's (1970) data*

Percentage practising	1970	1979
Female circumcision	66	92
Limb stretching	96	94
Head moulding	66	50
Hip moulding	100	84
Post partum taboo	100	94
Force-feeding	60	78

association between admitting to practising circumcision and stating the necessity for girls to be circumcised with the year of study (chi square (1) = 4.26, p<0.02). But whether this result, which implies an increase in female circumcision in ten years, reflects the true position, is not known.

2 Manipulation of the child's body

Most mothers manipulate their infants' limbs regularly, certainly up to the first three months of age, after bathing them carefully in water or in a herbal infusion (àgbo). A comparison with Lloyd's data shows that this limb stretching is still widely practised and there is no significant association with the year of study.

Head moulding is traditionally carried out to make the baby's head round, and the ears are pressed against the head, so that they will not stick out. Hip moulding makes sure that the baby has two dimples over the buttocks, which should have the desired round shape. There is no significant association between the year of study and either head or hip moulding practices.

3 Feeding

Previous research suggests that Yoruba mothers expect to breast-feed and do so.[6] But all mothers in this sample gave their infants bottle feeds as well. These held a variety of fluids ranging from formula to custard. In an environment like Oje, the dangers of poor hygiene, inaccurate mixing of formula and a possibly contaminated water supply make bottle feeding a hazardous practice.[7] In the past, long breast-feeding may have saved children's lives because the traditional weaning food contains 1 per cent or less protein and over 90 per cent water (Omolulu, 1974). Lloyd found that her subjects breast-fed for an average of 22.2 months. In this study, 17.2 months was the average. Possibly the reason for the reduction is that nowadays there are more apparently monogamous marriages and with the continued adherence to the post partum taboo on intercourse while nursing, it has been necessary for women to curtail the length of breast-feeding. But Jelliffe and Jelliffe (1978) present data from many societies showing that reduction in the length of breast-feeding is the pattern in most developing countries. The post partum taboo is adhered to almost as strongly as ever. The longer breast-feeding, together with the taboo on intercourse while nursing, is acknowledged to be an excellent method of birth spacing; but perhaps more important is the short time the child is allowed to feed on the breast. The mean duration of the breast-feed from my own controlled observations of sixteen breast-feeds was four minutes. Furthermore, 80 per cent of this sample was feeding its children on a diet inadequate in terms of protein, calories and vitamins.

Eighteen of Lloyd's thirty mothers admitted to force-feeding, compared with thirty-nine out of fifty for this sample. When asked why mothers force-fed their babies, 60 per cent responded that it was necessary to do so if the child refused food. A further 6 per cent said: 'We do not know the reason, but it has always been done', and 22 per cent said that although some people might do it, they did not themselves. Comparisons with Lloyd's figures would seem to indicate that force-feeding had increased in frequency although not significantly so.

To summarise, child-rearing practices traditional to the Yoruba have not changed radically in the ten years since Lloyd's investigation. However, the length of breast-feeding is reduced, hip moulding is less popular and only half this sample practised head moulding.

(b) CHILDREN'S MEDICINES

The subject of children's medicines in Oje can be used as an analogue of the 'contemporary traditional' person's approach to both traditional and Western beliefs, attitudes and practices[8].

Agbo is a general name for 'Any infusion brewed from leaves etc. for medicinal use' (Abraham, 1958). The different types of *àgbo* I have come across are those specific for fever, dysentery, rashes, oedema and convulsions. Each has a different recipe. Its use is widespread among this sample (76 per cent); indeed, thirty-one mothers gave their infants *àgbo* every day. However, only ten said that if their children had fever (malaria), *àgbo* was the sole treatment they would give. Home visits showed that mothers were giving their children a wide variety of pills and potions, from vitamins to chloramphenicol, on a regular basis. Oje Market mothers have a similar attitude towards both 'Western' and traditional medicines – cough mixtures are given as readily to prevent a cough, as they are to relieve it. Children who are not nowadays given *àgbo* exclusively are given some

'Western' preparation instead. Indeed, eighteen mothers believed that powdered baby milk was 'medicine' and therefore good for babies.

Oje market children are still given medicine every day in the traditional manner, but the mixture is not always *àgbo* alone, but may be both *àgbo* and a 'Western' preparation, or 'Western medicine' alone.

(c) A SIMPLE SCALE FROM TRADITIONAL TO MODERN

Mothers were categorised on a three-point scale as either 'modern', 'average', or 'traditional', according to their responses to items, as follows (see Table 7.3):

1 The amount of food purchased from vendors, compared with the amount prepared at home

It has been noted by Bascom (1951) that there has always been a tradition among the Yoruba of purchasing cooked food from vendors, whose trade it is to prepare food in their own compounds and either to wrap it in leaves, as they do with cold maize porridge (*eko*), or to carry it around in enamel bowls and sell it by the plateful, as with rice and stew. The more modern woman in this community has less time to prepare her own food, and Yoruba food can take a long time to prepare. Therefore, she buys more food than the average woman from food vendors. The traditional woman, however, still prepares most of her food herself (Burdin, 1976). Categories were defined by totalling the foods mentioned most often on each list the mother gave the interviewer. From the replies, two lists of food were compiled: foods bought and foods prepared at home. Those foods mentioned most often on each list were defined as average, in the sense that most women would either purchase them or prepare them themselves. Each mother was placed in a category according to whether she purchased more food than the average (modern), no more nor no less than the average (average) and those who themselves cooked a greater variety of foods than the average (traditional).

2 Whether the husband and wife eat together

Traditionally, women and children did not eat with their husbands and fathers (Bascom, 1951; Burdin, 1976). Therefore, those mothers who said they never ate with their husbands were labelled 'traditional', those who said that they sometimes did 'average', and those who said that they normally did were labelled 'modern'.

3 Taboo on intercourse while breast-feeding

Mothers who respected this taboo were labelled 'traditional'.

4 Length of breast-feeding

This variable was again divided into modern, average, and traditional. The mean age of weaning was 17.2 months, with a range of 7 to 24 months. 'Traditional' mothers were those who intended to breast-feed longer than 18 months; 'modern', those mothers who intended breast-feeding for less than 18 months.

5 Force-feeding

Mothers were divided between three categories: those who said they did force feed were labelled 'traditional'. Those who said that although it was a tradition that 'they had met in the world' and that they might force feed, if necessary, were called 'average', and those who said that they did not and would not force feed were categorised as 'modern'. Di Domenico and Burdin (1979) suggest that bottle feeding has replaced the traditional method of force-feeding among all but the most poor, non-literate families. Although the Oje mothers fall into this category, this study did not find bottle feeding was replacing force-feeding, as force-feeding is still widely practised in Oje.

6 The administration of traditional medicines to children

Mothers were placed into three categories: if they gave àgbo regularly every day (and some gave àgbo three times a day) they were categorised as 'traditional'; those who sometimes gave àgbo were categorised as 'average' and those who said they never gave àgbo were categorised as 'modern'.

The following variables were divided between those who carried out the practices and were labelled 'traditional' and those who did not, or would not, who were labelled 'modern': (7) *head moulding*; (8) *hip moulding*; (9) *limb stretching*; (10) *face and body marks*; (11) *female circumcision*. A Guttman scale was attempted, but was not successful because of the wide variability

Table 7.3 *Traditional practices*

		Traditional	Average	Modern
1	Food purchased	21	23	6
2	Husband eats with wife	26	10	14
3	Taboo on intercourse	47	0	3
4	Length of breastfeeding	9	26	15
5	Force feeding	33	6	11
6	Traditional medicine	31	7	12
7	Head moulding	25	0	25
8	Hip moulding	42	0	8
9	Limb stretching	46	0	4
10	Face/body marks	26	0	24
11	Female circumcision	46	0	4

n = 50

of response. In other words, one could not say that there was a scale from modern to traditional, using these data. Therefore, an alternative way of examining them was sought.

(d) THE MULTI-DIMENSIONAL SCALING ANALYSIS

The next step in the analysis was to submit these variables to a non-metric, multi-dimensional scaling technique, in order to find what dimensions arose and to see if there were patterns in the data that would be helpful in interpretation. The scaling technique used was the Guttman-Lingoes Smallest Space Analysis (SSA).[9] This technique uses a matrix of similarities based on the monotonicity coefficient, which is well able to cope with ties. Guttman (1968) says that SSA is more parsimonious than factor analysis, in the sense that it usually renders a space of fewer dimensions. The program used allowed for a four dimensional solution. The reasons why this analysis was chosen were: (1) a non-metric scaling technique was essential, as these data are categorical; (2) the SSA gives a monotonicity coefficient, MONCO, akin to a correlation coefficient (Guttman, 1968); (3) the solution gives a space diagram of the data, which can help interpretation. First, the monotonicity coefficients (MONCO) were examined. Table 7.4 gives the MONCO correlation matrix of the eleven traditional practices variables. As can be seen, the correlation between the body scarification variables (face and body marks and circumcision) was 1.000. The body manipulation variables give high positive correlations between head and hip moulding and limb-stretching, but no correlation between them and the scarification variables.

Examination of the traditional feeding variables (length of breast-feeding, and force-feeding) shows little correlation and a small negative correlation is shown between force feeding and àgbo giving (−.207). These variables are not associated with each other.

The traditional practices not directly concerned with children, (the buying of food, the intercourse taboo and whether the husband and wife eat together) show a positive correlation only between the taboo and the purchasing of foods (.826). MONCO does not, however, give significance levels for the correlations. These correlations suggest that the eleven traditional practices are not, on the whole, associated with each other. However, there were some rather interesting surprises. For example, one might have expected the intercourse taboo practice to be *positively* associated with the length of breast-feeding. In fact, they are *negatively* correlated (−.680): one explanation for this might be the greater pressure from the husband to renew marital relations. On the other hand, the body moulding variables, as expected, were correlated, as also were the scarification variables.

The Smallest Space Analysis (SSA), which is based on the MONCO correlations, was then examined to see if it could help articulate any underlying pattern in these practices and in the hope that it would throw further light on the results of the correlations. The goodness of fit, expressed by the coefficient of alienation, which varies from 0 to +1 (0 = a perfect fit), points to a three-dimensional solution (coefficient of alienation for a two-dimensional solution = .211; for a three-dimensional solution = .165). However, the data are better explained using a two-dimensional solution, for here two clear dimensions arise as are illustrated on the space diagram.

Figure 7.1 shows the smallest space analysis of the two-dimensional solution. The points on the space are labelled. The closer these points lie together, the stronger the positive correlation. As can be seen from this figure, two dimensions have been drawn through the space: Dimension I (Child Dimension) and Dimension II (Adult Dimension). Dimensions are defined in the same way as with factors in factor analysis,

Table 7.4   *MONCO correlations: traditional practices*

		1	2	3	4	5	6	7	8	9	10	11
Food purchased	1											
Husband eats with wife	2	—.380										
Intercourse taboo	3	.826	—1.000									
Length breast-feeding	4	—.164	—.026	—.680								
Force-feeding	5	.118	—.382	.707	.184							
Traditional medicine	6	—.122	—.213	.426	.019	—.207						
Head moulding	7	—.388	—.388	.132	.352	.101	.326					
Hip moulding	8	.721	—.230	—1.00	.259	—.205	.293	.767				
Limb stretching	9	.378	—.085	—1.00	.364	.133	.422	1.00	.547			
Face and body marks	10	—.315	—.328	.389	.442	—.045	.200	—1.00	—.747	—1.00		
Female circumcision	11	—.714	—.296	—1.00	.169	—.083	—.569	—1.000	—1.00	—1.00	1.00	

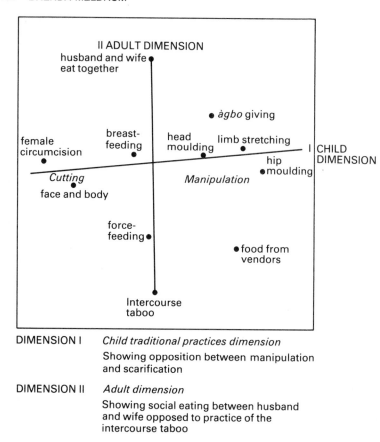

DIMENSION I   *Child traditional practices dimension*
Showing opposition between manipulation and scarification

DIMENSION II   *Adult dimension*
Showing social eating between husband and wife opposed to practice of the intercourse taboo

Figure 7.1 *Guttman and Lingoes Smallest Space Analysis: traditional practices – two-dimensional solution*

i.e., by consideration of the positive and negative loadings at each end of the lists of variables defined as dimensions or factors.

Dimension I for the two-dimensional solution is labelled 'Child traditional practices dimension', where body manipulations at one end are opposed to scarifications at the other. Dimension II is labelled 'Adult dimension', where adult social eating is opposed to the practice of the taboo on intercourse. Figure 7.1 illustrates the two-dimensional space and shows the clustering of the scarification and manipulation variables along Dimension I; it also shows that the following variables stand away from the dimensions: breast-feeding, force-feeding and *àgbo* giving.

(e) INTERPRETATION

Some practices of Oje Market women are more resistant to change than others, for example, the post partum taboo. However, eating with the husband is a modern practice that does not conflict with deeply held taboos and is thus more susceptible to change. Similarly with scarification: face scarification of tribal marks is an outward and visible sign of a traditional Yoruba practice and has all but died out; yet body manipulations can be practised at home, do not appear to have a detrimental effect on the children and, as has been observed, fall into an almost ritualised pattern of behaviour which appears to be enjoyable for mother and infant. However, the three feeding variables, length of breast-feeding, force-feeding and medicine giving, do not fall into any particular pattern. Yet the adult orientated practices fall in one dimension, and the child orientated practices of body manipulation and scarification along another and separate dimension.

We can conclude that those practices that show to the world that one is a traditional person, such as Yoruba tribal markings, will be the first to die out. A feeding practice, such as giving a bottle to a baby, shows that a mother is relatively 'Westernised' and this will be accepted readily. On the other hand, a taboo such as the prohibition of intercourse while breast-feeding seems deeply felt and rarely disregarded. But those practices that within the community do not label a mother either 'traditional' or 'modern', because they are widely accepted and practised (such as force-feeding and *àgbo* giving), will and do show a wide variability of response.

Thus, traditional feeding patterns, the giving of traditional medicine, taboos and manipulations form what Bartlett (1946) has called the 'hard' features of the culture.

Conclusion

The data give a description of the child-rearing practices of this group of mothers, as they apply to unweaned children. The description shows a group of women living in an undeveloped urban environment and bringing up their children in a mixture of traditional Yoruba and modern 'Western' ways. These data do not, however, delineate a more 'traditional' group within the sample, nor do they predict clearly which behaviours will change and which will remain 'traditional'. What they do suggest is that among this sample of contemporary traditional women, who come from a group which has been widely studied in Nigeria, there is no simple way of changing their behaviour towards more healthy practices, or better infant feeding. The reasons why the Oje Market children do not develop physically to the same level of growth as the children of elite Yoruba may seem obvious from a socio-economic point of view. But the Oje Market women want to do the best for their children and, even though it is very expensive, they buy tinned baby food, because they think it is both good for their children and that it has medicinal properties. Most clinics and hospitals in Ibadan try to persuade mothers to feed their children better, to breast-feed rather than bottle feed, to innoculate their children against disease and to conform to high standards of hygiene. But until we understand the reasons why mothers will choose, for example, to buy expensive tinned baby food rather than prepare fresh foods we will find it difficult to help them. Education by itself, although it makes a population literate, cannot cure the ills of inflation or clean up the urban environment. The problems are legion and the Nigerian government faces a daunting task in its attempt to liberate the population from poverty and disease. Perhaps one priority should be to install main drainage and ensure a safe and regular water supply.

In what ways can psychological research help? First of all, studies such as this are useful in generating hypotheses, but of themselves can do little besides point out the problems. This study was concerned with one group only. Future research into traditional Yoruba attitudes and practices would benefit from having at least three groups: perhaps an urban group, a rural group and an 'elite' group of mothers, such as has been used before (e.g. Ashem *et al.*, 1975). This would give a clearer idea of what practices die out and which remain. Secondly, research into the effects of different methods of helping mothers improve their child-rearing practices would be relevant. Which is more effective: teaching women when they attend antenatal clinics, or taking a target group and encouraging self-help, or for the helping agencies themselves to go into the compounds and demonstrate improved practices on the spot? Whatever ways are used, it is crucial that the positive and negative aspects of both traditional and 'Western' practices are made clear. Traditional practices such as long periods of breast-feeding and carrying the baby on the back have advantages which Western mothers are increasingly recognising.

Education in Nigeria is no longer the reserve of the elite. If children from environments like Oje Market are to compete with children from elite Yoruba families, both in schools and in the employment market, they will need help and further research into their pre-school environment can only illuminate ways in which this aid can be given.

Notes

1 See Abiola (1965), Lloyd (1971), Lloyd and Easton (1977), Ashem *et al.* (1975), Ashem and Janes (1978) and Durojaiye (1970). These authors compare children of elite parents with Oje Market children and some studies incorporate a third, rural, poor group.
2 Illsey (1967) and Draper (1977). Leiderman *et al.*'s (1977) book of readings (*Culture and Infancy*), of which Draper's is one, is an extremely useful and sensible examination of the effects of its culture and the environment on the infant.
3 See Burdin (1976); Orwell and Murray (1974); Omolulu (1974). The latter, writing of *ogi*, the maize pap, says it contains 90 per cent water and 1 per cent or less protein. It contains 30 calories per 100 millilitres, while breast milk contains 70 calories per 100 millilitres. By the end of the first year, the baby is fed primarily on pap, with only a few sucks from the breast.
4 Anya Oyewole (1976), in a paper on Social Paediatrics, delivered to a seminar at the Institute of Child Health, University of Ibadan, says: '*Child Mortality Rates in Nigeria:* No accurate figures are available but estimates range from: 40/1,000 live births in the highest SES group; 150+/1,000 live births in the lowest SES group. Compared with 19/1,000 live births in the population of the UK and 25/1,000 live births in the population of the USA.'
5 See Leiderman *et al.* (1977); Charles Super (1979) in Munroe *et al.* (1979) – a particularly good review of infancy and the effect of culture.
6 See Omolulu (1974); Ladipo (1975); MacLean (1966 and 1971); Burdin (1976); Orwell and Murray (1974); Di Domenico and Burdin (1979) among others.

7   Hendrickse (1965), writing while at University College Hospital, Ibadan, was one of the first to suggest that illiterate Yoruba women found it almost impossible to bottle feed successfully. Orwell and Murray (1974) said that a combination of breast and bottle feeding had been adopted by 7 per cent of Ibadan women.

8   'Contemporary traditional' seems to be an apt description of the Oje Market people; better, perhaps, than 'traditional', which has often been used in the literature to describe societies in the midst of change from traditional to 'Western'. I came across it in Ladipo (1975).

9   For an illustration of the way in which Guttman himself interprets MONCO and SSA, see Gutman (1968).

References

Abiola, E.T. (1965), 'The nature of intellectual development in Nigerian children', in *Teacher Education*, no. 6, pp. 37-58.

Abraham, R.C. (1958), *Dictionary of Modern Yoruba*, Hodder & Stoughton, London.

Ashem, B. and Janes, M.D. (1978), 'Deleterious effects of chronic under-nutrition on cognitive abilities', *Journal of Child Psychology and Psychiatry*, vol. 19, pp. 23-31.

Ashem, B., Janes, M.D., Olatawura, M.O. and Fasan, P.O. (1975), 'Systematic intervention: an alternative to conventional methods of promoting physical and cognitive growth in pre-school children in developing countries', paper prepared for the First Pan-African Nutrition Congress held in Ibadan.

Asuni, T. (1974), 'Socio-psychological aspects of the vulnerable child, risk and mastery: children of the modern elite in Nigeria', in E.J. Anthony and C. Koupernik (eds), *The Child and His Family: Children at Psychiatric Risk*, vol. III, Wiley, New York.

Bakare, C.G.M. (1972), 'Social class differences in the performance of Nigerian children on the draw-a-man test', in L.J. Cronbach and P.J.D. Drenth (eds), *Mental Tests and Cultural Adaptations*, Mouton, The Hague.

Bascom, W.A. (1951), 'Yoruba cooking', *Africa*, 21 (2), pp. 125-37.

Burdin, J.M. (1976), 'Social factors influencing attitudes and practices of child nutrition in Western Nigeria', unpublished MSc thesis, University of Ibadan.

Di Domenico, C.M. and Burdin, J.M. (1979), 'Breastfeeding practices among urban women in Ibadan, Nigeria', in D. Raphael (ed.), *Breastfeeding and Food Policy in a Hungry World*, Academic Press, New York.

Draper, H.H. (1977), 'Biological, cultural and social determinants of nutritional status', in P.H. Leiderman, S.R. Tulkin and A. Rosenfeld (eds), *Culture and Infancy: Variations in the Human Experience*, Academic Press, New York.

Durojaiye, M.O.A. (1970), 'Psycho-cultural constraints on formal education of the African child', Universities of East Africa Social

Sciences Conference, Dar es Salaam.

Forde, D. (ed.) (1950), *International African Institute's Ethnographic Survey of Africa*, London.

Goldberg, S. (1973), 'Infant care and growth in urban Zambia', in F. Rebelsky and L. Dorman (eds), *Child Development and Behaviour* (2nd edn), Alfred A. Knopf, New York.

Guttman, L. (1968), 'A general nonmetric technique for finding the smallest coordinate space for a collection of points', *Psycho-metrika*, 33, pp. 469-506.

Hendrickse, R.G. (1965), 'M for Misery. An account of some major paediatric problems in Nigeria', Paper presented at the WHO sponsored conference of professors of paediatrics in Africa, Kampala, February.

Illsey, R. (1967), 'The sociological study of reproduction and its outcome', in S.A. Richardson and A.F. Cuttmacher (eds), *Child-Rearing – its social and psychological aspects,* Williams and Wilkins, Baltimore.

Janes, M.D. (1967), 'Report on a growth and development study on Yoruba children in Ibadan, Western Nigeria', paper for a conference on rural nutrition, Dakar, Senegal.

Janes, M.D. (1970), 'The effect of social class on the physical growth of Nigerian Yoruba children', *The Bulletin of the International Epidemiological Association*, African Regional Meeting, vol. 20.

Janes, M.D. (1975), 'Physical and psychological growth and development', *Environmental Child Health*, special issue, 21, pp. 26-30.

Jelliffe, D.B. and Jelliffe, E.P.P. (1978), *Human Milk in the Modern World*, Oxford University Press.

Ladipo, P. (1975), 'Some observations on the study of the changing Yoruba family', paper presented to the conference of Social Research and National Development in Nigeria, University of Ibadan.

Lambo, T.A. (1960), 'Characteristic features of the psychology of the Nigerian', *West African Medical Journal*, no. 9 (3), pp. 95-104.

Leiderman, P.H., Tulkin, S.R. and Rosenfeld, A. (eds) (1977), *Culture and Infancy*, Academic Press, New York.

Lingoes, J.C. (1973), *The Guttman-Lingoes Nonmetric Program Series*, Mathesis Press, Ann Arbor.

Lloyd, B.B. (1970), 'Yoruba mothers' reports of child-rearing: Some theoretical and methodological considerations', in Philip Mayer (ed.), *Socialisation: The Approach from Social Anthropology*, Tavistock Publications, London.

Lloyd, B.B. (1971), 'The intellectual development of Yoruba children: a re-examination', *Journal of Cross-Cultural Psychology*, 2, pp. 29-38.

Lloyd, B.B. and Easton, B. (1977), 'The intellectual development of Yoruba children', *Journal of Cross-Cultural Psychology*, 8.

MacLean, C.M.U. (1966), 'Yoruba mothers', *Journal of Tropical Medicine and Hygiene*, 69, pp. 253-263.

MacLean, C.M.U. (1971), *Magical Medicines*, Penguin, Harmondsworth.

Meldrum, B. (in press), 'How poor Yoruba mothers feed their children', in C. Di Domenico (ed.) *Child-Rearing in Nigeria*.

Munroe, R.L., Munroe, R.H. and Whiting, B.B. (eds) (1979), *Handbook* of *Cross-Cultural Human Development*, Garland Press, New York.

Omololu, A. (1974), 'Nutritional factors in the vulnerability of the African child', in E.J. Anthony and C. Koupernik (eds), *The Child in his Family: children at psychiatric risk*, vol. III, Wiley, New York.

Orwell, S. and Murray, J. (1974), 'Infant feeding and health in Ibadan', *Environmental Child Health*, monograph no. 35.

Oyewole, A. (1976), 'Social, economic and environmental factors in the aetiology of malnutrition in young children living in Ibadan, Nigeria', research protocol for a PhD degree of the University of London.

Poole, H.E. (1969), 'The effect of Westernisation on the psychomotor development of African (Yoruba) infants during the first year of life', *Journal of Tropical Paediatrics*, 15, pp. 172-6.

Super, C.M. (1979), 'Behavioural development in infancy', in R.L. Munroe, R.H. Munroe and B.B. Whiting (eds), *Handbook of Cross-Cultural Human Development*, Garland Press, New York.

Tulkin, S.R. (1977), 'Dimensions of multicultural research in infancy and early childhood', in P.H. Leiderman, S.R. Tulkin and A. Rosenfeld (eds), *Culture and Infancy*, Academic Press, New York.

8 Handicapped children: an epidemiological study in Plateau State

Christopher A. Saunders

Introduction

This chapter is about children who have special needs – children who are physically handicapped, mentally handicapped or both. It reports a survey of children in Plateau State which aimed at identifying just how many children have what kinds and degrees of handicap. On that basis I go on to discuss how their special needs could be met. In many cases, existing 'ordinary' schools can be adapted to cope. In others, very specialised teachers and facilities are required and I discuss how these could best be provided by a flexible and decentralised system of special schools.

Although the principal aim of this study was to provide an estimate of the prevalence of various handicapping conditions in the child population of the Plateau State, and allow for the rational planning of special education provision for these children, there are factors which justify its inclusion in a volume concerned primarily with issues of child development and early education in Nigeria. The foremost of these is the size of the problem. In the sample of 6,000 children used in this study, 85 suffered from some form of handicapping condition which could affect their development, education and vocation in a significant way. This is a large number, but it represents only those identified by this particular survey method. If more sophisticated screening techniques had been used the number would have been far higher, particularly for problems relating to hearing loss and mild mental retardation.

It is therefore crucial that researchers and educationalists do not concentrate their efforts exclusively on 'normal' children. Handicapped children have special and urgent needs. If those needs are to be met we must know precisely what they are. How many Nigerian children have which kinds of handicapping conditions? How do these differ qualitatively and quantitatively from occurrence rates in the West? How might health and educational provisions be adapted to cope with and reduce the extent of handicap? These are the basic questions which I shall be considering in this chapter.

A further reason for linking studies of handicap with studies of child development and child-rearing practices is that recent work on the education of the disadvantaged and handicapped has increasingly emphasised the importance of early stimulation programmes. To date most of these studies have been carried out in so-called 'developed nations', but there have been clear demonstrations of how effective such programmes can be in developing countries, even when financial input is limited (Grantham McGregor et al., 1975). If this type of work is to be implemented in Nigeria in conjunction with other special educational programmes, a knowledge of children's early experiences in their home environment is important. For instance, the findings of Whiten and Milner (Chapter 3) highlight critical variables in traditional mother-child interaction patterns which they suggest possibly affect the young Nigerian child's readiness for education. The low frequency of behaviours falling into the 'modify interaction' category (see page 65) could have an exaggerated effect on the young mentally retarded child who requires more structure to his experiences than his non-handicapped sibling (Kiernan et al., 1978). The effects of this and other aspects of patterns of child-caretaker interaction in Nigeria will need to be carefully related to the differing needs of children suffering from mental, physical or sensory handicaps. In this way, positive features can be emphasised and other features improved in order to optimise development and school readiness in these groups of children. Such studies represent important topics for further investigation.

This chapter will concentrate on the fundamental issue of the prevalence of handicapping conditions in a specific child population, and will consider some of the methodological problems involved in this form of survey. As far as the author is aware, this project is the first such survey to be conducted in Nigeria. The few published reports of handicapping disorders which are available confine themselves mainly to clinical impressions of samples of handicapped persons in hospital settings without reference to the population from which they are drawn. For instance, Osuntokun *et al.* (1974) discuss EEG correlates of epilepsy in children referred to University College Hospital, Ibadan; and Lotter (1978) screened institutionalised children in Lagos and Ibadan in order to identify children with the syndrome of childhood autism. Such studies provide crucial information on aetiology and degree of severity likely to be encountered, but they fail to provide the overall picture of the problem which is necessary to plan an integrated service for the handicapped within a specific region. As should become clear in later sections, estimates based on the epidemiology of handicap in developed countries (where most of this research has been conducted) will provide a misleading picture of the frequency and type of occurrence likely to be encountered in Nigeria. In addition it is evident that even within one country regional variations in prevalence may occur, and that these variations might be quite localised and quite massive. Wilson (1964) identified substantial differences in the prevalence of visual defects due to localised infections, and Hinchcliffe (1973) reports on regional factors which affect the prevalence of hearing loss. This emphasises the need for research to be co-ordinated with programmes of provision.

The Department of Special Education, University of Jos, is one of the few departments of higher education in Nigeria engaged in the training of specialist teachers of the handicapped, and it is within this context that the survey was commissioned. The main emphasis of the study was to estimate the pattern of special education needs within the state, and highlight the differences between this and the pattern of needs found in developed countries. It is essential that these differences are recognised so as to avoid using limited resources to set up facilities modelled on a pattern inappropriate to the needs.

Survey method

The first requirement of a survey of this type is a reliable method of sampling the child population. In developed countries it is possible to sample from the school population with the knowledge that the vast majority of school-aged children attend school. Additional information can be obtained from social services and medical agencies. Data on the population density and housing conditions for particular areas is also available from local authority records, census abstracts and so on. In other words, developed countries have many sources of reliable information, and this information can be used as a base for epidemiological work.

In Nigeria there are few, if any, reliable sources of data from which to draw information on the characteristics of the population. This study attempted to solve the problem by collecting the necessary census information from the samples used in the survey. The samples therefore have to define the population characteristics.

The survey took the form of an interview with every head of household in six areas, four rural and two urban. The questions related to the size and structure of the household, and the tribe, religion, occupation and education of various members of the household. The final question asked whether any of the children in the household were handicapped in any way. If so, a further interview was conducted concerning these children.

The study was conducted in six stages:

(1) The interview schedule was compiled and translated into Hausa. Villages were assessed for suitability and selected. Interviewers were selected and trained.

(2) Interviews were conducted in four rural areas.

(3) A return visit was made to three areas to re-interview a proportion of heads of household. The re-interviews were conducted as a test of the reliability of the interview schedule with these particular population samples.

(4) The interview/re-interview data were examined and the interview schedule modified on the basis of this examination and field experience. Urban areas were assessed for suitability and selected.

(5) Interviews were conducted in two urban areas. The total number of heads of household in these two areas was approximately the same as the total number from the four rural areas.

(6) Return visits were made to the two areas to re-interview in a proportion of the households.

The interview schedule and reliability

The interview schedule was written in English and the interviewer training was conducted in this language. Towards the end of the training period the English version was translated into Hausa, and piloted in a local (non-sample) village. Questions asked of the head of household included his tribe, occupation, religion, the number of current, divorced or dead wives, their ages and tribes; the number of children to each wife, their age, their work and educational status, whether they live at home; the number of his children who have died, their age at death, and the cause of death; the number and age of other persons living in the household, and their relationship to the head of household. The final question asked if any children had any problems with moving their arms, legs or hands; or who had difficulty in seeing, talking, or hearing; or who were slow to learn things; or who acted in strange or peculiar ways.

The questions were included in order to obtain three types of information: biographical detail which would contribute to the definition of the sample population; detail of the head of household's children and other children living in the household, which would indicate the size of the child population within the sample; and one question which identified any handicapped children within that sample.

In order to test the reliability of each of the schedule items, re-interview data was collected and differences between responses in the first and second interview noted. Table 8.1 presents the percentage agreement on the key items in the schedule. It can be seen that except for the number of wives of the head of household who have died or been divorced, and the number of children fathered by the head of household who have

Table 8.1   *Percentage agreement of schedule items*

	Rural	Urban		Rural	Urban
Tribe	92	97	Children - living	87	95
School	91	90	- dead	44	29
Employment	89	97	Sex	99	99
Religion	87	100	Mother	87	93
Wives - living	96	97	Age	35	53
dead/divorced	61	48	School	86	93

died, responses from the urban sample tend to be more reliable than those from the rural sample. Except for the above two items and the given age of children, all items have a greater than 85 per cent agreement.

Biographical information: As can be seen from Table 8.1 some questions seem to present little problem, e.g. head of household's tribe, religion, employment and schooling. Disagreement in these cases is probably largely a function of interviewer error. The naming of current wives showed few differences between interview and re-interview, but the number of dead and divorced wives showed great discrepancy (61 per cent and 48 per cent agreement). This was possibly a function of perceived importance of the question from the point of view of the interviewee, although other factors may also have contributed.

The number of living children was a critical question because an accurate record of the size of the child population was necessary for calculating the rates of prevalence of the various handicapping conditions. The agreement was relatively high for this item (87 per cent and 95 per cent) and the existing discrepancies were, for the most part, explicable. In several cases children said to be own children by the head of household in one interview were included in the 'other person's children' category in the other interview – an interesting point which may reflect attitudes to children and relationships in an extended family culture. Most of the other cases of discrepancy were with adult offspring who had left home. Therefore only a small number of the children within the target population (age group 0-16 years) failed to appear in one interview when mentioned in the other. Thus assessment of the total child population within each community is fairly accurate and the small discrepancy they create is unlikely to affect the overall prevalence calculation by a significant degree.

Age of children: the second problem which is critical to the study concerns the given age of the children. Because the study's main emphasis is on the educational implications of handicap it focuses only on the prevalence of conditions occurring in the 0-16 year age band. It soon became obvious during field-work that many interviewees had little use for the Western concept of age. Situations arose in which the age of the child was given as greater than the age of the mother; or the mother would give birth to several children within the same year – but not by multiple birth as this was usually mentioned as a significant event.

If the age given is a highly unreliable statistic then the total of children within the age group 0-16 years in each sample population is also unreliable, as is the inclusion or exclusion of handicapping conditions on the basis of age. The agreement for age was 35 per cent and 53 per cent which is extremely low. It should be noted that similar problems were encountered in the classification of official census data of Nigeria, which produced disproportionate age distributions, and tendencies for people to give ages ending in zero (Umoh, 1972). Varied reasons for errors in age reporting in developing countries are listed in *Demographic Year Book 1977* (UN publication).

A closer examination of the given ages of children provides a less alarming picture than that suggested by the low agreement figures. Analysis of the ages given for children in the interview/re-interview shows that only 16 per cent (rural) and 9 per cent (urban) of ages given were discrepant by more than three years, and for 5 per cent and 1 per cent of named children discrepancy in the given age shifted them into or out of the target population of children younger than seventeen years. It is this shift between the two age groups which is the significant point for the study, because a shift bias in one direction or the other will affect the overall size of the target population. However, with a relatively small proportion of children moving from one group to the other, if there is any bias it is likely to have an insignificant effect on the total population size.

The data on the reliability of given ages indicates that although the level of agreement between first and second interview is poor, in most cases this discrepancy is relatively small (less than four years). However it is important to note that agreement does not equal accuracy. Interviewees may merely have been consistent in their errors, and a child aged fifteen years may have been given an age of eleven years in both interviews. Thus the question of given age must be considered with extreme caution, particularly in studies where it is used as a dependent variable. In such cases objective methods of age identification should be used (Jelliffe, 1966).

Child mortality: an item of considerable relevance to the study, but one which proved to be highly unreliable, was that concerned with children who had died. Mortality rate is obviously very high in countries where there is limited access to medical facilities. Figures in excess of 15 per cent within the first year of birth are quoted by WHO (*Demographic Year Book, 1977*). However, reliable statistics are not readily available, particularly for the rural areas of developing countries. This study found only 44 per cent and 29 per cent levels of agreement in answer to this question. Discussion of this point with various people led to the suggestion that to many people of the Plateau area a baby was not considered to be part of the family until after the naming ceremony had taken place. The death of babies younger than this would often not be mentioned. Attitudes to death are understandably complex and private and not readily discussed with strangers. Indeed, the only unpleasant incident which occurred between interviewer and interviewee in over two thousand interviews occurred as a result of asking this question.

Prevalence, incidence and mortality rates: it is important to distinguish between incidence and prevalence rates of the various handicapping conditions. Incidence refers to the rate of occurrence of a particular disorder; while prevalence refers to the number of persons suffering from that disorder in a given population. Thus the incidence of a certain condition at birth may be high: perhaps two in every thousand children (2/1000) may be born with or contract the condition. If the majority of the children suffering from it die within a few months, the prevalence of this condition in the child population as a whole will be low, perhaps only 0.1/1000. Such a difference between prevalence and incidence is likely to pertain to handicaps closely associated with additional medical disorders, such as cerebral palsy, spina bifida, and so on.

With other handicaps not specifically associated with additional problems, such as congenital hearing loss or sight defects, there is likely to be little or no difference between incidence and prevalence rate. Children suffering from this type of condition will have a similar chance of survival to any non-handicapped child in the same population, and they will therefore be represented in each age cohort of that population. Thus if one child in every thousand suffers from one of these defects the incidence rate of the condition will be 1/1000, while the prevalence rate in the same population is also likely to be 1/1000.

It should now be clear that any difference between incidence and prevalence rates is closely associated with child mortality rate. The implications of this association, specifically with regard to educational and medical provision, will be drawn precisely later in this chapter. What needs to be emphasised now is the importance of determining infant mortality rate because this will be the crucial statistic for the long-term prediction of trends in prevalence. As outlined in the last section, this study was unable to obtain any reliable information on this factor. There is an obvious need for further research to substantiate the existing crude estimates.

Recognition and identification of the handicapped

There seemed to be little problem in identifying handicapped children by means of the interview. There was no instance of a handicapped child being identified subsequent to the household being interviewed. And there was little evidence to suggest that parents failed to recognise handicapping conditions which would have been obvious to parents in developed countries. The only exception to this is possibly with children who suffer from petit mal epilepsy. As is discussed in the appropriate section (page 220), only four of Osuntukun's sample of 96 cases of epilepsy suffered petit mal fits. The reason for so few referrals of this condition was considered to be a function of lack of awareness of the clinical symptoms of petit mal among the general population. Although there is little documented evidence to support this view, it seems a highly probable explanation. Even in the European context it has been estimated that only about 50 per cent of all cases are referred, and so a similar but less extreme lack of recognition pertains in developed countries (Gulliford, 1971).

Cases of significant, as opposed to severe, hearing loss, and cases of mild mental retardation are also likely to be difficult for Nigerian parents to identify. But this seems to be a universal problem, and one which is a function of the nature of the two disorders. For instance in Europe, where routine medical examination of infants is commonplace, and where parents are perhaps more aware of developmental milestones, a significant proportion of these disorders is identified late in the child's school career if at all. It would therefore be unrealistic to expect either of these conditions to be identified reliably in large groups of children by an interview based survey. More sophisticated techniques would be required. For instance, in order to detect children suffering from mild mental retardation some form of educational assessment would be necessary; a version of the Sweep Frequency Test is likely to be the most effective screening technique for cases of significant hearing loss (provided that detection of loss rather than diagnosis of the condition is all that is required (Wilber, 1979)).

More obvious to parents, but still presenting some difficulty, is the problem of moderate and severe visual disability. In Europe routine school-based sight tests identify problems in young children, and these defects are then usually rectified easily and cheaply with corrective lenses. In Nigeria there is no routine screening, and even when the problem is identified the defect cannot readily be corrected because the expense of lenses puts them out of the reach of most of the population. As with hearing, screening of the child population is the only effective method of identifying children with mild and moderate sight defects.

These four conditions represent the major problems of identification with an interview based survey. Identification of severe disability seemed to present few problems. Terminology and suggested causation were occasionally bizarre by European standards, but there seemed to be no problem of recognition.

On one occasion a father of a handicapped child did refuse to be interviewed. However, the child was identified by the headman of the village who supplied us with the relevant information. Frequently, during the course of an interview, the interviewee would discuss neighbours' children who were known to have problems. In addition the author checked with the head teacher of the local school to ascertain which of his pupils he knew of as having problems. This ensured that there were several cross-checks in the identification of obvious and severe handicaps.

Diagnosis and severity

When a case was identified the parents were given a second interview in order to assess the degree of the child's handicap. The questions asked concerned the child's abilities and limitations within the community; the attitudes of the parents, siblings and peers to the child; when appropriate about self-help skills, mobility and communication skills; whether the child attends school now, or whether this will be possible in the future; the possible cause of the handicap and when the parents first noticed the problem. On the basis of the replies an attempt was made to classify the type and severity of the handicap, and in obvious cases suggest a diagnosis. In the majority of cases the researcher also saw the child and attempted to verify the replies. However, this was not always possible given that several of the handicapped children were not living with their parents at the time of the interview. In some of these cases parents were able to send for the children and return visits were made in order to see them. In one such case the child showed no evidence of a handicapping condition. Certain confusions had arisen during the interview and the parents had either exaggerated symptoms of bedtime crying and tantrum behaviour, or the interviewer had misrepresented replies such that the researcher was under the impression that the child might be demonstrating behaviour problems and possible retardation. On seeing the child and asking further questions no such condition was evident.

This case clearly illustrates some of the drawbacks of assessing handicapping conditions by interview, and from it stems the particular frustration that most interviews had to be conducted through an interpreter as I could not converse in Hausa. There was only one instance of a parent in the rural areas having sufficient command of English to be interviewed directly. In the urban areas there were more, including a trained nurse who was conversant with the medical details of her child's problem. However, except for these few instances all handicap interviews were conducted in Hausa, and this created translation problems. The major safeguard was that the most reliable interviewer stayed with the project for the two-year duration and was the only person to act as interpreter of handicap interviews. But the few alternatives possible, such as the use of graduate assistants or tape recorded interviews which could be independently translated, were impractical from the point of view of budgetary or time constraints or both.

Classification of handicaps: handicap was defined by a functional assessment of the child and the classification made on the basis of disability. Often diagnosis could be made when the condition was obvious, such as in the many cases of polio and the few cases of cerebral palsy. However, in the statistical presentation these cases are reduced to type of impairment (i.e. physical, mental, hearing, sight, multiple, epileptic, speech defect) and degree of severity.

Classification of severity could be seen as somewhat arbitrary. It was made on the basis of whether the researcher judged the disability to be such that it would seriously interfere with the child's education in the current conditions offered by primary schools. Thus the handicap of one child is his disability in the context of the Nigerian primary school system, and would not necessarily be his handicap in the context of the system of education found in developed countries. Children classified as suffering from severe handicap would find difficulty in competing with their non-handicapped peers in school. Children suffering from mild conditions would find little difficulty if teachers made some allowances for their problems. It will be of value to consider a number of examples which illustrate the classification of one disability, that of physical handicap. Similar criteria were used for the other forms of disability.

(1)   Paraplegic children who find difficulty in walking without aid because of the effects of polio should not experience much educational disadvantage in as far as polio will cause only motor disability, leaving cognitive and perceptual skills unaffected. However, in these cases, particularly in rural areas, distance between home and school will affect whether they attend primary school regularly. In addition, it is questionable whether many schools would be able to adapt their educational provision to allow these children to compete adequately in the job market. Thus severe physical disability is a major handicap for the child with respect to his chances of obtaining education and his chances of that education being geared to his particular needs. Such children would be classified as suffering from severe physical handicap.

(2)   Children affected by polio to the extent that they are mobile without aid, but have some physical limitation, would be classified as mildly physically handicapped.

(3)   Children demonstrating obvious signs of having suffered polio, but where the effects on mobility are minimal (e.g. the wasting of one leg causing the child to limp), would not be

classified as a handicap and therefore not be included in the body of the data.

The interviewers

The interview team for the rural area consisted of six people. They had a minimum education of grade 4 primary, and were all able to read and write. They were fluent in both English and Hausa, and all had at least one other language. Their training lasted four weeks and consisted of:

(1) a discussion of the purpose of the survey, and the reasons for including the various items of the interview schedule;

(2) video-taped recordings of different handicapping conditions and discussions relating to these;

(3) role play sessions involving part and complete interviews, with checks on the individual's accuracy in completing the schedule;

(3) practice interviews in a local non-sample village.

In the four rural areas it was found that the team of six was too large. In each of the areas the majority of interviews were conducted in the first few days of work. After that many days were spent tracing the few remaining interviewees, which meant that the team was fully occupied for less than half of its time. The need for close supervision made it impossible to split the team such that one group could be independent of the other for part of the time. Consequently, the interview team for the urban area was reduced to two persons, and this was found to be satisfactory.

Method of working

The same steps were used for each sample area, the first being to meet with the Secretary of the Local Government Council (LGC) in order to explain the aim of the study. A choice of townships or areas was made and the Secretary or delegated member of the LGC introduced us to the village or area headman. Permission to work in the community was sought from him, and in the case of distant LGCs accommodation was arranged for the team. Before our arrival the purpose of the study was announced to the community.

The need to interview every head of household in each of the selected communities was of considerable importance to the study. Only by doing this could a true estimate of the size of the population be made. If the team interviewed only those heads of household who made themselves readily available a self-selected sample would be taken. This would be likely to contain the majority of households with handicapped children and be likely to miss other households with non-handicapped children: a situation which would obviously inflate prevalence figures.

This problem presented the major practical problem to the study, and several methods were employed in an attempt to solve it. During the rural study the team relied on a local person to act as a guide. In some places the team was taken through the area compound by compound, interviewing whichever heads of household were available at the time. Return visits were then made to interview any persons who were missed. In other places the headman called his people to meet us, and interviewing took place in a central area. This latter method was efficient but only successful in smaller villages. When used in a larger township, such as Lakushi, with 260 compounds, it was not effective. In this township over 100 interviews were conducted in the first few days. However, after that the team averaged about 10 interviews per week. The headman had difficulty in knowing which people, or even how many, were necessary to make up the full complement. Using the compound to compound method demonstrated that over 100 interviews were still missing after five weeks work.

Before beginning interviews in the urban areas a man local to the area was employed as a full-time member of the interviewing team to act as a guide. His status as an employee rather than a volunteer allowed the team greater control over the organisation of the interviewing than was possible in the rural study. The second improvement was to map the compounds prior to working in a particular area. Interviews and compounds were given corresponding numbers which enabled the team to check its progress. This, of course, did not guarantee complete coverage because often several households lived within one definable compound, or seemingly several compounds made up accommodation for one household. However, it was a significant improvement on the methods used in the rural areas, and in fact one which should have been used for the larger townships.

Selection of areas

The three LGCs used in the rural study were Keffi, Shendam and Mangu. These LGCs were suggested by the Permanent Secretary for Education, Jos. They represent three different regions in Plateau State, with Mangu on the plateau and Keffi and Shendam in low-lying regions.

Following discussions with the Secretaries of the three LGCs a number of small townships were suggested for the study. Visits were made to assess suitability, with the main criteria being size and rural character of the communities. In addition it was necessary for the townships to be primarily farming communities in order to provide good contrast with the urban sample.

The following townships were finally selected (small neighbouring villages were included when time permitted): Keffi LGC – Gitata; Shendam LGC – Poeship and Lakushi; Mangu LGC – Kantoma.

In the selection of an urban settlement the obvious choice was Jos. However, choosing suitable areas within Jos posed the particular problem of finding ones which had well defined boundaries and yet were still integrated within the main urban development. Two areas in Jos were eventually selected, Jenta Adamu on the north-western edge, and Angwan Soya on the northern edge.

Characteristics of sample areas

Excluding Kantoma and the neighbouring villages, each of the rural townships was dependent upon a farming, trading economy. Kantoma and its neighbours are situated in a tin mining area, and a proportion of the population combine work for the Tin Mining Company with farming.

Each of the townships had its own primary school which served the township and the neighbouring areas. Gitata had its own rural health clinic, and Kantoma was served by the Tin Mining Company's clinic. Kantoma alone had electricity, supplied by the Company to houses occupied by their employees.

In contrast to this the urban areas had a hospital service and both primary and secondary schools. Many houses were connected to mains electricity and, unlike the rural areas, water was piped to central points in the neighbourhood. Some of the wealthier compounds had their own water taps. A greater variety of local and imported produce was available to those who could afford it.

The interviews revealed many differences between urban and rural samples particularly in terms of employment, education and tribal distribution. These are worthy of separate comment.

Employment: a wide variety of occupations were pursued in the urban areas, ranging from unskilled work such as labouring, through trades and work in the armed forces and police to teaching, clerical and civil service posts. In the rural areas work was confined mainly to subsistence farming with the exception of mining in the village of Kantoma.

Education: predictably there were differences between the urban and rural areas in the level of education received by children and heads of household. In rural areas 14 per cent of all heads of household had received primary education compared with 51 per cent in the urban areas. Included in these figures are the 2 per cent and 11 per cent who had gone on to secondary education. With regard to children between the ages of six and sixteen years, 50 per cent of children in rural areas and 80 per cent in urban areas were attending either primary or secondary schools at the time of the interview. It is likely that the majority of urban children will receive some form of education given that a significant proportion will enter primary school after six years of age, and will leave before sixteen years (see Oyewole, Chapter 6 in this volume). It is equally as likely that significantly fewer rural children will receive some form of education than their urban counterparts. However, the trend towards education for all children is obvious by comparing the current proportions in education with the proportion of parents who received it. This is an important issue when discussing the need to establish special education facilities.

Tribal distribution: tribal distribution in this part of Nigeria is very complex. It has been estimated that as many as 100 distinct tribal groups are native to the Plateau and surrounding area (Meek, 1925). The distribution of the tribes in the survey indicates that rural areas tend to have specific tribal groupings, while the urban areas are more cosmopolitan. This latter point was demonstrated not only by the number of different tribes but also by a fuller representation of the three main groupings – Hausa, Yoruba and Ibo.

Results

Table 8.2 illustrates the size of the survey. The numbers of children include both the children of the head of the household and other children living in the household at the time of the interview. This is the total child population used to calculate the prevalence of handicapping conditions.

The overall results are tabulated in Table 8.3. They show the number of cases of each handicapping condition found in the six areas, and the combined prevalence rate for these conditions for the urban and rural samples. At the outset of the survey a basic premise was that there would be a significant difference in the prevalence of at least some of the handicapping disorders between the urban and rural areas, and Table 8.3 has been set out to illustrate these differences. However, the rate of occurrence of any of these disorders is too small to test for statistical difference, and so the results can only be discussed in terms of overall rates and possible differences.

If the results are considered from the point of view of the prevalence of severe handicapping conditions (mental handicap, severe physical handicap, blindness and deafness), there is an overall prevalence of 5.0/1000 in urban areas and 5.75/1000 in rural areas. This is likely to be an accurate reflection of the size of the problem in the sample communities, and other communities with similar social and geographical characteristics.

A number of general points need to be emphasised concerning these findings. Some of these will be discussed in more detail

Table 8.2 *Size of sample populations*

Area	No. of interviews	No. of children between 0 and 16 years
Gitata	325	1431
Poeship	222	752
Kantoma	258	780
Lakushi	253	825
Total	1058	3788
Jenta Adamu	435	1407
Angwan Soya	369	1006
Total	804	2413

Table 8.3 *Prevalence of handicapping conditions*

	Rural		Urban	
	No. of Cases	Prevalence	No. of Cases	Prevalence
Mental handicap				
severe with PH	2	0.50 ⎫ 1.50	4	1.66 ⎫ 3.32
severe without PH	4	1.00 ⎭	4	1.66 ⎭
Polio				
severe	6	1.50 ⎫ 2.25	2	0.83 ⎫ 1.66
mild	3	0.75 ⎭	2	0.83 ⎭
Other physical handicap				
amputation	1	0.25 ⎫ 1.00	1	0.42 ⎫ 1.25
congenital or unknown diagnosis	3	0.75 ⎭	2	0.83 ⎭
Epilepsy				
petit mal	—	— ⎫ 0.25	—	— ⎫ 0.83
grand mal	1	0.25 ⎭	2	0.83 ⎭
Hearing disorder				
deaf	5	1.25 ⎫	2	0.83 ⎫
loss with discharge	8	2.00 ⎬ 4.50	11	4.58 ⎬ 6.66
loss without discharge	5	1.25 ⎭	3	1.25 ⎭
Visual handicap				
blind	2	0.50 ⎫ 2.00	—	— ⎫ 1.25
partially sighted	6	1.50 ⎭	3	1.25 ⎭
Speech disorder				
varied	1	0.25 0.25	3	1.25 1.25

Prevalence rate = number of recorded cases per thousand children.

under the heading of specific handicaps or in the discussion of implications.

(1) The study collected data on the prevalence of conditions affecting the child population. It does not reflect prevalence in the population as a whole. In the adult population certain conditions are likely to be less prevalent because life expectation associated with these conditions is poor. This applies generally to mental and multiple handicap, and specifically to conditions like cerebral palsy, spina bifida and hydrocephalus. However, other conditions are likely to be more prevalent, particularly visual handicap, hearing disorder, and certain forms of physical handicap. In these cases either infection and disease can lead to

the development of disorders in adult life, or conditions which are classified as mild disorders in the younger age group will become progressively more severe with the onset of age.

(2) The survey is unlikely to have been successful in detecting all cases within the sample population. The types of condition overlooked are probably relatively mild, but they are the same conditions which, in some cases, may be progressive and thus represent substantial problems for individuals in later life.

(3) The prevalence of severe mental and multiple handicap was found to be less than the overall prevalence usually ascribed to developed countries. However incidence is likely to be much greater. The high infant mortality rate is likely to account for this discrepancy.

(4) Children suffering from the effects of polio represent a significant proportion of the total number of physically handicapped children. The figures of 2.25/1000 and 1.66/1000 reflect the prevalence of the effects of polio. The incidence of the disease is far higher, given that certain children will suffer minimal or no effect, and others will die as a result of it.

(5) Severe hearing loss and visual disability have comparable prevalence to that found in developed countries. The degree of handicap which results from these conditions is likely to be more severe in most cases because of the lack of remedial aids available to the majority of Nigerians at the present time.

(6) The prevalence of less severe hearing and sight defects is likely to be higher than that found in developed countries because of the high incidence of minor infections which lead ultimately to permanent disorders. In developed countries these conditions are, for the most part, treatable; but in Nigeria this treatment is not readily available.

Discussion

Mental handicap: a number of studies have been conducted in UK which give comparable figures of prevalence for the various categories of mental handicap. A review of some of these is given by Tizard (1972). For convenience, the data given in these studies can be related to two categories of mental handicap, the severely subnormal (with IQ scores below 50), and the mildly subnormal (with IQ scores between 50 and 70). Of the twelve studies reviewed by Tizard the mean prevalence rate per 1000 for the severely subnormal is 3.8 (with a standard deviation of 0.65). Tizard estimates that the severely subnormal category represents only one quarter of the total population of classifiably subnormal children. On the basis of this estimate the prevalence rate for subnormal children will be in the range of 15/1000. Kushlick and Cox (1973) put this figure at nearer 24/1000, although they qualify this by saying that only a small number of the expected 20/1000 children with IQs of 50 to 70 attract the attention of special services.

There are two important distinctions to be made between the severe and the mildly subnormal groups:

(1) In Tizard's review specific reference is made to the Aberdeen study conducted in 1962. Among other things the data clearly illustrates an absence of social class gradient for children diagnosed as mildly subnormal. In other words, the incidence of mild subnormality is strongly associated with families of low social status and poor educational attainment living in conditions of relative poverty, while the incidence of severe subnormality is evenly distributed across all social classes.

(2) In the Wessex study Kushlick and Cox (1973) report that the majority of severely subnormal children have obvious clinical signs of the disorder causing the handicap, even if the aetiology is unclear. The mildly subnormal usually show no clinical signs of the disorder causing the handicap.

No specific attempt to identify mildly retarded children was made in the current study because of the difficulties involved when using an interview-based method. In developed countries prevalence figures show an age related effect because identification usually occurs during early school years. This is due largely to lack of clinical signs which make the condition immediately obvious in the first two or three years from birth, and the dependence on educational attainment as a major criterion for diagnosing the problem. It is therefore unlikely that Nigerian parents would be able to identify such children, and even if a minority could, little or no reliability could be attached to the method of identification. However, there are also philosophical and practical issues involved with the problem. It has been argued that the concept of mild retardation is spurious until the condition begins to put the individual at a disadvantage relative to his peers (Robinson, 1978). This situation will not occur in

Nigeria until UPE is well established and job opportunities for the majority become dependent upon educational attainment. Until this occurs the problem of mild retardation will be relatively small and unless combined with additional disabilities will rarely be classified as a handicapping condition.

Table 8.3 presents the prevalence of mental handicap found in rural and urban areas. All but two of the fourteen cases identified were clearly classifiable as suffering from severe mental handicap. Of the two exceptions, one was mildly hemiplegic, presented certain behaviour problems, and was socially immature. The other was hyperactive and exhibited bizarre behaviours.

The literature presents few studies of the epidemiology of mental handicap in developing countries. Tizard (1972) predicts that given the poor obstetric and antenatal care which prevails in developing countries, the incidence of severe mental handicap is likely to be very much higher than figures given in UK studies. However, high infant mortality is likely to reduce the prevalence to below UK rates.

The results of this survey are consistent with this prediction. Two points need to be emphasised. First, the prevalence in the urban samples is higher than in the rural samples. Although this is not a statistically significant difference it is a difference which would be expected given the greater availability of medical facilities to the urban sample than the rural, and hence better chances of survival for those infants suffering from medical conditions associated with severe mental handicap. Second, the figure of 3.32/1000 from the urban sample is close to the current prevalence rate of 3.75/1000 in the UK. The figure of 1.50/1000 for the rural sample is less than half this rate, and because approximately 80 per cent of the population of Nigeria live in rural areas (Segal, 1972) the overall prevalence of severe mental handicap will be substantially lower than UK rates – though this figure still represents major educational and vocational problems.

Down's Syndrome: with regard to specific causation the most prominent condition in the UK is Down's Syndrome, representing between 20 per cent and 30 per cent of all cases of severe mental handicap (Kushlick and Cox, 1973; Berg, 1974). The incidence of Down's Syndrome is closely linked to maternal age, and the relative change in the distribution of child-bearing age has been shown to have a significant effect on this incidence rate. Over the last few decades in Europe and in North America a decline in the proportion of maternities in the high age range is seen as a significant factor accounting for a decrease in the incidence of Down's Syndrome – for instance in Northern Sweden rates decreased from 2.2/1000 to 0.85/1000 (Gustavson *et al.*, 1977), and in the USA from 1.67/1000 to 1.10/1000 (Stein and Susser, 1977).

Incidence in Nigeria is likely to be similar to the early high rates recorded in Europe and the USA. There are few studies available to support this. Axton and Levy (1974) report a rate of 1.67/1000 from a maternity clinic in Rhodesia. Prevalence rates will be very much lower than this because of the susceptibility of these children to pneumonia and cardiac problems (Berg, 1974). This, in combination with the lack of sophisticated medical facilities, will give rise to a high mortality rate in this group of children. The author's experience in Nigeria supports this view. No Down's Syndrome children were recorded among the sample populations used in the survey, and only two cases were noted during visits to various institutions throughout the country.

Cerebral Palsy: within the group of mentally handicapped children eight had some form of motor dysfunction (see Table 8.3). In two cases the mental handicap was clearly the primary disorder, with the motor dysfunction a minimal disability. A third child was severely hydrocephalic. At two years of age no assessment could be made of her mental ability, but the likelihood is that she will suffer some degree of mental retardation.

The remaining five children were diagnosed as suffering from cerebral palsy. This condition is classifiable as primarily a physical handicap, although it is often associated with mental retardation (Kirman and Bicknell, 1975).

As with Down's Syndrome children, there is likely to be a large discrepancy between incidence and prevalence in Nigeria. Incidence is likely to be high – Asirifi (1972) estimates that in developing countries it will be twice as high as the rate in developed countries – and prevalence low. There are a number of reasons for this:

(1) In the majority of cases cerebral palsy is caused by either pre-term delivery, birth trauma, or toxaemia of pregnancy (Davies and Tizard, 1975). These problems will be rife in

Nigeria, where obstetric and maternity care, even when available, are often not used by the majority of women (Odebiyi, 1977). Consequently incidence of cerebral palsy is likely to be high.

(2)   As with Down's Syndrome, there is a strong association between high maternal age and incidence of the disorder (McManus et al., 1977). In developing countries child-bearing often continues well into the high-risk age group.

(3)   The problem of meningitis encephalopathies associated with childhood diseases such as measles and chicken pox also affect incidence of cerebral palsy in infancy, particularly in situations where little or no medical treatment is available. This is likely to be a major cause of cerebral palsy in Nigeria and similar countries (Asirifi, 1972).

(4)   Prevalence of cerebral palsy is likely to be low owing to the susceptibility of this type of child to diseases during infancy, and the usual practice in rural areas of not allowing children with obvious congenital abnormalities to survive (Asirifi, 1972; Mba, 1978).

Changes in health education and obstetric and maternity care are likely to bring about associated changes in incidence. A study conducted in Western Australia (Dale and Stanley, 1980) indicated a peaking of the rate at 3.7/1000 in 1967, and then a steady decline to 1.2/1000 by 1975. They suggest that the main factor affecting this decline was improved obstetric care and management of the neonate, and preventive programmes aimed at pre-term births. Under these conditions of improved care, the survival rate of affected neonates and infants is likely to be high. This, of course, underlines the main differences between incidence and prevalence of cerebral palsy in the developed countries and Nigeria. No figures are available for incidence in developing countries. It is likely, however, that the rate will be higher than the 3.7/1000 given by Dale and Stanley, but prevalence will be much lower. The results of this survey indicate 0.75/1000 for both rural and urban areas (three cases in the former, and two cases in the latter). These figures would be consistent with the poor survival expectations of this group of children.

Polio: Polio is still a major cause of physical handicap in Africa, and it is a disease which should be and hopefully will be eradicated with an internationally co-ordinated vaccination programme. A recent survey in Malawi (WHO Report, 1980) found a prevalence of 6.5/1000 for all detectable cases of polio. Using a 20 per cent correction factor to allow for complete recovery and deaths, the incidence was estimated at 8.2/1000. The prevalence of severe cases (children unable to walk, or only able to walk with an aid) was 1.9/1000.

Table 8.3 gives figures for the prevalence of severe and mild effects of polio in the Plateau State survey. Severe effects had a prevalence of 1.5/1000 in rural areas and 0.83/1000 in urban areas. The rural figures are similar to those found in Malawi. The extent and effectiveness of national vaccination programmes will obviously account for some degree of national and regional differences in the incidence of the disease.

Other physically handicapping conditions: other physical handicaps amounting to 1.0/1000 and 1.25/1000 for rural and urban areas respectively included one case of an accident leading to amputation of the hand, and one case where treatment by traditional medicine led to severe disability in the lower limbs. The remaining five cases were either congenital handicaps or conditions of unknown diagnosis, all of a relatively severe nature. One of these children was suffering from an apparently progressive condition which was not responding to treatment. At the time of interview the child was finding walking difficult. This particular case was included because the condition seemed permanent. Other cases were excluded if the child was suffering from a treatable condition which was giving rise to temporary disability. This, however, was a somewhat arbitrary decision given the problems entailed in medical treatment in rural areas. For instance, a child living near Gitata was suffering from a severely ulcerated hip. He could only walk with an aid, and then with great difficulty. The researcher had taken him to the rural health clinic where a course of antibiotics was administered, but after three weeks the condition had not improved. Arrangements were therefore made for hospital treatment, but on arriving to take the child, the parents told the researcher that they were unhappy with the decision and would take him once again for traditional medicine. Prognosis was poor for this child and illustrates how poor treatment of minor conditions can lead to permanent disability.

Epilepsy: The prevalence of grand mal epilepsy was found to be 0.75/1000 in urban areas and 0.25/1000 in rural areas. These rates were derived from only three cases and so care must be taken in interpreting the results. Studies cited by Osuntokun *et al.* (1974) suggest that prevalence of epilepsy could be higher in African countries than in developed countries. In fact epilepsy in the UK is very prevalent. In a NHS report cited by Gulliford (1971) the prevalence rate was 8.0/1000. However, only about 50 per cent of cases were known to the authorities, and of these only a small proportion suffered frequent grand mal fits.

The three cases identified in the survey suffered frequent grand mal fits. No cases of petit mal were recorded. This is consistent with the findings of Osuntokun *et al.* (1974). Only 4 per cent of the 96 cases reported in their study suffered petit mal fits, although as they and others have suggested it is possibly because of a lack of awareness of the clinical symptoms that petit mal cases are not referred to hospitals. Of all the disorders identified in the study, epilepsy was probably the least understood and accepted by the parents. In each of the three cases the children seemed intelligent and healthy with no signs of additional problems. All three children attended school and yet in the three cases the parents described their children as 'crazy'. They believed that devils and ju ju accounted for their children's condition and only further magic could relieve them of it.

Deaf and partially hearing: In developed countries there is a high prevalence of children with significant hearing loss. Dale (1967) reports a routine screening test carried out on school children in Surrey, England, where 77/1000 children had significant hearing loss. Ear infections leading to conductive hearing loss were probably more common in the UK than they are today because improvements in health care have reduced the types of infection that often lead to such loss (Gulliford, 1971). In developing countries where this level of care is still limited prevalence of ear infection, particularly otitis media, is extremely high. In a study of Indian school populations the prevalence ranged from 163/1000 to 186/1000 (Kapur, 1976), with between 70 per cent and 80 per cent of these cases having evidence of acute or chronic otitis media.

The effect of significant hearing loss on both the educational and social functioning of the child varies. In many cases the loss is intermittent, this being reported particularly in the cases of exudative conditions. In cases of mild and moderate loss the child's intelligence and ability to adapt will determine the degree of handicap (Gulliford, 1971). However in many cases this ability to adapt is in itself a cause of problems because the loss is frequently not obvious to parents or teachers. This factor means that audiometric screening is the only reliable method of establishing the prevalence of this disability, and only those cases of chronic otitis media, where frequent discharge often accompanied by pain draw the child's and parent's attention to the problem, are likely to be detected in an interview based survey.

Results presented in Table 8.3 give prevalence in rural areas as 2.0/1000 for exudative ear infections, while the rate in urban areas is 4.5/1000. These figures, however, do not reflect a true difference in prevalence of this disorder, but rather a focusing of interest on the problem by the researcher. Throughout the first part of the study conducted in rural areas interviewers asked parents whether any of their children had difficulties with hearing. If such children were identified some form of verification was required as to the extent of the hearing loss, i.e. under what circumstances was the child able to hear, and when did the child experience difficulties. Because of the relative frequency of exudative ear infection in rural areas, in the urban study the researcher asked specifically if any young children showed signs of frequent discharge. Of the eleven cases four from the urban sample were infants and included only on the basis of their discharge. No behavioural verification of hearing loss could be obtained.

In spite of this change in strategy it is obvious from comparing these figures with those of the published screening tests referred to above that the survey is likely to have detected only a small proportion of children in this category, albeit the more chronic cases. However, these limitations were expected at the outset of the project.

A further eight cases of hearing loss (without discharge) were detected, giving a prevalence of 1.25/1000 for both rural and urban areas. These children included one case where the problem was possibly genetically determined since the father also suffered from hearing loss; and one case in which the problem was caused by a large swelling or growth beneath one ear. One child had both hearing and visual defects, and one had speech problems accompanying the hearing loss.

With no objective measures available to compare degrees of

severity it is impossible to divide the cases into children suffering from a mild or moderate degree of loss, and those children suffering from such a severe loss as to require hearing aids and/or specialised training in order to function adequately in an educational setting. This latter group of children form the extreme end of the classification of significant hearing loss. Anderson (1973) quotes the prevalence of these children as 0.6/1000. This is consistent with the USA's National Center for Health Statistics findings of 1/1000 for the age group 0-17 years (Hicks and Glenn, 1979). Some cases identified in the Plateau State survey would almost certainly fall within this category. For instance, one child was reported to rely heavily upon visual cues including lip-reading in order to understand speech.

A total of seven cases of profoundly deaf children were identified, giving a prevalence of 1.25/1000 in the rural areas, and 0.83 in urban areas. These rates are similar to those found in developed countries. Anderson (1973) reports a rate of 0.5/1000 for children in the UK, while Dale (1967) reports the rate as being nearer 1.0/1000. Less difficulty was involved in making an objective statement as to whether a child was profoundly deaf as opposed to whether he was partially hearing. Hearing loss in combination with lack of speech were the important indicators.

Of the seven cases identified five were of school age, but only one of these children attended school, and this was the school for the deaf in Jos. None of the parents of the other deaf children were aware of this special education facility. One child in particular had developed a sophisticated sign system which was understood by many of the villagers. He was a well integrated boy and a dominant member of his peer group (although a contributing factor may have been his relationship to the village headman, and the fact that he lived in the headman's compound). In contrast, one child seemed poorly integrated. She was badly dressed compared with her siblings, and seemed to be the one person in the compound given the most menial jobs and to be the subject of general derision.

Visual handicap: the problem of the blind has long attracted attention if for no other reason than its prominence among the population of beggars, particularly in Moslem areas (Daramola, 1976). Wilson (1964) has reported on the surveys carried out on regional differences in the prevalence and aetiology of blindness in Africa. In Africa south of the Sahara, prevalence of blindness for the total population (i.e. children and adults) is 5.0/1000 in areas where the main causes are cataract, glaucoma, measles, smallpox, and minor infections. In areas where trachoma is endemic the figures are nearer 8.0/1000, and where onchocerciasis (river blindness) and keratomalacia occur prevalence reaches 10/1000.

Thus the prevalence of blindness is subject to considerable regional variation depending upon the causative factors prevailing in that area. Although it is unrealistic to designate one condition as being the most prominent cause, it has been suggested by Wilson (1981) that in much of Asia and Africa cataract accounts for at least 50 per cent of blindness, while Sandford-Smith and Whittle (1981) indicate that measles in combination with dietary deficiencies is the significant cause of childhood blindness in many parts of Africa, and in Northern Nigeria in particular accounts for over 50 per cent of all cases. Here the distinction needs to be made between blindness in the population as a whole and blindness in the child population. Obviously with increasing age the prevalence rate also increases, and the prominence of particular causes will change. The nature of the relationship between these factors is difficult to ascertain from the literature, but it is clear that the incidence of diseases likely to affect the sight of children in Nigeria is far higher than that experienced in developed countries. Wilson (1964) reports findings that in Nigeria and Ghana about 12 per cent of the blind are under fifteen years of age, compared with 2 per cent or 3 per cent which is usual for Europe and North America (Kirchner and Peterson, 1979).

This survey found the prevalence of blindness to be 0.5/1000 in the rural areas, which is slightly lower than the predicted average rate of the findings reported by Wilson (1964). No cases were found in the urban samples, but this is not inconsistent given the relatively low overall rate.

The identification and classification of visual disability is relatively simple in cases of severe impairment. However, the prevalence of these conditions is low relative to the overall prevalence of visual impairment in the population. Difficulties arise when attempting to assess whether a child who suffers some degree of impairment is in fact handicapped by this condition, and how the handicap manifests itself in the educational setting. The whole problem is confounded by the difficulty in obtaining effective remediation, particularly prescriptive lenses.

As previously stated, the only reliable means of obtaining objective measures of the prevalence of visual impairment is to use a screening technique with large numbers of children. This would provide the necessary information for assessing the various types and degrees of impairment. These figures could then be related to degrees of handicap likely to be experienced at the various levels of disability. As far as the author is aware no such study has been conducted in Nigeria. It can only be assumed that the rates are likely to be relatively high compared with developed countries because of the higher rates of infections, vitamin deficiencies, and lack of available medical treatment for conditions such as cataract. In this study only children suffering from severe impairment were included in the data. If a child had difficulty in recognising people standing within ten feet of him or difficulty in seeing book print he would be included. Children suffering from conditions likely to be progressive without medical treatment, particularly cataract, were also included. Children who suffered lesser degrees of impairment were not included because of the difficulty of assessing the degree of handicap pertaining to these conditions. For instance, two children in the total sample had lost the sight in one eye due to accidents but neither were included in the data because the disability would probably represent a relatively minor handicap.

On the basis of these criteria Table 8.3 shows a rate of 1.5/1000 and 1.25/1000 for rural and urban areas respectively. Of the nine cases identified, four were suffering from cataract and one child, mentioned in the previous section, from a dual visual and hearing handicap. The remaining four children suffered from severe disabilities of unknown causation. The author considered that each of these children would require special considerations if they were to function adequately in the classroom.

Speech disorders: the survey identified one child in the rural samples and three children in the urban samples suffering from articulation and speech disorders. This gave prevalence rates of 0.25/1000 and 1.25/1000 respectively. In two cases the children suffered from specific speech disorders involving an inability to formulate sentences correctly, and so a classification of disphasia would seem appropriate. The remaining two children both suffered from severe stammer. The reason for including these children was that both had been excluded from school for periods of time because of their articulation difficulties – so both can justifiably be classified as suffering from an educational handicap. Whether this was a reflection of the teachers' attitude or the severity of the handicap is open to question.

Interpretation of prevalence rates

The main relevance of this study is that it provides the basis for the planning of special education facilities within Plateau State. It is hoped that it may also be of use to other regions within and outside Nigeria. However, care must be taken in interpreting the results because local and massive regional variations can exist, and the implications may differ according to cause. For example, Adamrobe in Ghana is often referred to as the 'deaf' village. Here deafness has a prevalence of 100/1000 and is genetically determined (David et al., 1971). Not surprisingly Adamrobe featured as the base for one of Ghana's first schools for the deaf (Markides, 1976). Another example can be taken from Wilson's report on blindness in Africa south of the Sahara (Wilson, 1964). In this the mean prevalence rate for blindness is given as 5/1000, while in areas where onchocerciasis (river blindness) occurs it is given as 10/1000 – a one hundred per cent increase in prevalence.

These two examples provide an interesting contrast in as far as the deafness in Adamrobe cannot as yet be considered a treatable condition, and consequently the high prevalence rate must be taken into account in the planning of long-term provision for the deaf. However, the implications differ in areas which are subject to high prevalence of visual defects due to river blindness. The condition causing blindness can be controlled, or populations living within the area where transmission occurs can be moved. Consequently emphasis is on prevention, and the planning of local provision should be seen in terms of a significant reduction in future prevalence rates. This changing profile of prevalence should be taken as the rule rather than the exception, and it is possible to predict six major influences: *preventative medicine, curative medicine, epidemics, provision of technical aids, change in social conditions* and *increased educational provision.*

(1)   Preventative programmes can have both local impact as in the case of river blindness, or far reaching general effects as will be the case with a successful WHO programme to combat polio. Obviously in these cases the direct effect of such programmes is a reduction in the incidence and therefore the prevalence of the respective conditions.

(2)   Improved antenatal and obstetric care should have a significant effect on the currently high incidence of brain injury at birth. However, such programmes are likely to run parallel with improved curative medical programmes. These latter programmes will probably have the effect of increasing the survival rate of children suffering brain injury. Thus in combination there should be a reduction in the incidence of such conditions as cerebral palsy and severe mental handicap, but an increase in the prevalence of these conditions.

(3)   Epidemics or the peaking of endemic diseases can have a significant impact on the prevalence of conditions affecting particular age cohorts within a given population. For example, the results of the Malawi study (WHO Report, 1980) suggest a peaking of the incidence of polio every six to seven years. Similar phenomena are evident in developed countries. The 1964-5 rubella epidemic increased the prevalence of deafness in combination with visual handicap by 2.5 per cent above the national average in the USA. This increase still has a significant effect on the demand for special provision for that particular age cohort (Hicks and Glenn, 1979). Similar specific demands are likely to occur in developing countries across the whole range of handicapping conditions once special provision becomes generally available.

(4)   There is currently a high prevalence of disorders of hearing and vision in developing countries. Similar conditions in Europe or USA would not be regarded as great handicaps because corrective lenses or hearing aids can significantly improve the individual's ability to function both in educational and social settings. Increased availability of such aids will reduce the handicapping effect of such disabilities even though they do not affect the prevalence of the conditions themselves. Projects similar to the one run by the Christoffel Blinden

Mission and supported by Intermediate Technology in Nairobi, which plans to make corrective lenses and frames cheap enough to be bought by the local population (Mallet, 1980), should have a significant impact on this handicap.

(5) Certain related syndromes have been shown to be associated with both dietary deficiencies and the high consumption of specific foodstuffs, particularly cassava. Hinchcliffe (1973) reports a number of studies which demonstrate that, among other things, the syndromes involve both optic atrophy and sensorineural hearing loss. Improved communication and transport could bring about less dependence on specific locally grown foods and thereby affect the incidence of these disorders.

(6) As ordinary educational provision improves and UPE takes effect there is likely to be increasing recognition of children with learning difficulties. These may be the result of either below average general intelligence or learning difficulties specific to one set of abilities (such as reading, language or mathematics). These problems are defined primarily by educational rather than social criteria, and consequently require a relatively sophisticated education system before they can be identified. The prevalence of these problems is likely to increase as a function of improvements in the education system. Initially improvements will have the effect of creating categories of handicap which do not at present exist in the majority of developing countries.

The above points illustrate some of the more obvious effects of medical, educational, and technological intervention on the handicapped population, and emphasise the change in frequencies and types of handicap likely to occur. They indicate the need for regional prevalence studies to monitor the effectiveness of intervention programmes of one form or another, and also highlight the dangers of relying on static data for long-term planning of provision.

Conclusions

It has been emphasised throughout that an interview-based survey has methodological limitations for detecting certain types of disorder, particularly mild forms of visual and hearing impairment, and mild mental retardation (though the validity of the latter classification has been questioned in the current

Nigerian context). It has also been suggested that these conditions are likely to have a high rate of prevalence, although there is little documented evidence to support this. The types of conditions which the survey could identify reliably were either severe disorders e.g. mental retardation, multiple handicap, blindness, deafness or grand mal epilepsy, or obvious disorders, particularly physical handicap.

With these limitations in mind, three points need to be emphasised:

(1) There is no evidence in the data to suggest that any particular handicap has an unusually high rate of prevalence. However, this does not mean that there is no possibility of locally high rates of one or more of these conditions within the state. In fact it is quite likely that such variations in localities do exist.

(2) By combining the urban and rural figures the overall prevalence rate of handicapping conditions was found to be 13.98/1000. However, only a small number from this total group suffer from conditions which definitely require specialist teaching and specialised equipment for satisfactory education. This group of children would comprise those who were deaf, blind or mentally or multiply handicapped, and the total prevalence of these conditions amounts to 3.7/1000. (If the difference in prevalence between urban and rural areas for mental and multiple handicap is a true difference, rather than a function of sampling error, the overall prevalence for the state is likely to be lower than 3.7/1000. The data suggests that the rate in rural areas, which represent the majority of the population, is lower than that of urban areas.) The distinction between the group who will definitely require specialist teaching and those who could be integrated into the ordinary school system is made from an educational viewpoint and does not suggest that the latter group, representing a prevalence of 10.28/1000, all suffer mild handicapping conditions. Many of these children were classified as severely handicapped, particularly those suffering from visual and physical disabilities. But the problems involved in teaching these children are of a practical nature, and they focus on the adaptation of existing facilities and teaching materials, to suit the individual child's needs, rather than the use of new forms of material, such as those required by blind children, or highly specialised training techniques as would be required by

deaf or mentally handicapped children.

(3) From a medical point of view, untreated deformities resulting from polio are often progressive. The damage to the ear caused by otitis media leads to increased hearing loss; cataract left untreated leads to serious defects of vision and so on. When so-called mild disabilities are progressive they may result in educational problems later on in the child's school career, and will almost certainly result in more severe handicap later in life.

With a total population of approximately 2,027,000 persons (*Nigerian Standard*, 19 June, 1979) and an overall prevalence of 13.98/1000 cases in the child population, it would be possible to estimate the approximate number of special education places required by the state, and simply to make separate provision for them. However, this would be neither practical nor desirable because, as I said before, the majority could be integrated into the ordinary education system. This is happening to some extent at the moment, but the quality of education received is often inadequate, due in many cases to oversights by the teacher. The onus should therefore be on developing the ordinary teachers' awareness of problems related to dealing with children suffering from visual defects, hearing loss, physical disabilities and so on. The obvious time for this would be during the teachers' initial training. This system could then deal with the 10.28/1000 children who are handicapped, but who do not require highly specialised materials or training. In Plateau State this number would be approximately 5,210 children (using the figure of 2,027,000 as the total population, with an estimated 25 per cent of this population being between six and sixteen years of age). The remaining group who will require special education facilities would number approximately 1,875 children.

An additional component in the programme should be the development of support services for the practising teacher in ordinary schools. These would be best run on a regional basis, and probably in the form of a peripatetic referral service. This service could advise individual teachers and provide practical help where necessary. For instance, ideally there should be a physiotherapy adviser who could help with the provision of simple mobility aids such as those illustrated by Huckstep (1975). Integrated provision has the cost effective advantage of making use of the existing education system which should be capable of dealing with about three quarters of the handicapped children identified in this survey. It would also curb the current tendency to segregate children who, though disabled, could cope with education in ordinary schools if given minimal aid. This tendency is particularly applicable to polio children who attend the schools for the physically handicapped in Nigeria (Cope, 1979). I recognise that transport problems for physically handicapped children, particularly those in rural areas, can leave little alternative besides residential schooling. But this is a poor alternative given the expense of such placement and the more doubtful educational value of segregated education.

Given nearly 2,000 children who will require specialist teachers and facilities not readily available in ordinary schools, it would seem reasonable to suggest a decentralised system of placement. For instance about 20 schools or units could be established throughout the state, each one dealing with all categories of handicap. This system would have several advantages:

(1) It would reduce the number of residential placements necessary.

(2) It would enable children with secondary or multiple handicaps to benefit from the expertise of a variety of specialists.

(3) It would provide a local base for the peripatetic and advisory teachers servicing the ordinary schools.

(4) It would enable pupils to remain close to their family and community.

The above system is one which emphasises integrated education. It should form the basis of a flexible service designed to cater for the needs of today's handicapped children, at the same time as being ready to meet the predicted expansion and change without need for major reorganisation.

Acknowledgments

This project was funded by the Research Grants Committee of the University of Jos, and the Ministry of Education, Plateau State. Particular thanks go to Professor J. Cooper and Mr Ron Corkhill of the Department of Special Education, University of Jos, for their valuable assistance during the field work, and to Dr C.C. Kiernan for his advice on the write-up of the report.

References

Anderson, E.M. (1973), *The Disabled Schoolchild. A Study of Integration in Primary Schools*, Methuen, London.

Asirifi, Y. (1972), 'Aetiology of cerebral palsy in developing countries', *Developmental Medicine and Child Neurology*, vol. 14, pp. 230-2.

Axton, J.H.M. and Levy, L.F. (1974), 'Mental handicap in Rhodesian African children', *Developmental Medicine and Child Neurology*, vol. 16, pp. 350-5.

Berg, J.H. (1974), 'Aetiological aspects of mental subnormality: pathological factors', in A.D.B. Clarke and A.M. Clarke (eds), *Mental Deficiency – The Changing Outlook*, 3rd edn, Methuen, London.

Cope, C. (1979), former course tutor in physical handicap, dept. of special education, University of Jos, personal communication.

Dale, D.M.C. (1967), *Deaf Children at Home and at School*, University of London Press.

Dale, A. and Stanley, F.J. (1980), 'An epidemiological study of cerebral palsy in West Australia 1956-75', *Developmental Medicine and Child Neurology*, vol. 22, pp. 13-25.

Daramola, S. (1976), 'Educating the visually handicapped in Nigeria: Some theoretical and practical considerations', *West African Journal of Education*, vol. 20, no. 2, pp. 171-7.

David, J.B., Edoo, B.B., Mustaffah, J.F.O. and Hinchcliffe, R. (1971), 'Adamrobe – a "deaf" village', *Sound*, vol. 5, pp. 70-2.

Davies, P.A. and Tizard, J.C.M. (1975), 'Very low birth weight and subsequent neurological deficits', *Developmental Medicine and Child Neurology*, vol. 17, pp. 3-17.

Demographic Year Book 1977, UN, New York, 1978.

Grantham McGregor, S.M. and Desai, P. (1975), 'A home-visiting intervention programme with Jamaican mothers and children', *Developmental Medicine and Child Neurology*, vol. 17, pp. 605-13.

Gulliford, R. (1971), *Special Educational Needs*, Routledge & Kegan Paul, London.

Gustavson, K.H., Holmgren, G., Jonsell, R. and Son Blomquist, H.K. (1977), 'Severe mental retardation in children in a northern Swedish county', *Journal of Mental Deficiency Research*, vol. 21, pp. 161-80.

Hicks, W.M. and Glenn, S.P. (1979), 'Deaf-visually impaired persons: incidence and service', *American Annals of the Deaf*, vol. 124, no. 2, pp. 76-92.

Hinchcliffe, R. (1973), 'Neuro-otolaryngology in West Africa,' in W. Taylor (ed.), *Disorders of Auditory Function*, Academic Press, New York.

Huckstep, R.L. (1975), *Poliomyelitis: A Guide for Developing Countries – Including Appliances and Rehabilitation for the Disabled*, Churchill Livingstone, Edinburgh, London and New York.

Jelliffe, D.B. (1966), *The Assessment of Nutritional Status in the community*, WHO Publication, no. 53, Geneva.

Kapur, Y.P. (1976), 'Hearing loss in the Indian population', *Sound*, vol. 1, no. 1, pp. 20-1.

Kiernan, C.C., Jordan, R. and Saunders, C.A. (1978), *Starting Off*, Souvenir Press, London.

Kirchner, C. and Peterson, R. (1979), 'The latest data on visual disability from N.C.H.S.', *Journal of Visual Impairment and Blindness*, vol. 73, no. 4, pp. 151-3.

Kirman, B. and Bicknell, J. (1975), *Mental Handicap*, Churchill Livingstone, Edinburgh, London and New York.

Kushlick, A. and Cox, C.R. (1973), 'The epidemiology of mental handicap', *Developmental Medicine and Child Neurology*, vol. 15, pp. 748-59.

Lotter, V. (1978) 'Childhood autism in Africa', *Journal of Child Psychology and Psychiatry*, vol. 19, pp. 231-44.

Mallet, A. (1980), Administrator, Intermediate Technology, personal communication.

Markides, A. (1976), 'Education for hearing impaired children in Ghana', *Teacher of the Deaf*, vol. 74, no. 435, pp. 19-27.

Mba, P.O. (1978), 'Issues of social adjustment and societal attitude: a comparative perspective', paper presented to the World Congress on the Future of Special Education, Stirling, Scotland, 1978.

McManus, F., Range, M. and Whittaker, J. (1977), 'Is cerebral palsy a preventable disease?', *Obstetrics and Gynecology*, vol. 50, pp. 71-7.

Meek, C.K. (1925), *The Northern Tribes of Nigeria*, Oxford University Press.

Odebiyi, A.P. (1977), 'The socio-cultural factors affecting health care delivery in Nigeria', *Journal of Tropical Medicine and Hygiene*, November 1977.

Osuntokun, B.O., Bademosi, O., Familusi, J.B. and Oke, P. (1974), 'Electroencephalographic correlates of epilepsy in Nigerian children', *Developmental Medicine and Child Neurology*, vol. 16, pp. 659-63.

Robinson, N.M. (1978), 'Mild mental retardation – does it exist in the People's Republic of China?', *Mental Retardation*, vol. 16, no. 4, pp. 295-9.

Sandford-Smith, J.H. and Whittle, H.C. (1981), 'Corneal ulceration following measles in malnourished Nigerian children', *Child: Care, Health and Development*, vol. 7, pp. 91-101.

Segal, B. (1972), 'Urbanisation in tropical Africa', in S.H. Ominde and C.N. Ejiogu (eds), *Population Growth and Economic Development in Africa*, Heinemann, London.

Stein, Z.A. and Susser, M. (1977), 'Recent trends in Down's Syndrome', in P. Mittler and J.M. de Jong (eds), *Research to Practice in Mental Retardation*, vol. III, Biomedical aspects, University Park Press, Baltimore.

Tizard, J. (1972), 'Epidemiology of mental retardation. Implications for research on malnutrition', *Symposia of the Swedish Nutritional Foundation XII*.

Umoh, O.E. (1972), 'Demographic statistics in Nigeria', in S.H. Ominde and C.N. Ejiogu (eds), *Population Growth and Economic Development in Africa*, Heinemann, London.

WHO Report (1980), 'Expanded programme on immunisation: poliomyelitis prevalence survey', *Weekly Epidemiology Review*, no. 8, February, 1980.

Wilber, L.A. (1979), 'Threshold measurement methods and special considerations', in W.F. Rintelmann (ed.), *Hearing Assessment*, University Park Press, Baltimore.

Wilson, J. (1964), 'Africa's blind children', in A. Taylor and F.H. Butcher (eds), *Education of the Blind in Africa*, The Caxton Press (West Africa), Ibadan.

Wilson, J. (1981), 'Seminar on blinding malnutrition amongst children: an introduction', *Child: Care, Health and Development*, vol. 7, pp. 81-4.

Index